WEB OF DECEPTION

WEB OF DECEPTION

MARGARET VALENTA

PRESCOTT, ARIZONA

Library of Congress Control Number: 2019919803

ISBN 978-0-578-61316-1

Book design by Longworth Creative, LLC

First Edition
Printed in the United States of America

To

MY CHILDREN
Diane, Michael, Gregory and Brian

GRANDCHILDREN

GREAT-GRANDCHILDREN

"Family isn't defined only by last names or by blood. It's defined by commitment and love. It means showing up when they need it most. It means having each other's backs. It means choosing to love each other even on those days when you struggle to like each other. It means never giving up on each other."

– Dave Willis, author

CONTENTS

ACKNOWLEDGEMENTS

I want to thank everyone who listened, advised, and edited my memoir—especially:

David Whittlesey, computer expert and friend, who gave wise counsel and computer expertise throughout the entire five-year process of writing the book.

My class teacher, Elaine Jordon who patiently instructed, directed and motivated me to bring my story to its conclusion.

Classmates: Connie, Judy, Carol, Kathleen, Judith and Bobbie who offered many suggestions and morale-boosting comments.

To Vaughn Delp-Smith, the wise teacher who edited my story.

My beloved daughter, Diane Koch, who provided her continual support throughout the five years, from rough drafts to story end.

Verna Killbarger, best friend and enthusiastic cheerleader, who spurred me on.

My cousin, Barbara Bondar, writer, who from the beginning saw my potential and encouraged me to write my story.

Grandson Brian Koch and his wife Tayva who asked me to write about my life so their children would know family history.

Great Granddaughter, Alissa DeBord, who helped put me on Facebook and Instagram.

All of you contributed your time and your interest. You gave of yourselves. I return my most sincere THANK YOU!

PREFACE

One of the reasons I wrote this book is for people to realize when things go terribly wrong, they can overcome it.

There's always a way. The road you take may not be easy.

When you persevere, in the end, you will realize it was worth the struggle.

Drugs, alcohol or suicide is never the answer.

"It's not what happens to you, but how you react that matters."

– Epictetus

1

THE MEETING

THE MEMBERS OF 'THE MEETING' did not celebrate Christmas. They only read the story from the Bible during a December service. My sister and I never heard of Santa Claus, never had a Christmas tree and our family never sent Christmas cards or exchanged gifts.

The Christmas I was three years old, my mother's brother, Uncle Ray, came from Detroit where he lived, to spend the holidays. Uncle Ray, not a member of The Meeting, was upset that my sister Virginia and I didn't have a Christmas tree with presents under it. He told my mother it was sad we didn't know anything about Santa Claus, which their eleven brothers and sisters enjoyed so much as children.

Uncle Ray sat me on his knee and said, "I'm going to tell you all about Santa Claus."

When he finished talking about Santa and the night before Christmas, I believed every word he said and I was so excited.

"Uncle Ray, will Santa Claus bring me a dolly?" I asked.

That night, after my sister and I went to bed, we could hear Uncle Ray talking to Mama and Daddy. Several times we heard raised voices, unusual in our house. The next day, Uncle Ray and our family went into the woods and cut down our very first Christmas tree. We only had lights on the tree, and a star at the top, but to me it was the most beautiful tree I had ever seen.

It was the first Christmas that my sister and I got a present and we both got a doll. My doll had blonde hair and blue eyes just like mine, and Virginia's doll had brown hair and blue eyes like hers.

I felt as a child, I had missed out on the fun and pageantry of the Christmas season. Looking back, I know this was a hard decision for Daddy to make. As the years went by, Christmas became the most important time of the year for me. To this day I always put up a Christmas tree.

***

I was born on March 31st 1933 in Sault Ste. Marie, a small town in the upper peninsula of Michigan.

My father was the preacher of a church called 'Gospel Hall' which originated in England. The small congregation, of about forty, called it, "The Meeting". They never referred to the Gospel Hall as a church because they believed churches worshiped idols, which was a sin. They believed they were the only Christians going to heaven.

The Meeting was free from all superficial embellishments. There were no musical instruments, crosses, statues, flowers or adornments of any kind. The congregation sat on hard wooden chairs. At the front, was a raised platform where my father stood, and behind him was the baptismal tank where a new member, professing they were saved, would be totally emerged in water.

The women wore their long hair pulled into a bun at the back of the neck. They never wore pants, shorts or jewelry except for a plain wedding band. The Gospel Hall dogma taught that you had to remain plain, not prideful, which was a sin. Hats and gloves were required for women and girls at all Meetings. Men wore suits and everyone carried a Bible. The members of the congregation were forbidden to drink alcohol, smoke, play cards, dice games, dance, wear makeup, gamble or belong to any organization. Movies were called "The Devil's Playhouse," and it was a sin to attend. Members of The Meeting were called brothers and sisters. It was a Bible church that preached hellfire and damnation.

Sermons were terrifying to me as a child. They preached if you weren't "saved," your parents would be taken up in the night, to heaven, and you would be left behind to go to hell, where you would burn forever. You would long for a drop of water to cool your parched tongue. I stayed awake for hours worried that my parents would disappear. In the middle of the night, I'd kick off my blanket and yell, "Daddy, I'm cold," so he'd come into my bedroom and I'd know they were still there.

Every day we had prayers before breakfast and lunch, then a verse from the Bible after the meal. At dinner-time we had prayers before and after. Then every night, instead of going outside to play, we went into the living room and took turns reading the Bible out-loud, starting with Genesis. That's how I learned to read.

I was not allowed to play with boys, or the girl down the street who was Catholic. My sister Virginia was three years older, and I don't think she ever played with me. She loved to read and kept to herself with her books. That was her escape then and is to this day.

I had no one to play with until I was four. One day I decided to wheel my doll buggy down the street. When I got to the corner, a little girl, a year younger than me, came out of her house to look at my doll. Her name was Arbutus Cook. I asked her, "Do you go to Sunday School?"

"No," she replied.

"Good." I said. "Now I can play with you."

I knew Arbutus didn't attend The Meeting. If she didn't go to any Sunday School, she didn't go to the bad churches, so I could play with her. She and I remained childhood friends playing hide-and-seek, kick-the-can, hop-scotch, marbles and skip rope.

My mother's family weren't members of the Gospel Hall, they were Episcopalians. The Gospel Hall was my father's family religion. He was very strict in what he believed was right, but my mother was not as strict in some things. She'd read children's books to me my father didn't approve of.

Some afternoons, I'd sit on my mother's lap as she'd read to me. Not only did she read Mother Goose Rhymes but wonderful fairy tales. Stories about Cinderella, Snow White and Rapunzel were my favorites. I spent hours dreaming about them and of a knight in shining armor who would come and rescue me.

My father's sister, Aunt Ruth, was my Sunday school teacher at the Gospel Hall. Only children went to Sunday school, and there weren't many of us. When she told the Bible story about Noah and the Ark and how only the animals on the ark would be saved from drowning, and only Noah's family that built the ark would be saved, I raised my hand and said, "But, Aunt Ruth, why would God drown all those baby bunnies, kitty cats, puppy dogs and little babies? Isn't one of the commandments 'thou shalt not kill?' Why is *he* doing it?"

"You'd better be careful that God doesn't strike you dead for saying that," she said.

Every time I would raise my hand in a question, *and* I *questioned everything*, she tried her best to ignore me. I must have frustrated her to no end.

One night the meeting was having a program that all members attended. The Sunday school children chose a verse to recite in the program. Each child walked up to the raised portion of the hall and did their best to remember a verse. Being four years old and shy, I picked the shortest verse I knew.

Daddy asked me, "What verse have you chosen to recite?'

"It's a secret," I replied.

Dressed in my best Sunday dress, long white stockings and polished shoes, I walked up the few steps to the podium, took a deep breath, and recited my verse, "Jesus wept."

If they gave out a grade for Sunday school, I'm sure I would have got the lowest grade possible. As the years went by, and I was teased and ridiculed in and out of school, because of my parents' religion, I rebelled against The Meeting more and more. When I was sixteen, in the middle of a Sunday night Meeting, I walked out, walked home and refused to go to Meeting again.

2

THE DEVIL'S PLAYHOUSE

WHEN I WAS FIVE YEARS OLD, it was time to start kindergarten. In 1938, there were no pre-schools and most children started school without a basic knowledge of numbers, colors and reading. Michigan started school the day after Labor Day.

If children lived in the country, they rode the school bus and everyone else walked to school. To get to Garfield school, I'd have to walk two blocks and across a long bridge that was over a swift moving canal. Families had only one car which the father took to work. It was rare that a mother worked.

As September approached, my mother said, "You'll be starting kindergarten soon and it will be in the afternoon after lunch."

"I don't want to go to school. Grandma Gordon said I shouldn't go because I'd learn wicked ways."

"Every child goes to school, your sister goes to school, so I don't want to hear anything more about it," she said.

The thought of leaving home terrified me. I was extremely shy in my early years, hiding behind my mother when introduced to anyone new.

All school-girls wore dresses or a skirt and sweater. The boys wore dress pants and button-down shirts. The shoes for both boys and girls were lace-up dress shoes. Tennis shoes and flip-flops were not worn in those days.

On the day I started school, I had on my best dress, which hung down over my knees, long brown stockings and brown leather shoes. Other girls wore white ankle-socks but I wasn't allowed to wear them. I had to wear the long brown stockings every day except white ones on Sunday.

That afternoon, when it was time to go, my mother took my hand and walked me to the kindergarten. I protested all the way. As we entered the classroom, I saw an elderly, plump, unsmiling lady and about twenty-five children sitting on the floor in the room. I tried to hide behind my mother but after she talked to the teacher for a minute, my mother untangled me, said goodbye, and walked out the door.

I ran to the door calling, "Mama, Mama don't leave me."

Miss Kemp, the teacher, told me to be quiet and sit down on the floor by the other children. I cried the entire afternoon and didn't speak to anyone that day and for several months thereafter.

My sister had to walk to school with me every day. I would drag behind, not wanting to go. She'd yell at me, "Margaret, keep up, so we won't be late." After a couple of weeks, she refused to walk with me anymore. It didn't bother me to walk by myself and I always managed to get to the kindergarten room just before the bell rang.

Kindergarten was all about learning how to play. We didn't learn anything like reading, writing or arithmetic. We had a band, using no instruments, only things that made noise. I played the sticks. Billy played a triangle. Miss Kemp told him he was off key. How he could be off key is a mystery to me to this day. In the middle of the afternoon we all laid down on mats and took a nap.

World War II started on Sept 1st, 1939, when I entered first grade. Many of my classmate's fathers went off to war. We learned to say the Pledge of Allegiance, standing, turning to the flag that was in every classroom, placing our hands over our hearts. We would recite it before class every day until we graduated from high school.

While I was in grade school, the United States entered the war on December seventh 1941 when Hawaii's Pearl Harbor was bombed by the Japanese. Sault Ste. Marie became one of the most critical places in the United States for attack by the enemy. The ships going through the locks, transporting iron ore down the Great Lakes to war factories in Detroit, Chicago and other places, put the city in great danger, so the Air Force, Army, National Guard and Coast Guard established bases in the Sault.

We had bomb shelter drills at school. When the alarm sounded, we filed to homes surrounding the school and went into their basements, where we would sit on the floor with our head between our knees. It was very frightening.

At home, when a siren sounded, we had to black out our windows to show no light so it didn't attract war planes. We went to the basement and waited for the all-clear sound. My father was the watch-captain for the neighborhood, leaving home to patrol every time a siren went off.

All families were issued books of ration stamps. You couldn't buy anything without a stamp. We were very limited as to what we could buy and some items were not available at all. We had a vacant lot on our block, and all the families decided it should be turned into a garden to grow food. These gardens were called, 'Victory Gardens.' My father was in charge of the lot and all the families were honest and took their turn tending their portion. My father helped the people that didn't know how to garden.

I was twelve years old when the war ended on September 2, 1945.

***

I gradually felt better about school, although I dreaded being called on to answer questions, or go to the blackboard to solve a math problem. I had that feeling for most of my school years.

I was forbidden to join Brownies and then Girl Scouts which all of the girls in the class joined. On the day of the scouts' meeting, when they all came to school in their uniforms, I didn't want to go to school and would sometimes fake being sick so I wouldn't have to go. No one at school belonged to The Meeting, and I felt I was different. I wanted so much to be like everyone else.

I gradually became friends with several girls in my class and I walked to school frequently with Billy McPherson who lived up my street.

One day, when I was in the fifth grade, a classmate, Joyce, asked me to go with her to a Roy Rogers movie at the Saturday afternoon matinee. I knew my parents would never let me go. It cost ten cents. I had a ten-cent weekly allowance but I bought a comic book every week with it. I would sneak the comic book, which I wasn't allowed to read, into the house under my sweater and hide it in my room. I told Joyce I couldn't get the money and had spent my allowance. She said she would lend me the ten cents.

It took me only a second to decide to accept the money and go to the movie. I thought, 'all the kids at school went to the theater, why can't I?' I was tired of being ridiculed for not being able to go to fairs, carnivals, the circus or the movies. I knew The Meeting members wouldn't be there, so my parents probably wouldn't find out about it. I told my mother I was going to the library and would be back in a couple of hours.

Since I had never been to the movies, I was excited but also afraid because The Meeting called it 'The Devils Playhouse.' As we went into the theater, I looked around for the Devil, even though I knew that The Meeting was wrong to think that the Devil was in there. When the lights turned down and the maroon curtains parted, the movie began. I immediately forgot about the Devil because I was amazed at what I was seeing. It was the most exciting story! The horses were beautiful as they raced across the big white screen. Roy Rogers was handsome and outsmarted the villain. I loved every minute of the thrilling story, and I couldn't see any reason why I was forbidden to go. I thought it was much better than a comic book and planned to go again.

That night I had a nightmare. I dreamed the Devil was walking down my street, coming to my house. In my dream, I ran to the front door, shutting and locking it. The door slowly opened and I heard the Devil's footsteps coming closer. I shut the door locking it again. The door opened. In a panic, I slammed the door, locked it and pushed against the door with all my might to keep it closed. It opened. I could smell the Devil's putrid breath as his hand reached in to grab me. I awoke, screaming in terror. I had this dream for most of my young life, although I continued to go to the movies.

3

DANCING

THE SUMMER BEFORE entering Junior High, seventh grade, my friend Ginny invited me to her thirteenth birthday party. No one ever invited me to a party before. I'd never had a birthday party. I worried I wouldn't be allowed to go. After I begged and pleaded, my mother agreed. I asked her if she could buy Ginny a Nancy Drew mystery book for her present. She bought the book and helped me wrap it in white tissue paper and tie it with a pink ribbon from her sewing basket. I was excited and could hardly wait for the party.

Ginny lived across town. Since the party was on a Saturday afternoon, my father told me he would drive me to the party, and to call him when the party was over, so he could come and pick me up.

When I arrived at the party, there were ten girls sitting in a large, sunny, living room. Everyone was talking and laughing and they all said hello when they saw me. I shyly handed Ginny her present and sat down on a vacant chair, not knowing what to do.

Ginny's mother suggested we play some games and she set up a game of Musical Chairs. After we played it for a while, we played Pin The Tail On The Donkey and Blind Man's Bluff. Then Ginny put a dance record on the phonograph and the girls danced with each other while I watched.

Ginny's older brother, who was in high school, came into the room. He said to me, "Why aren't you dancing?"

"I never danced before, so I don't know how," I said.

"Well, let's fix that." Taking me by the hand, he proceeded to show me how to dance. First, he showed me the box step, then he showed me how to jitterbug. I thought the jitterbug was the most fun of all! Catching on quickly, I could keep up with him while we danced to a fast record. Ginny's mother stood in the doorway watching us. When the record ended, she applauded and said, "Well done." By the end of the afternoon, I had lost my shyness. When the party ended, I called my dad to come and get me.

When my dad arrived, Ginny and her mother walked me to the car. Her mother said to my father, "You should give Margaret dance lessons, like ballet. She has a natural ability and would make a great dancer. She picked up on how to dance quickly and has the form of a dancer."

My dad drove away in silence. I was horrified. I didn't know what to expect because my dad believed dancing was a sin. Daddy didn't smile, had a stern look on his face and I wondered what he would say when we got home.

When we went into the house, he told my mother, "Dorothy, Margaret was dancing at the birthday party even though she knew it was wrong. It was a mistake to allow her to go."

I said, "There were only girls invited to the party and the girls danced together. I don't see anything wrong with that. Why can't you be like other parents? I hate being different."

"My rules are for your own good. If you don't like it, we'll send you to the Children's Home," my dad said.

In those days, there was a Children's Home for unwanted children and a Poor Farm for old people, mostly men and injured veterans, who didn't have any money. On Sunday afternoons, after Sunday school, we went to the Homes and my father preached. Then my mother played the piano and we sang hymns. The people at the Poor Farm and the Children's Home looked forward to our coming. I felt sorry for them, but I didn't want to end up in either place.

After lecturing me about dancing, my dad sent me to my room. I closed the bedroom door and hummed to myself as I practiced the dance steps I'd learned. I defiantly told myself, 'it's not wrong to dance and I'll dance every chance I get. If they send me to the Children's Home I'll just run away.' I have a love of dancing to this day.

A couple of months after seventh grade started, I had a terrible stomach ache all day in school. I could hardly wait for the school day to end. When I arrived home, I headed upstairs to use the bathroom. When I pulled down my panties, I found blood in them. I was shocked. I couldn't imagine how I had cut myself. I got a mirror and looked to see where the cut was. I couldn't find any. The blood kept dripping on the mirror. I thought, 'I must be really, really sick inside.' My mother wasn't home and I didn't know what to do. I sat on the toilet and started to cry. My sister, Virginia heard me sobbing.

"What's the matter with you?" she asked.

"I'm dying," I wailed.

"What so you mean you're dying?"

"I'm bleeding to death!"

Because she was three years older, she knew exactly what was wrong. "You're not dying and Momma will explain it to you when she gets home."

She went to her room and came back with a strange looking pad and told me to put it in my pants.

I stayed on the toilet until my mother came home a short time later. Momma gave me a strap that went around my waste and down my stomach and back-side to attach to the pad to hold it in place, plus a pamphlet to read. Not knowing anything about the female body, I didn't understand a word it said. Momma's sister, Aunt Edna, who lived two doors from us, stopped by. My mother told her I had just started my period and didn't know what was happening.

Aunt Edna said to my mother, "Dorothy, why didn't you tell Margaret about what was going to happen when she got to this age?"

Then she turned to me, "All women go through this but don't talk about it to anyone. It's not polite."

I asked her, "How long does this last?"

"Until you're about fifty-five years old."

I was shocked and wondered how I would have enough blood to continue this horrible thing for forty-two more years.

4

LIFE'S CHOICES

I always felt like an outsider at school, from the first day I started kindergarten through junior high. I thought everyone was smarter than I was. I hated school. My parents believed it was wrong to give compliments on appearance or achievements because it would make you prideful, which was a sin. Their reluctance left me feeling very insecure.

High school was going to start in just one week. I was worried about the reaction my parents would have about what I planned to do. I rehearsed it in front of my mirror over and over the entire week and was afraid of what the consequence would be.

The morning I was going to start high school, ninth grade, I took one last look in the mirror, left the bedroom, went down the stairs, walked into the kitchen for breakfast, with *lipstick* on. My father looked at me in surprise.

Before he could utter a word, hands on my hips, I dramatically said, "You can beat me and chain me to the bed.

I'm wearing lipstick like the other girls. I'm not going down the street to the corner and put lipstick on like Virginia does. I'm going to wear it from home."

My sister gave me a glaring look.

My father looked at my mother, then me, and said, "You can wear lipstick but nothing else on your face. No lipstick on Sunday and you can only wear light colors, not that dark purple stuff."

Even though the dark purple was popular, I knew it didn't look good on me because I'd tried it. I told him I agreed. Looking back, I'm sure my dad knew I meant to wear lipstick regardless of how he felt, so made the compromise. I never wanted to wear any other make-up but lipstick until I was in my sixties.

***

When I was in the tenth grade, we had an assembly in the auditorium for all the high school students. At the assembly, they introduced the new band, choir and orchestra teacher, Mr. Dieke. The music department was in sad shape with not enough students playing key instruments in the band. The former music teacher, who played the violin, had little interest in the band and concentrated only on the orchestra.

Mr. Dieke was hired from Michigan State University. When he walked across the stage and was introduced, I thought, 'my, he's so handsome.' He was a tall, slender man, with wavy brown hair and brown eyes. He seemed to be in his twenties, a quiet serious man. He announced that anyone who played a musical instrument, should come to the band room after school and talk to him. Tryouts for choir would be the following day.

After the assembly ended, I ran to my two best friends, Diane and Joyce and told them we should join the band and choir.

Diane looked at me shocked and said, "But we don't play an instrument!"

I said, "If others can learn to play an instrument we can too. It will be so much fun to be in the marching band at all the football games. We'll go on the school bus to the out of town games and march in the town parades, like the 4th of July. Most of the instruments are available on loan in the music department and they supply our uniforms."

I pleaded with them to come with me. They finally agreed. After school, the three of us went to the band room. It was a very large room to hold the ninety-piece band. I wondered where I'd be sitting and what I would play. I walked up to Mr. Dieke and told him we wanted to join the band.

He asked, "What instrument do you play?"

I replied, "Oh, anything."

I could see the surprise in his eyes at my response and his effort not to laugh. Turning to me with a twinkle in his eyes, he said, "I do need someone to play the trombone."

To Joyce he suggested the bass clarinet and Diane the saxophone. He said, "I'm guessing you girls really can't play any instrument. If you're willing to learn, with a lot of effort and practice, you'll find it quite enjoyable."

The school had the three instruments available, and Mr. Dieke scheduled times for each of us to have our first lesson.

The next day, we tried out for choir. Diane and I were in the alto section and Joyce soprano. Carrying the trombone, I went home and told my parents I had joined the band and choir and I was going to play the slide-trombone.

Daddy said, "You don't know how to play the trombone. What on earth are you thinking?"

"Well, I played the piano after lessons, so I can learn to play the trombone too. Mr. Dieke is going to give me free lessons."

I was excited about having my first lesson and seeing Mr. Dieke. He told me about the slide-trombone, the different positions for the notes on the slide and the tension of the mouth on the mouthpiece to form the notes. My first attempt to blow into the horn, made the most pitiful sound you would ever hear. I thought, 'I'd probably get a better sound blowing into a pickle jar.' I practiced before school, at lunch hour, after school and after dinner. I practiced so much I had a red ring around my mouth from my mouthpiece. My practicing drove my sister crazy.

"I can't stand this racket," Virginia said.

Daddy said, "Don't let it bother you, she'll never last."

That was all I needed to hear to prove that I could do it. Most of all I wanted Mr. Dieke to be proud of me. In three months, the three of us were in the band, and Joyce and I were also in the orchestra.

Six months later, at my lesson, Mr. Dieke told me to challenge the first chair trombone player at the next band practice. At practice, shyly, I challenged him, just to please Mr. Dieke. Winning the challenge surprised me. I never imagined I would be playing first chair.

Mr. Dieke formed a dance band with eleven of his best students, including Joyce and me. Mr. Dieke played the saxophone with the band. We played at the school dances, were applauded and I loved it.

My mother always went to the programs at the school when the band and orchestra had concerts. Mama was quiet, serious and soft spoken. She enjoyed music and played the piano. She had a beautiful voice and sang alto when the congregation sang hymns at The Meeting.

My father never attended the high school programs. However, he bought me a trombone, so I would have a better instrument to play.

The day I walked into the music department to join the band would change my life forever. It gave me confidence and made me happier to be in school.

Life is choices. Because of my decision to join the band, that choice would cause me much sadness, heartbreak and pain.

5

FIRST DATE

DURING MY TIME IN THE BAND, I developed a friendship with the first chair trumpet player, Pat Henderson. Pat was the same age as I was, nice looking, average height, straight brown hair, blue eyes and a cleft in his chin. He had an older brother and younger sister. His father was the court prosecutor, his mother was a schoolteacher, and they were Catholic. We were in several classes together as well as music.

Whenever the band went on the school bus to out-of-town football games, Pat wanted me to sit next to him, and we usually sat in the back of the bus. Since it was late at night when we were returning from the ball game, he would put his arm around me and I would fall asleep on his shoulder.

I had never dated before and neither had Pat. Although, when I was in the ninth grade, a basketball player, a few grades above me, walked me home from an after-game dance. He put his arms around me and gave me a kiss, putting his tongue in my mouth. Horrified, I pulled away from him and ran into the house. I ran upstairs as fast as I could and gargled with mouthwash, afraid I would get pregnant.

Since I didn't have any brothers, wasn't allowed to play with boys as a child, never saw my father without clothes on, I had no idea what naked boys looked like. We had no classes in school that explained reproduction so I didn't know how you got pregnant. It was a subject that was taboo in our house. That innocent ignorance had consequences.

Later that year, the American Legion was having a dance for teenagers and Pat asked me to go with him. He said, "I don't know how to dance but I'd like to try." We both played in the high school dance band, so we never got a chance to dance with each other at school dances.

"I'd love to go," I said. "It should be a lot of fun and you'll catch on to slow dancing in no time. You're musical and all you have to do is listen to the beat and move your feet. I'm game if you are."

Since I was only in the tenth grade, I was afraid my parents wouldn't let me go on a date, especially with a Catholic. I told them I had to go to a school function, and because it might snow, Pat Henderson was going to drive me there.

"He'll pick me up at seven and I should be home by ten-thirty," I said.

On the day of the dance, I decided to wear my navy-blue pleated skirt, pale blue angora sweater, silk stockings and flat dress shoes. In the forties, high school girls didn't wear high heels.

Since it was winter, I wore a heavy jacket but no hat

because I didn't want to mess up my long hair that I had curled and fussed over for a long time.

The American Legion had hired a band and decorated the area around the dance floor with strings of colored lights. The view of St. Mary's river was spectacular from the many windows. A sign said we could buy soft drinks at the bar.

A lot of my classmates attended. In those days, if you didn't have a date and a boy didn't ask you to dance, girls danced together hoping boys would cut in.

Pat and I sat at a little table on the edge of the dance floor with Joyce and her date. As the first slow dance started, I took Pat's hand and led him onto the dance floor. "There's a lot of people on the floor, so no one will notice us. Move your feet from side to side in time with the beat, then move around as you want and I'll follow. It's easy."

After a few stumbles, Pat caught on. He couldn't jitterbug, my favorite dance, but he could dance the slow dances fairly well. Joyce's date, Rus, couldn't jitterbug either so Joyce and I danced the fast numbers together while Pat and Rus watched.

After a couple of hours dancing, Pat said, "How about going to Murphy's Drive-In for hamburgers."

"I'd love to go," I said. "Their burgers are delicious."

Murphy's Drive-In was a popular hang-out for teens. Parked next to the building was a large truck with snow removal blades on the front of it to keep the drive-in area as clear of snow as possible. A girl, bundled up for winter weather, ran to the car to take our order.

While we waited for her to bring the burgers to the car,

Pat held my hand and talked about when he went to the Catholic grade school. We finished the hamburgers quickly because it had started to snow.

The Sault, being in the center of the Great Lakes, in Michigan's Upper Peninsula, got a lot of lake effect snow. Snow banks were extremely high. While Pat was driving, he suddenly leaned over and kissed me on my cheek and slammed into a snow bank. He tried to back out but his wheels just spun. The car was stuck.

"My dad's going to kill me." He said. "I'll never get the car again. I was only supposed to drive from my house to the dance."

There were no cell phones. I tried to think of what we should do. I said, "We can't stay here waiting for someone to drive by to help you, we'll freeze. There's a house not far from here with their lights on. We can walk to it and ask for help."

"Let's do that," Pat said.

The snow covered our shoes and stockings and I felt like my feet and ears were going to freeze as we tramped through the snow in sub-zero temperatures. It never occurred to me to stay in the car and Pat never suggested it either.

A man answered the door. When we explained we were stuck in a snow bank, down the road, he said, "I think I can shovel you out. Let me get my shovel."

When we finally started driving home again, I worried we were going to be late and what my parents would say. Pat was silent as he drove, so I knew he must be worried too.

When I arrived home, before my mom or dad could

ask why I was late, I said, "Pat drove into a snow bank and it took a while to get us out. That's why I'm late."

"You better get your wet shoes off and get to bed before you catch a cold," Mama said.

As I climbed the stairs to my bedroom, I thought, 'I hope he'll ask me out again. It was fun to dance with him. This is one date I'll ever forget.'

6

MY WORLD CAME TUMBLING DOWN

DURING OUR JUNIOR AND SENIOR YEARS, Pat and I continued to date. Once, when he asked me to go to a dance, I got up the courage to tell my mother where we were going. I wanted my parents to know we were dating and not have to make things up when I went out. I was afraid of their reaction but it was fine with my mother, although my dad never said how he felt. He was never around when Pat came to pick me up.

Since Pat was raised in a Catholic home, his parents wanted him to date a Catholic, not someone with my family's strict Bible religion. When he told me that his parents didn't like him dating a non-Catholic, I was surprised that we continued to date. It wasn't in Pat's personality to question authority and fight for what he wanted or believed in.

Pat's father gave him an old truck to drive and he drove it on most of our dates. We went to movies, picnics at Soldiers Lake and dances we weren't playing for. We were

Margaret Gordon   *Pat Henderson*

Sᴀᴜʟᴛ Hɪɢʜ Sᴄʜᴏᴏʟ Cʟᴀss ᴏғ '51

always together at out of town games when we played in the band and traveled on the school bus. My parents never told me when to come home. They trusted me to be home at a reasonable time, which I always was.

When he took me home, Pat would park at the side of the house and we would kiss for a while before I went in. I worried that my dad would look out the window and see us, and I'd never be able to go out with Pat again, but I thought it was worth the risk because I liked his kisses.

In my junior year, I won a scholarship to Interlochen National Music School where I would spend the summer. Pat didn't like it that I won the scholarship and he didn't. I had been playing the trombone for only a few years, and he'd played the trumpet since he was in grade school. Pat was an amazing trumpet player. I could tell he resented my award.

"I suppose you won because they knew my parents could afford to send me to Interlochen if I wanted to go," he said. He looked angry as well as disappointed.

***

Toward the end of our senior year, we were making plans for our future. Pat's dad insisted Pat become a lawyer and attend the university in Detroit, where he'd gone to college. Pat wanted to be a music teacher.

I asked, "Why don't you tell your dad you don't want to be a lawyer?"

"I did. My father said he won't pay for my education if I don't go into law."

"You would make a terrible lawyer," I said. "I'd be a better lawyer than you. I spent four years arguing, persuading, and questioning my parents to make them see things my way. That's what it takes to be a lawyer, and that's not you."

"I had no choice, so I enrolled in law. I'll leave for Detroit a few days after graduation to go to summer school," he said.

Soon after that, I told to my father, "I want to go to college."

"Absolutely not," he said, "Girls shouldn't go to college. You'll get married and have a family. It's a waste of money. I don't want to hear any more about it. That's final."

The day of our graduation, my mother invited Pat to dinner. She took some pictures of Pat and me in our cap and gown. I wore a pale pink, knee-length party dress under my graduation gown because Pat and I were going to a friend's house-party afterward.

Pat showed me a note his mother handed him before he left his house. It was addressed to Patrick Gordon. His mother criticized him for spending so much time with me and the note was very critical of him. I could tell that Pat was hurt by it.

After graduation, we went to the party. When we arrived, the party was in full swing. The punch was spiked. I had never had a drop of liquor in my life, and I thought it tasted really good. I had many glasses, and I thought my tongue was going numb when I tried to talk. I had a difficult time standing up and walking as the room spun around. Every now and then, things seemed to slide sideways.

Pat said, "Why don't we get out of here and go to my cabin. I have the key. It's a nice night and we could walk on the beach."

We left and drove to the cabin at Lake Superior, about

twenty-five miles out of town. I had a hard time staying awake. It was cold in the cabin and Pat got out a blanket. He put it over us as we cuddled on the sofa. As we were kissing, he reached under my skirt and it felt like my panties were being pulled down. I wasn't sure what was happening. Pat said he loved me and after college we would get married. I felt confused. I couldn't imagine what he was doing and thought, 'I shouldn't have had so much punch.'

A few days later, Pat's parents sent him to Detroit to start college in the summer. I took a job in a flower shop. I learned how to make arrangements for weddings and funerals. I loved working with the flowers. I planned to save all my money so I could go to the University of Michigan. With a scholarship, the money I would save, I believed college would work out.

Two months later, I felt like I was getting the flu. I threw-up one morning when I got up. When I got to work, the smell of the flowers made me sicker and I went into the bathroom and threw-up again. I told the owner I must be coming down with something and went home. Pat and I wrote to each other every day and I wrote to him that I thought I had the flu. After three days of not keeping anything down, my sister came into my room.

She asked, "Are you pregnant?"

I said, "No! How could I be?" I thought about the evening at Pat's cabin. I felt panic. What had happened that night?

Back then, they didn't have pregnancy test strips. I had to find out if my sister was right, so I looked in the phonebook for a doctor. I found the name of a female doctor and made an appointment. I had never had a complete examination by a doctor before and I didn't know what to expect.

When I went into the doctor's waiting room, the girl at the desk asked me the reason for the visit. Not knowing what to say, I said, "It's personal."

She gave me some forms to fill out and then I was shown into a room with a high, strange- looking, long bed with a sheet over it. I sat on the end of it.

When the doctor, who had a kind, pleasant face, came into the room, she asked me, "When did you have your last period?"

I said, "Two months ago, but I'm never regular."

She said, "I'd like to exam you. Undress completely and put this gown on, I'll be back in a minute."

When she came back, she told me to lie back. She put my feet in stirrups at the end of the bed. I was so embarrassed when she sat down at my feet and lifted the gown, that I started to cry.

She said, "I'm afraid you're pregnant. May I ask who the boy is?"

Between sobs, I said, "Pat Henderson. We planned to get married after he finished college."

She said, "Margaret, in this situation, records show that the boy does not usually marry the girl. Especially in affluent families. I would be surprised if the Hendersons would allow it. You are both underage. He has to have his parents' consent. You have two choices, give the baby up for adoption or keep it. In your best interests I advise you to give it up for adoption. For your nausea, if you drink some Coca Cola and eat crackers, it may help. The nausea can last for three to six months. If that doesn't help, ask the pharmacist at the Karmelcorn Drug Store to give you some coke syrup from their soda fountain and take a teaspoon of it twice a day. I'm not charging you for the visit. Stop at the desk and I'll give you some information you should consider about adoption."

I was terrified. How do you have a baby? What is going to happen to me?

As soon as I got home, I called the Greyhound Bus and asked what the fare was to Detroit. It would take all that I saved, plus some from my sister. I told her I was pregnant and not to tell our parents. I needed to tell Pat.

I called Pat, and said, "I'm taking the bus to Detroit in the morning, can you pick me up at the bus station?"

He said, "I'll be there. It'll be great to see you."

I told my parents I was going to stay at Joyce's for a few days. Although I was sick all the time, I managed to hide it from my parents.

While I was on the bus, the swaying made me sick. I thought the bus ride would never end. I worried the entire way about how I was going to tell Pat I was pregnant and wondered what he would do about it. Would Pat be mad at me? I wondered if it hurt to have a baby. I didn't know what to expect because no one had ever said how you had a baby.

When I arrived, Pat came toward me as we departed the bus. Taking my overnight bag from me, he put his arm around me, giving me a kiss.

He whispered in my ear, "Are you pregnant?"

I started to cry.

He said, "Don't cry, we'll get married and it will be all right."

7

DECEPTION

THE BUS TERMINAL was in the downtown area of Detroit. I had never been in a big city before and was amazed as I stared up at the rows of tall buildings.

Pat said, "I thought we could get a hotel room for the night and plan what we should do."

"I feel sick from the bus ride," I said. "Can we go to a restaurant, so I can get a soda and some crackers? The doctor said it will help with my nausea."

"There's a place close to the campus, and I want you to see the University."

As we drove, Pat talked about the university, what classes he was taking, the difficult law classes, the band. He added that he still would rather be a music teacher.

He never mentioned our situation.

He pulled into a parking place at a small restaurant that was mostly filled with students. We found a booth at the back of the restaurant. I ordered a coke and asked if I could have some crackers. Pat settled on a hamburger with fries.

As I sipped my cola, I said, "I really don't think it's a good idea to get a hotel room tonight. I don't feel good. My mother's sister, Aunt Mildred, lives in Detroit. I thought maybe she would let me stay with her until we made our plans. I copied her telephone number from my mother's address book. I can call her from that telephone booth by the bathroom. She should be home from work about now."

Pat gave me a nickel and I went to the phone booth.

When she answered, I said, "Aunt Mildred, it's Margaret Ann from the Sault. I'm in Detroit visiting a friend at the University. I wonder if it would be possible to stay with you for a couple of days."

She said, "Margaret Ann! How delightful! I'll be happy to have you." After she gave directions to her house, I told her the bus ride had made me sick, not to worry about dinner and I would be there in a little while.

When we arrived at Aunt Mildred's, I introduced her to Pat. We talked for a few minutes, then Pat said, "I have to leave to study. I'll call you tomorrow after my one o'clock class." As I walked him to the car, he added, "My class will end around two and then I'll call. I'll come to your aunt's so we can make plans before she gets home from work."

After he left, Aunt Mildred said, "You look so pale and tired, you should lie down for a while."

I was so exhausted, I slept until morning and didn't hear Aunt Mildred leave for work.

As I waited for Pat to call, I wondered if we could fake

our age to get married, or find a state where we could get married at seventeen. Maybe a southern state.

When it came closer to two o'clock, I thought, 'where will we live? How will we pay for an apartment, school and baby? I'll have to get a job. Would Pat's dad still pay for his education? If not, we could both work and save money so he could still go to college. Our parents will be shocked. Especially my parents. They'll probably never speak to me again.' The more I thought about the situation the more concerned I became.

At two o'clock, I sat by the telephone, anticipating Pat's call. Two o'clock came and went. Then three, four, five, and I began to worry. I waited by the phone, getting more anxious.

When Aunt Mildred came home from work and made dinner, I tried to choke down some food to be polite. I hardly ate anything before I had to rush to the bathroom to throw-up. I thought, 'thank goodness, the bathroom is far enough away so she can't hear me.'

That evening, as Aunt Mildred talked about having had breast cancer with radical surgery, her love of music, her divorce, I could hardly concentrate on what she was telling me. I kept listening for the telephone.

When I finally went to bed, I couldn't sleep, wondering what had happened. In the morning, after my aunt left for work, I decided to call the university and leave a message for Pat.

Finally getting the right department, I heard a woman say, "Yesterday, the Henderson's came and withdrew him from school. *He's gone.*"

I was shocked. As I put the telephone down, I sat there stunned, staring at it. I felt sick.

Pacing the floor, I thought, 'why didn't he call me, leave some kind of message? How can he be so cruel! He must have told his parents I'm pregnant. What am I going to do now? Did they take him home, or to another college?'

My aunt had left her work number and I gave the operator the number. When my aunt answered, I broke down and started to cry, "Aunt Mildred, I'm in trouble and I don't know what to do."

"I sensed something was wrong," she said. "I'll be right home. Whatever the trouble is we can work it out.'

When she came home, I said, "I'm pregnant and Pat has disappeared without saying a word to me. His parents came to Detroit and withdrew him from school. *Please,* don't tell my parents. I'm sure they'll throw me out. What am I going to do?"

"They have to know, dear," she said. "I'll call your mother. It'll be alright. Go and lie down before you fall down. You're distraught and it won't help."

She talked to my mother for quite a while, and when she hung up she told me my mother was coming on the next bus. I wondered why my father didn't come too and drive her to Detroit.

The next day, when my mother arrived, she hugged me with tears in her eyes. She asked no questions, did not reproach me.

She just said, "We're going home."

8

THE DEADLY SOLUTION

WHEN WE ARRIVED BACK HOME, my father didn't say anything to me about my pregnancy, but he looked sad.

Years later, my sister said, "When Aunt Mildred called, and Mama told Daddy you were pregnant, he said, "Margaret can't come home. She made her bed, so she can lie in it. She'll have to go to a home for unwed mothers." After a heated argument, Mama said, 'if that's the case I'll leave for Detroit and not come back.' Then he relented and said you could come home."

I soon learned the Henderson's brought Pat home from the University and he was staying at their cabin at Lake Superior. Our cabin was about a quarter mile further down the lake. When we went to our cabin, I walked down the beach and went by his place, hoping Pat would come out and talk to me. He never did.

I tried telephoning him but his mother answered and said, "He's not here. Do *not* call again!"

I confided in my friends, Diane and Joyce, that I was pregnant and what had happened in Detroit. Although they were sympathetic, they didn't know what I should do, or how I could get in touch with Pat. Diane said, "He's such a jerk!"

Pat's best friend, Anthony, telephoned me. He said, "I'm playing in the city band and Pat's also in the band playing his trumpet. He told me you're pregnant and his parents forbid him to see you. It's hard to believe that Pat's acting the way he is. We're playing in the park on Saturday evening. I wanted to let you know."

I was so glad Anthony called me. I went to the park to hear the band concert. I'm sure Pat saw me but after the last song played, he left in a hurry.

In August, Anthony called again and told me Pat had returned to college. It upset me that Pat didn't try to get in touch with me while he was home. I felt I just had to go on without him.

A week after Pat left, I got a call from his mother. She wanted me to come to her house and talk. I was surprised and hoped they had relented and would let us get married. They lived on the same street as we did, about three blocks away. As I walked the tree lined street to their house, I believed it would turn out well after all.

When I arrived, Mrs. Henderson seemed nervous but smiled and asked how I was. In their living-room, she directed me to a chair and sat opposite me. Mrs. Henderson was a slim woman, average height with short brown hair. Not what I would call a pretty woman. She gave the appearance she was someone that liked to be in control.

She said, "Margaret, you and Pat are so young and he

has to get an education to succeed in life, so getting married is out of the question. However, I have a solution. We heard of a doctor in Ann Arbor that will perform an abortion. It's perfectly safe since you are only about two to three months pregnant. It's for the best. We will give you two thousand dollars if you will agree, and we'll pay all the expenses."

I looked at her, speechless. They were a Catholic family whose church believed abortion was a sin! Finding my voice, I said, "You want to kill a baby! Your grandchild! What kind of people are you! I will never take a penny from you. I'm keeping the baby and you will never see it."

As I was getting up to leave, she said, "You realize you will probably never get married because no one will want an unwed mother with a child."

I walked out and slammed the door.

In September, I got a letter from Pat. "In November, after my eighteenth birthday, I'll come and get you. It's legal to get married at eighteen. I'm back at Detroit University and flunked out of law. I couldn't concentrate worrying about our situation. I'm enrolled in music and hope to be a music teacher."

I was relieved when I read his letter. I'd always believed he would make things right and we would be together. I was right. My worries are gone.

I was five months pregnant in November. Pat's birthday came and went without a word from him. One evening, the door-bell rang. I went to the door and Pat stood in the doorway. I threw my arms around him and cried, "You came, you came."

He said, "We can drive over the border to Wisconsin

and get married. We can't get married here because my father's the prosecuting attorney and he'd find out when we went to the courthouse. We both need to have a copy of a blood test to get a marriage license."

My friend Diane worked at the clinic where I saw the doctor. I immediately called her and told her what was happening. "I need a copy of my blood work and Pat has to get a blood test," I said. "We have to keep it from his parents, so we need to do this right away. Is there a way you can help us out?"

"If Pat can be at the clinic before it opens tomorrow, I'll make arrangements for his blood work. It would have to be before seven."

Pat said, "I'll be there."

I showed him the sweaters, booties and hat I'd knit for the baby. Since I didn't know whether we were having a boy or girl, I'd made them in white. In those days there were no ultra-sounds, so the baby's sex would be a surprise. I felt disappointed when Pat didn't say anything when he saw the baby's things.

Before Pat went to sleep in the guest room, my father told him he would put him through college. "If I had a boy," he said, "I would have sent him to college, so I'll consider you the son I never had."

I was surprised, and pleased that Daddy offered to do that. I was happy that Pat could continue going to college and thankful for my dad's generosity.

In the morning, refusing breakfast, Pat said, "I'll see you in about an hour." Then he headed for the clinic.

I packed a small suitcase, put on my best maternity skirt and blouse, and sat in the rocking chair facing the front door, my suitcase beside me. As I sat there, I felt relief as well as anxiety, hoping once we were married, his parents would accept it. I wondered where we would live. Should I come home after we get married and Pat go back to the University? Maybe we should keep it a secret for now.

I thought, 'I wish last night we had discussed what we would do after we got married, but I was so overwhelmed with his sudden appearance I wasn't thinking.'

Eight o'clock in the morning came, nine, ten and no Pat. I thought, 'it must have taken more time to get the result of the blood test than we figured.'

I continued to sit in the rocking chair, waiting for him to come for me, only leaving for the many trips you have to take to the bathroom when you're pregnant. Eleven o'clock came and went. I refused to think he deserted me again. I believed he would come any minute.

The telephone rang. My mother answered and after speaking for a few minutes, hung up and phoned my father and told him to come home.

Turning to me, she said, "Diane called and said that Pat never showed up at the clinic." I stared at my mother in disbelief. I was *sure* he wouldn't leave me like he did before.

"Maybe he went to get something to eat," I said. "Maybe he went to see his friend Anthony to tell him what we're doing. I'm sure he wouldn't have come all this way from college and just leave without saying a word to me." After a few minutes, added, "It's winter, maybe his car slid off the road and he's hurt."

My dad, who'd come home, shook his head and sighed as he looked at my mother. "I'll drive around. It's not far to the clinic. I'll check everywhere and see if something has happened."

Several hours later, my dad returned. "He's nowhere. I checked all the roads, checked the hospital to see if they had any recent accident victims. He must have returned to school."

I remained sitting in the rocking chair waiting for Pat. I was sure he was going to come and rescue me.

At nine o'clock that night, my father said, "Margaret, get up out of that chair and go to bed. You must face it. He is *not* coming. He's gone."

Looking at my father and mother, I said, "I'm keeping this baby. I will not give it up for adoption. I'll work and support it." Picking up my suitcase, I walked up the stairs to my bedroom, closed the bedroom door and said to myself. "There is no knight in shining armor, like I dreamed about in fairytales. No-one will ever rescue me. I'll do this all by myself. I don't need anyone at all."

9

TOWN GOODNESS

In 1951 and 1952, having a baby out of wedlock was rare in Sault Ste. Marie, Michigan. In the Sault, as well as the rest of the United States, the pregnant girl was usually sent to a home for unwed mothers, or hidden away.

In our small town, everyone knew what was going on in other people's lives. Soon most of the town knew the story about Pat and me. The amazing thing was, the people rallied around me and turned against the Hendersons. It surprised me because Mr. Henderson was a well-known attorney, Mrs. Henderson operated an antique store and was a substitute teacher. They belonged to the country club and were well known in town. I was the disgraced unwed mother.

In November, shortly after Pat returned to the University, I received a call from a young man named George Mara, who'd played in the high school band with me. He invited me to come to his home for dinner one Sunday afternoon.

When I arrived, he and his wife greeted me warmly.

They let me know they cared and supported me. They had a wonderful roast pork dinner, and I couldn't get enough of the delicious food. Before that day, I was sick to my stomach most of the time, but after the dinner, I was never sick again. I'll never forget them and how they reached out to me.

A few days later, another unusual thing happened. The owner of the two movie theaters in town, Mr. De Paul, telephoned me. He told me his cashier, at his largest theater, was going to be gone for a month. He wondered if I would be interested in working while she was gone. He would pay me fifty cents an hour. That was high pay for a woman in the Upper Peninsula. I was surprised, because I was five months pregnant. In those days, employers didn't let a pregnant woman work after she started to show.

I was eager to make some money to pay my medical expenses. When I'd left my job at the flower shop without warning to go to Detroit, that job ended, so I accepted the cashier job. I thought, 'more people will probably come to look at me than the movie.' My parents never said a word about my working at the "Devil's Playhouse".

After the month ended, Mr. De Paul asked me if I would work in the office, copying items from a ledger into a card file. I worked until a week before the baby was born. I later learned it was a made-up job he didn't need me to do, but Mr. De Paul and his wife wanted to help out.

I was expecting the baby March 3rd. My parents supplied a used bassinet and I decorated it with white eyelet lace, reaching to the floor. I had cloth diapers, baby clothes and several blankets, gifts from town people I didn't even know. No-one in my father's church reached out to me.

On the first of February, a woman telephoned and identified herself as a registered nurse. She asked if she could come to our house that evening to talk to me about my delivery. I told her that was fine, thinking the doctor must have sent her, and I was finally going to find out what to expect. When I previously had asked my elderly doctor how you had a baby, he said, "You will go into labor, go to the hospital and the nurses will monitor how far along you are. Then, when the time is right, you will be taken into the delivery room and I will assist you."

Not knowing the female anatomy, or having had classes in school about it, and no discussions at home, it still wasn't clear to me exactly what was going to happen. All I knew was my stomach was getting huge while the rest of me was thin. I wondered how on earth you get the baby out of there. I was too shy to ask the doctor any more questions.

When the nurse arrived, she introduced herself to my mother and me. Her name was Rose and she was an attractive, outgoing woman in her thirties. She said, "I'd like to be your private nurse when you go into labor. I talked to the hospital and they agreed. If I'm working when it's your time, they will have someone cover for me and I can be of service to you."

"Thank you so much but I can't afford it," I said.

"Oh no, I don't expect you to pay me, I just want to do it for you. Since no-one can be in the labor room with you, like your mother, I thought it would be easier for you to have someone with you all the time, right through delivery. A friend of mine, Nancy Evans, who lives in the block behind you, told me about your situation and I wanted to give you all the help I could."

I was overwhelmed. My mother said to her, "You are such a kind, thoughtful person. It would be wonderful if you can do that for Margaret. Since no-one is allowed in the labor or delivery room but medical staff, it will relieve my mind."

Rose gave us her home telephone number and said, "Call me as soon as labor starts and I will take over from there. If no-one answers my phone, call the hospital because I'll be at work."

I thanked her for helping me, and for the first time I felt a little less frightened.

On the 21st of February, early evening, I had a sharp pain that made me cry out. My mother came running, and said, "It's ten days early, but you might be going into labor." Not long after, another pain racked me. Picking up the telephone she called the registered nurse.

Rose said, "Bring Margaret to the hospital, I'll be waiting for her."

My father drove us. The pain was terrific and it terrorized me. When we arrived at the hospital, Rose was waiting for us. My father left to return home, and my mother said, "You're in good hands and I'll be in the maternity waiting room."

"Can't you come with me?" I pleaded.

"No. You'll be alright. Rose will take care of you."

Putting me in a wheelchair, Rose wheeled me to the private room she had arranged on the maternity floor. I put on a hospital gown; she helped get me into bed, then examined me. At first, I was embarrassed, but the pain soon made me not care.

"The first thing I have to do is shave you, then give you a mild enema."

I was shocked! Horrified, I said, "Why would you do such a thing!"

"We do that to all maternity patients. It's necessary," she said.

Soon the word got around town that I was in labor and in the hospital. My former high school home-room and math teacher, Miss Joslin, came to the hospital and stayed with my mother in the maternity waiting room the entire time I was in labor.

I don't know what I would have done without Rose. She encouraged me, talked me out of jumping out the window, and after many hours of intense pain, she wheeled me into the delivery room.

My baby girl was born in the afternoon on February twenty-second. I named her Diane Grace. Diane, after my best friend, Diane Tucker Dobbins. My sister Virginia's middle name was Grace.

About four hours after delivery, I heard a rustling sound coming down the hall. Into my room came a nurse carrying my baby in a brown paper bag, like they have in a grocery store. She told me not to take the baby out of the bag for cleanliness. As soon as she left the room, I took her out to see the rest of her. She was a pretty baby with blue eyes. What little hair she had was blonde. She weighed over seven pounds.

The doctor told me it was healthiest to bottle-feed the baby, so they bound by breasts tightly to try to keep the milk from flowing. I could hardly breath. When the milk came in, my breasts hurt so much I could hardly lift my arms.

The binding lasted for several months. In those days, most mothers bottle-fed their babies.

As soon as she was allowed, Miss Joslin came to see me with a bouquet of flowers and a beautiful poem for Diane.

I was in the hospital for seven days. It was the usual length of time you stayed after you had a baby. They kept you in bed most of the time.

When the doctor came to examine me before he released me, he said, "You aren't built to have children. Your pelvic area is very narrow, that's why you were in hard labor for so long and have so many stitches." He handed me instructions on how to take care of the stitches, which were extremely painful. I felt like I'd been shot with a cannon ball. He gave me formula instructions for the milk, and the hospital gave me several bottles of formula to take home.

When my father and mother came to get me, Daddy immediately fell in love with Diane. He carried her out of the hospital and said, "What a pretty little girl."

When I got in the back seat of the car, he handed Diane to me. No seat belts or child seats in those days.

When we arrived home, my mother said, "I think you need to change Diane's diapers, and I'll heat up a bottle of formula for her."

Never having changed a baby before, I found putting a diaper on a squirming baby more difficult than when I put a diaper on my "Betsy-Wetsy" doll as a child. On my first attempt, afraid of sticking her with the safety pins, the diaper was too loose. When I picked her up, the diaper slid down to her ankles. The next time I tried was a success. Putting plastic pants over the cloth diaper, and swaddling her in a receiving blanket, I made her ready for the bottle.

I sat on a soft pillow in the rocking chair with Diane as I fed her the formula. After she drank most of it, my mother showed me how to burp her. She immediately fell asleep. Even though the pain from the stitches was terrific, I remained sitting with her. As I rocked her, looking into her sleeping face, I thought, 'everything I went through was worth it, just for this moment.'

Rose came to the house to check on me several times and made sure my stitches were healing. I told her I didn't know which was worse, the birth or the pain from the stitches.

Even though I was reluctant to leave Diane, three months later, when I could finally sit comfortably, I took a job with the Bell Telephone Company as a "Number Please" telephone operator.

10

SINK OR SWIM

DURING THE TIME I worked at the Bell Telephone Company, I had to walk past Pat's home. I couldn't help but glance at his house to see if he was home from college. I wondered why he didn't care for his baby or me when we'd been so close in High School. He'd promised we'd get married after he made me pregnant, and it hurt to think now he didn't care at all.

All summer, when I returned home from work, I put Diane in her baby-buggy to take her for a walk, and since we lived on the same street as Pat, I went by his house again. I began to realize something had to change, that I couldn't go on this way.

My decision to leave Sault Ste Marie, my friends and family, was a painful decision. I knew I had to leave for my daughter's sake as well as mine. I couldn't continue to wonder where he was, or why he'd left me to face things alone. I didn't want Diane to grow up in the Sault without a father and the town's knowledge of my situation.

I had to go far away, so far, I could never go home again.

My choice to move to Phoenix, Arizona, was mainly because of my sister and Uncle Ray.

My sister, Virginia, was an avid reader, and she loved the Zane Grey western novels about the Wild West. The setting was Arizona. During her entire senior year in high school she talked about how exciting it would be to live in Arizona. Virginia and her best friend Gladys, decided they would go to Phoenix when they graduated. However, Gladys married her high school sweetheart right after graduation, so my sister didn't go.

Uncle Ray, my mother's brother, had been living in Phoenix for 10 years. He and Aunt Stella, moved there because Uncle Ray had a lung condition, and Phoenix was known as the best place to recover. I had a special regard for him ever since he told me about Santa Claus when I was three years old and changed the way we celebrated Christmas.

Just because Uncle Ray was in Phoenix, I didn't expect him to be burdened with my daughter and me. I had to find a place on my own, but knowing he was there would ease my mind that someone I knew was nearby.

Since May, when I started to work at Bell Telephone, I saved my money as much as I could. In December, I researched how to move from Sault Ste. Marie to Phoenix. I thought the best time to go would be in March when Diane would be a year old. The Greyhound Bus would be too long a trip with a year-old baby, so the only other option was to fly, but there wasn't an airport in the Sault. A friend at work told me her father flew TWA on business out of

Detroit. When I called TWA, the only flight they had, non-stop to Phoenix, was out of Chicago. I would have to take the Greyhound Bus to Chicago.

In January, I decided to tell my parents my plan. I knew I couldn't expect any financial support from them if I moved away, because I was brought up with the saying, "if you make your bed you lie in it," though they provided for me while I was at home. My mother took care of Diane while I worked, and they didn't ask for any rent. I paid for the necessary things for my baby, like doctor visits for her inoculations. The formula was cheap to make and there were very few expenses. I spent nothing on myself so I could save my money.

One evening, after dinner, I told my parents of my plan to go to Phoenix to live.

"I think that would be a good idea," my mother said. "Your Uncle Ray lives there. It would be a new start for you."

My father never said anything or asked any questions.

That night, I wrote to Uncle Ray and explained why I wanted to move to Phoenix. I asked him if he would send me the Phoenix Sunday paper, because I wanted to look at the ads to find a place to live and see what jobs were available. I told him about my plan to fly TWA out of Chicago in March. I explained that I didn't expect him to be responsible for Diane and me. I'd make it on my own.

He immediately wrote back and told me not to come: "I will not help you. It's very hot in Phoenix and you'll not like it. I haven't room for you to stay here. How can you afford to live by yourself with a baby? I'm not working. Stella works at a restaurant and we don't have a car. It's a bad idea, so stay where you are."

His letter surprised and disappointed me. I don't know what I expected but that wasn't it. I wondered why he wouldn't be glad to see me after all these years. He could have at least sent me the paper. I realized I couldn't rely on anyone but myself. I never showed my mother the letter because I didn't want her to be disappointed in her brother.

I was determined not to be discouraged and made up my mind to go ahead with my plans. Picking up the phone, I told the telephone operator I needed to call the newspaper in Phoenix, Arizona. She connected me and I asked them to send me the Sunday paper. When it arrived, I found a small house for rent for forty dollars a month, furnished and utilities included.

After much thought, I called the number in the ad and the landlord answered. I knew I'd have to make up a story about why I was moving and about myself. "Hi," I said, "My name is Margaret Gordon, I live in Sault Ste. Marie, Michigan and plan to move to Phoenix in March. I have the Phoenix Sunday newspaper and saw your ad. I'm nineteen, almost twenty, and I have a year-old baby. I'm a widow. My husband was killed in an auto accident. My uncle lives in Phoenix and I'm flying there to work for him. I would very much like to rent the house."

He said, "Send me the first month rent by Western Union. Let me know the date and time you will arrive and I'll meet you at the house."

"My uncle is unable to pick me up at the airport. Is there a bus I can take from there?"

"Let me know the date, time, airline and flight number. I'll pick you up at the airport."

I called TWA and made a reservation for March seventh. The flight cost sixty-nine dollars which I'd pay when I arrived at O'Hare airport. I sent the rent by Western Union, gave notice to Bell Telephone, called the landlord and gave him the flight information. He told me he would supply linens, kitchen ware and would look for some kind of bed for my child.

When it came time for me to go, I choked down tears, as I said goodbye to my family and friends. I tried not to show my anxiety about the future, knowing I could never afford to go back home again. I would either sink or swim.

My mom and dad drove me to the bus station with my baby and three small suitcases. My mother told me that when I got settled she would send a box, with a few more things if I needed them. The Greyhound driver said I could get a taxi to the airport from the bus station, so not to worry about handling the luggage with a baby.

Arriving at O'Hare airport, it took me a while to find out where to go to get the flight. There were no jet planes. I was flying on what they called a prop plane. I had never been on a plane before, and I was terrified. When it was time to board the plane, I climbed up something that looked like a stepladder to get into the plane. There were two seats in each row, on both sides of the airplane. The flight attendants were young beautiful women in pretty uniforms with very short skirts, high heels and a little hat. I had to hold Diane on my lap for the six-hour flight.

As the plane revved up for takeoff, the sound was loud and the plane shook. I thought it was going to fall apart. I tried not to show my fear because I didn't want to upset

Diane. Fortunately, she was a very good baby and seldom cried. We were served a meal and snacks. I was glad no-one smoked around us, although by the time we got to Phoenix the plane was blue with smoke. The lady sitting next to me thought Diane was the best little girl and helped entertain her. The flight attendant came by often and took her for little walks.

I arrived in Phoenix, at the age of nineteen, with my one-year old daughter, Diane, and fifty dollars in my pocket.

The landlord was waiting, holding a sign with my name on it. He was a tall, middle-aged man, with blonde short hair. When we arrived at the house on Roosevelt and Tenth street, it was a shock. I tried not to show how alarmed and disappointed I was. It was a tiny white shack in the poor, mostly black, section of town. Going in the only door, I found it was one large room and a small bathroom with a tub, sink and toilet.

On the floor of the little house, the linoleum was so worn you could hardly see the pattern, which was pretty awful anyway. On one end of the room was a sink with a garbage can under it, small refrigerator, tiny electric stove with a little cupboard above. It held two each of plates, bowls, cups and glasses and two each of silverware. Inside the oven was one pot and a frying pan. Across a corner of the room was a short wire-line with hangers for clothes. There were two windows with curtains, one in the living area and a torn one over the sink. A gas heater was in the wall and a swamp cooler on the roof. I'd never heard of a swamp cooler.

The furniture consisted of a single bed, small table with

two chairs, and a worn overstuffed green chair. The landlord, Mr. Woods, had found a crib for Diane that he'd placed against the bed.

After Mr. Woods showed me how to work everything, he offered to drive me to the grocery store, about a block away. I gratefully accepted. I bought a quart of milk for twenty cents, a loaf of bread for twelve cents, peanut butter at twenty-nine cents, a can of Franco American Spaghetti for ten cents, dry cereal, animal crackers and a pail for Diane's soiled cloth diapers. The total came to two dollars and ten cents. I had forty-seven dollars and ninety cents left. I thought, 'that should hold us until I get a job. I'll just drink water and leave the milk for Diane. I have to get a job, I just have to!'

The three suitcases fit nicely under the bed. One suitcase held Diane's cloth diapers, clothes and a few toys. The second suitcase held my clothes and hygiene items. The third held a small alarm clock, two wash clothes, two towels, Diane's blanket, a tiny picture of a little girl that was on the wall of my bedroom as long as I remembered, my high school year book, my first doll, my favorite book as a child, "Little Women," and a picture of my family and our dog, Blondie.

After putting the groceries away, and hanging up my few clothes, we went to bed.

As I laid in bed, I thought about the day: saying good bye to my parents and leaving my friends, I felt lonely and sad, I wondered if I'd made the wrong decision to leave, even though I knew in my heart I had to do it. I thought of my first plane ride, my surprise that it didn't break apart and fall out of the sky and the poor little shack we lived in.

On the positive side, the place was clean. The landlord, Mr. Woods, was nice and helpful. *Tomorrow* I *will find* a *job. We will be ok.* I *don't need anyone.*

11

COCKROACHES AND NEIGHBORS

I SUDDENLY WOKE to a rattling sound. I heard a giggle and turned to see Diane, standing in her crib, shaking the side and looking at me.

Morning had come. I could see the sun shining through the tear in the curtain. As I lay there, I looked around the room. My eyes caught a movement on the sink. There was a huge black bug crawling across it, the most gigantic, hideous bug I'd ever seen! It had six legs and antennas on its head. I'd never seen anything like it before. Was it poisonous? Did it bite?

I panicked! Grabbing Diane out of her crib, I ran out the door. Across the street, an elderly man was walking down his driveway to pick up the newspaper.

"*Please* help me," I cried. "There's an enormous bug in my house. I don't know what it is. I'm afraid it's poisonous and will bite. Can you help me?"

As he walked over to me, I was embarrassed to be in

my pajamas and bare feet holding Diane.

He said, "I'll see what I can do. Where is it?"

"It's on or near the sink, which is to your right when you go in the door."

I stood outside the open door and watched, too afraid to go in. With several swats of his newspaper, he killed the bug.

"It's a sewer roach," he said. "They're not poisonous and won't bite. You need to keep all your drains covered so they can't come up. You've never seen a cockroach before?"

"No, the only bugs I've seen in Upper Michigan are mosquitoes big enough to carry you off. Thank you so much for coming to my rescue. I just moved in last night. I'm Margaret Gordon, and this is my daughter Diane."

"Tom Whiting. I'm glad I could help."

"Is the downtown area of Phoenix far from here?" I asked. "Can you tell me how to get there? I'm looking for a job and someone to watch Diane while I look."

Tom said, "When you get settled this morning, why don't you come over and meet my wife Anna? I'll tell you how to get to town, and we can see about that cute little girl of yours."

After I changed Diane, gave her breakfast, put on a skirt and blouse, looked in the mirror, fluffed my hair, put on lipstick and then we went across the street to the Whitings. They lived in an old, large, stone house with a big porch across the front. I thought, 'their lawn must be dead because it's all brown.' In Michigan, you didn't see dead lawns. Everything is green as soon as the snow melts.

Answering the door, Anna, a tiny woman, introduced

herself and invited us in. She had brought out toys they had for their grandchildren, and taking Diane's hand, sat down with her to play.

Tom had on cowboy boots, jeans, plaid shirt, and a cowboy hat on his balding light brown hair. I asked him, "Are you a cowboy?" I'd never seen a cowboy before except in the movies and had been hoping to see one.

He laughed and said, "No, I was a plumber before I retired."

I said, "Where is the desert? I thought Arizona was all desert. Is it far from here?"

"You're on it," he said.

"If I'm on it, where are the sand dunes?"

"Phoenix isn't that kind of desert. Yuma has the sand dunes."

Anna spoke up, "Tom told me you wanted to look for a job today. Why don't you leave Diane here with us while you look? We don't have anything planned. We'll give her lunch, so you can take your time looking."

Tom said, "Downtown is on Central Avenue, go ten blocks straight down this street and you'll run into it. There's a bus stop at the corner and it will go to Central. It costs ten cents to ride the bus."

I knew I couldn't afford the ten cents, so I'd have to walk. Diane was having a great time playing with the toys and seemed content. I thanked them for keeping Diane, said goodbye, promising I'd be back soon.

As I walked the ten blocks, many things came to my mind. I thought, 'I'm so lucky I met the couple across the street. If it wasn't for that cockroach I probably wouldn't have. I'll have to write to Mama and tell her about the beautiful weather. Phoenix is so warm, the sun bright, without a cloud in the blue sky. I left in freezing weather with wind and snow. I hope I never see snow again. I have to get a job, I don't care what it is. I'm not skilled at anything. I wonder how much they pay women in Phoenix. I hope it's more than the thirty-five cents an hour I started with at Bell Telephone. I need soap for Diane's diapers, and it will cost to have someone look after her. I wonder if the Whittings would do it?'

When I came to Central and turned onto the street, the first building I came to was a bank. It was a large brick building, the Farmers and Stockman Bank. In the window was a sign that said, "Applications and interviews for the bookkeeping position will be held today between ten-am and two-pm."

As I stared at the sign, I thought, 'I didn't like math, and I've never done any bookkeeping before, but if someone else can do it, why can't I?'

I went in, stopped at the first desk I came to, and said, "I'm here to apply for the bookkeeping position."

She said, "Fill out this application form and take a seat, the manager will be with you in a few minutes."

As I filled out the form, I knew I'd have to lie to get the job. I just had to do it.

After a short time, the manager called me in. A pleasant looking man. His dark, straight hair was slicked back. Dressed in a suit, I wondered why he would wear it when Phoenix was so hot. Looking over the form, he asked, "Where were you employed as a bookkeeper?"

"At the First Federal Bank in Sault Ste. Marie, Michigan. I really enjoyed it. I just moved to Phoenix yesterday and I'm anxious to go to work."

Glancing at the application he said, "You are a young widow with a child? Why did you decide to come to Phoenix?"

"My husband was killed in an automobile accident during a snow storm. I can't take the snow and cold in Michigan anymore. My uncle lives in Phoenix. He thought I needed a change and warmer weather."

"I know what you mean about the snow and cold. I'm from Wisconsin. When this job opened up I was happy to get away from the cold weather." Glancing again at the application, he added, "Did you work with the Burroughs Bookkeeping Machine at the First Federal Bank?"

"Yes, I did," I lied. "It's quite a machine."

"I need someone right away. Fortunately, you know how to use the Burroughs Machine. The position pays fifty cents an hour, and we provide health insurance. After three months, the pay increases to fifty-five cents an hour after a performance review. You'll work from eight to five with a half-hour lunch. Would you be able to start tomorrow?"

"Yes, I can do that."

We talked about the weather in Wisconsin and Michigan. I had a feeling that was the bond that landed me the job, or maybe it was because I said I knew how to use that machine.

Walking home, I was beginning to panic. I thought, 'What is a Burroughs Bookkeeping Machine? How am I going to figure it out? Will it be hard to do? What will happen if I can't figure it out? I guess all they can do is fire me. I can't let that happen. I need the job.'

When I arrived back at the Whiting's home, Diane was glad to see me, showing me a stuffed dog she was playing with. "Was she any trouble?" I asked.

"She was no trouble at all," Anna said. "Diane is such a happy, easy-to-care-for little girl."

The Whitings were surprised that I found a job so quickly. I told them where I was going to work, about the job, leaving out the part that I didn't have any idea how to do it.

I asked them if they would be interested in taking care of Diane while I was at work.

Anna said, "We did talk about it, and we would be willing to take care of her. It will give me a little extra spending money. Don't worry about giving Diane breakfast or lunch, she can have what we have. You will have to leave early for work, so that will make it easier for you."

"How much will you charge?" I asked.

"Do you think five dollars a week will be too much?"

Very relieved, I said, "No, five dollars will be fine."

That night I sat at the little table and tried to figure out my money situation. I would make four dollars a day, twenty a week, so that would be eighty dollars a month, less what they take out for taxes. I will have to pay forty for rent, twenty for Diane's care. That will leave me less than twenty a month for food and everything else. I still have the forty-seven dollars and ninety cents. I have to be careful not to spend it and keep it for emergencies.

I thought, 'I'll have to wash our clothes and Diane's diapers in the bathtub and hang them outside. I can't afford a laundromat. Rain or shine, I'll have to walk to work.'

I'll work it out. I *will do it.*

12

THE DREADED BURROUGHS

BEFORE GOING TO BED, I set my alarm clock for five am. I didn't know how long it was going to take to get Diane ready to go to the Whitings and walk ten blocks to work. I didn't want to be late on my first day at the bank.

I hoped Diane could adjust to Anna taking care of her instead of my mother. I thought, 'Diane seemed happy with Anna while I was looking for a job. The Whitings seem like a nice couple. Their place is clean and homey. I'm lucky Diane's easy to take care of, quiet and entertains herself. She shouldn't be any problem for them. I'll try not to worry about it. I have to work, I don't have a choice, I have to leave her.'

As I walked to the Farmers and Stockman Bank, I tried to hold down the panic I felt at starting a job I knew nothing about. Would I be able to figure out that dreaded Burroughs Machine? How hard would it be? I told myself, 'if others are able to do it, you can too, so stop worrying about it. Just do it.'

When I arrived at the bank, the receptionist introduced me to the other bank employees and showed me around the different departments. It was a large bank. In 1953, if you had any banking to do, you had to go inside the bank to do it.

She took me to the desk where I would be working, and my heart sank. On the desk was a very large machine. It had many rows of keys with numbers and symbols on them. I had no idea what the symbols meant. Across the top, was a roll bar to hold two ledger pages. Next to the bar was a large roll of tape. On the left side of the desk was a bin that held many ledger files, and next to it was a long tray with checks. On the right side was a tray of signature cards.

I stood staring at the desk taking keep breaths as I struggled to hold back my tears. I felt overcome. Someone came up behind me. Turning, I saw it was the manager.

Seeing my bewildered face, he said, "By your look, I bet you must have worked with the older Burroughs. This model came out just this year."

"This doesn't look the same at all. I must have worked with the older model," I said.

Going to the desk next to me, he said, "Betty, come and sit with Margaret today. She worked with the older Burroughs. You'll need to show her how the newest model works."

I let out a sigh of relief. Some of the panic I was feeling, lifted. I couldn't believe how lucky I was that he came by, just at the right moment.

Betty Kemp was my age, nineteen, pretty, with brown hair and kind brown eyes. She was a bookkeeper and patiently showed me what to do. It was as hard as I imagined it would be. I took down notes, so I could study them when I got home. By the end of the day, Betty and I were good friends.

Everything went fine on Diane's first day with the Whitings. When we got home, I heated Franco American Spaghetti for dinner, and afterward we played for a while. Giving her a tub-bath, some of my tension of the day lifted. I read one of Diane's little books to her. Then, after putting her to bed, I memorized all my notes. Just before falling asleep, I felt hope that I'd be able to work the machine and do the bookkeeping job.

As summer came, the heat was unbearable. What a contrast it was to the summer temperature in Michigan's Upper Peninsula! I was surprised that the nights didn't cool off and was glad the landlord showed me how to work the swamp cooler, but most of the time it felt either too cold or too warm in the little house. It surprised me that on rainy days, there was no relief from the heat, and the swamp cooler didn't seem to work at all. In Michigan, when it rained it cooled off.

One morning, when I brought Diane to the Whitings, they told me it was 110 degrees outside. It would go higher during the day. As I walked the ten blocks to work, one of my leather sandals began to flop. The thin leather in the sole had separated because of the hot cement on the sidewalk. I had to drag my foot so I wouldn't trip or lose the sole of the shoe and burn my foot. Embarrassed, I hoped no-one would notice me, and when I got to work, I put rubber bands around the shoe to hold it together.

Every day, Betty's father dropped her off at the bank on his way to work. When Betty saw my sandal with rubber bands on it, she insisted they drive me home. I was embarrassed about having them see where I lived, although Betty must have known how poor I was, because I wore the same few things over and over and only ate a peanut butter sandwich for lunch.

When Mr. Kemp drove me home, pulling up in front of my house, he said, "We'll drive you home every day. It'll be no problem. You shouldn't walk this far in temperatures over a hundred degrees. You could have a heat stroke."

My job at the bank was going well. After my three-month performance review, I got my five-cents an hour increase. The extra five-cents meant on Sunday I could take Diane, once a month, on the bus to Encanto Park. It was a large, pretty park with a lake in the center, walking trails and a golf course. We brought a piece of bread, so Diane could throw little pieces to the ducks on the lake. When they all came quacking, I was surprised she wasn't afraid of them. I had to watch her carefully so she didn't end up in the lake with the ducks. Afterward we would sit on a park bench and eat our peanut butter sandwiches before taking the bus home.

When the first of September came, I was surprised it was still hot. Upper Michigan could have snow in September. I wondered if it would ever get cool in Phoenix. 'However,' I thought, 'I'd much rather have heat than snow.'

***

For several months I'd been having severe problems with my monthly period. I had extreme pain and heavy flow. Betty sensed something was wrong. After telling her what it was, she told me I should see a doctor.

"I can't afford to, maybe it will pass," I said. "I've always had trouble with severe pain, even before I was pregnant. Maybe you just flow more after having a baby."

"You have insurance," she said. "Usually you can make arrangements for installment payments on the balance the insurance doesn't pay. You won't have to pay it all at once."

The next month it was worse. Betty gave me the name of a gynecologist, Dr. Donald Lee, who she said was the best doctor for females in Phoenix.

"You really need to see him," she said. "I'm telling you as your friend, go!"

I called for an appointment and was scheduled for Thursday the following week.

Dr. Lee was a handsome man, in his early thirties. His manner was all business. After I explained my problem, and he examined me, he said, "You need to have a D & C. It will require a four to five-day hospital stay. I want to schedule you for surgery next Monday morning at St. Joseph's Hospital." He explained what a D & C was, what he would do and why I had to stay in the hospital.

"*No*," I said. "I have to work. I have a baby under two-years old to take care of. She only has me. There's no-one else. Can't you just give me some medicine?"

"I'm afraid not," he said. "It's not a question of whether to do it or not. It's something that has to be done. You're in danger of hemorrhaging, which can be life threatening. The need to have this type of surgery sometimes happens after you have a baby."

I stared at him speechless. I couldn't think of what to do.

"This will correct the problem you're having," Dr. Lee said. "If you have a child, you need to stay healthy. This won't just go away. The nurse will be in shortly to give you your pre-surgery instructions. I will see you Monday at St. Joseph's." Turning, he walked out the door

When I arrived back at work, I told Betty, "The doctor wants to operate. He said I needed a D & C and has scheduled me for surgery on Monday. I don't know whether to call him and cancel it."

"Margaret, you have to do it," she said. "Tell the bank manager what has happened and you need to take a couple of weeks off. The insurance should cover most of it. You need to get better."

"What if I die," I said. "What will become of Diane? I don't have any life insurance. She will have nothing. What will happen to her? We're all alone here."

"You shouldn't worry about dying. I told you, Dr Lee is the best women's doctor in Phoenix. You'll be okay. Just do it."

"I guess I really don't have a choice," I said. "At least I have three days to prepare. Honestly, Betty, I'm terrified. When I was nine, I almost died when my appendix ruptured and I had to stay in the hospital a long time. My mother isn't here. I'm all alone."

That evening, there was a knock on the door. Betty, her mother and father, stood in the doorway.

Her mother said, "Betty told us what's happened. We'd like to take care of Diane while you're in the hospital. After you're released, we insist you come to our house until you can go back to work. Friday, when Al drives you home, he'll collect your things. You can stay with us this weekend, and we'll drive you to the hospital on Monday."

I couldn't believe how kind they were. I felt grateful and relieved.

The Kemps were an outgoing family, Roseanne, the mother, blonde, a little plump, loved to entertain. The dad, Al, dark-haired, tall, a good sense of humor, worked as a mechanic at the Harley Davidson Motorcycle Shop. Kip, Betty's seventeen-year old brother, tall and dark-haired like his father, went to high school and had a motorcycle. In the evenings, he loved to ride down Central Avenue with his motorcycle friends.

Four days after the surgery, the Kemps brought me back to their home. A few days later, when we sat down to dinner, I said, "I should go back to work Monday. I'm going to have to pay the doctor and hospital the balance after the insurance makes their payment, so I can't afford to be off work any longer."

Mr. Kemp smiled and said, "We'd like you and Diane to stay with us. We're all attached to Diane, she's no problem at all. It will make life easier for you if you stay here. You'll have transportation to and from work, Diane will be taken care of, and we'd love to have you. If you can pay us sixty dollars a month, I think that will cover any additional costs and give my wife more money to spend on things she can't live without. You and Diane can continue bunking in Betty's room. I promise we'll feed you more than peanut butter sandwiches."

I was surprised at their generous offer, and I gratefully accepted. My rent was paid to the end of the month, so I would have a few days to collect the rest of my things and let Mr. Woods and the Whitings know I was leaving. I had been living in the little house for seven months.

The decision to live with this wonderful, kind family, would affect my entire future—and bring me fear and terror for the next twenty-three years.

13

JOE

HALLOWEEN WAS APPROACHING, and the Kemps planned a have a party. Neighbors were invited as well as Kip's friends and Betty's boy-friend. As guests arrived, I was introduced to three of his motorcycle riding buddies who were in the Air Force stationed at Luke Air Force base. One was Joe Valenta. Joe was twenty-three years old, three years older than me, average height, slim, very nice looking, with beautiful, large, brown eyes and black hair. He was friendly in a quiet way. Joe took a liking to Diane and showed her how to bob for apples. Holding her above the tub, she tried her best, but her mouth was too small to grab an apple. After Joe gave her one, she followed him around the rest of the evening.

As the party ended, Joe said to me, "Would you like to go to dinner on Saturday? There's an Italian restaurant I like to go to."

"I'd love to," I said.

"You'll have to ride on the back of my motorcycle."

"I never rode on one before, but it should be fun."

On Saturday, Joe came early to pick me up. He brought Diane a ball, and they tossed it back and forth for a while. As Joe and I rode to the restaurant, I thought, 'this is exciting.' Suddenly, a huge bug hit me right in the eye! By the time we got to the restaurant my eye was shut. It was swollen, running, and turning black. I went into the restroom to hold cold water on my eye but it didn't help. As we ate dinner, I must have been a sight.

Joe said, "Too bad I didn't have an extra pair of goggles for you to wear. When you're in a car, bugs smash on the windshield and make a mess. That what happens sometimes on a cycle too. My reflex was to duck and it hit you instead of me. Sorry about that."

First dates don't work out for me. My only other first date was with Pat, and that didn't work out well either. I should have paid attention.

During the fall and winter, Joe and I continued to see each other.

Joe told me about himself. He was from a small town, Crete, Nebraska. He was the oldest of six boys and two girls. The grandparents immigrated from Czechoslovakia. He was Catholic and went to a Catholic school, which had all grades in one-room. When he was in the third grade, the nuns struck his knuckles with a ruler when he answered sixth grade questions, telling him to pay attention to the third grade and not the other grades.

Joe was completely deaf in one ear. His mother told me—when she visited several years later—that when Joe was two, he had an earache, and cried all night. Finally, she got so angry when he wouldn't stop crying, she struck him in his ear, causing the infection to go into the bone which never healed. The entire inside of his ear had to be removed. The infection in the bone drains from his ear to this day.

The family was very poor. His mother made most of their clothes from articles given to her from the Catholic charities. Joe made toys for his five brothers, two sisters, and himself, from pieces of wood, and anything he could find. When a neighbor's kid would get into trouble, his mother made Joe go to a tree in their yard and cut a switch. She then switched Joe and his brothers so they would never do what the neighbor's kid did. He couldn't play with other children, except his siblings, and in the summer worked at his Uncle Joe's dairy farm.

On my twenty-second birthday, Joe asked me to marry him. I told him the real story about Diane, and he said, "That's in the past, I would still like to marry you and adopt Diane."

Relieved, I told him I'd love to get married and it would be wonderful if he'd adopt her. We set our wedding date for Saturday, May seventh, 1955. He gave me a tiny diamond engagement ring that I thought was beautiful.

"I'm Catholic," he said, "so you'll have to go to instruction and bring our children up Catholic."

"That's fine," I replied. "I don't mind going to instruction, bringing the kids up Catholic, but I don't want to join *any* church."

I immediately wrote to my parents. I told them about Joe, and our plans to get married on May seventh. I wrote: Joe doesn't drink, never uses foul language and will make the best father in the world. He always includes Diane on our dates, gives her little rides on his motorcycle and she loves it. I was surprised the loud noise of the cycle didn't frighten her.

They sent a letter, telling me they were coming to the wedding, were going to drive, and planned to arrive on May fifth. They were going to stay with Uncle Ray, who I now saw occasionally, after my mother told him I was in Phoenix and where I was staying.

Joe wrote to his parents. When he told them, he was marrying a woman with a two-year old child, he never told me what they said. They weren't going to come to the wedding, but his brother planned to come. I took it for granted that his parents weren't able to make the trip.

Joe was discharged from the Air Force in April. He traded his motorcycle in on a used car and found a job at Reynolds Aluminum Company as a janitor.

I went to the church for instructions, and because I didn't join the church, we were to be married in the rectory.

We found a small, older, furnished house to rent, not far from the Kemps. It had two small bedrooms, full bath, small living room and large kitchen. A wringer washer and stationary tub were outside on the patio, and clothes-lines stretched across the fenced backyard. It had an uncovered driveway with a large shed at the end. Joe was glad there was a shed so he could have a place to build model airplanes.

When my parents arrived, Diane and I were excited to see them. I introduced them to the Kemps, and when Joe came after work, he greeted them warmly. They brought many gifts from family and friends. We spent the evening catching up on things and telling them about our plans for the wedding. Betty, and Joe's brother, Don, were going to stand up for us. I showed Mama my strapless, white wedding gown I bought at Korrick's department store on sale. It was full skirted and came just above the ankles. The veil came to my waist. My dad was going to give me away.

The day before the wedding, Joe's Air Force friend, Ed, came to the Kemps and said he wanted to talk to me alone. I wondered what he wanted. We went outside and sat on the patio.

He said, "Margaret, I don't know how to say this, I've been wrestling with it for some time. What I need to tell you is, you shouldn't marry Joe. He has a violent temper. At times he's completely out of control. When Joe, myself and another Air Force guy went on a motorcycle trip, Joe became so angry at something that was going on with his cycle, he put all of our lives in danger."

I was shocked!

"What are you talking about," I said. "I've never seen a sign of a temper, and I've been going with him for quite a while."

"If things don't go Joe's way he becomes enraged," he said. "I've never seen anyone get as angry as he does. When he drinks his temper is worse."

"I don't believe you," I said. "I know Joe, and he's nothing like you described. He never drinks alcohol when he's with me."

"Well, I had to say something. I had to warn you. I'm sorry I didn't say something sooner." As he got up and started to walk away, he turned toward me and said, "Good luck, you're going to need it."

I immediately told the Kemps what Ed said. They were surprised, and Al said, "Joe never shows signs of being angry around us. He's always polite and mild mannered. Maybe Ed was jealous or angry at Joe and wanted to get back at him."

"Joe never drinks, never raises his voice or gets angry," I said. "He plays with Diane and plans things we do to include her. I think he'll make a wonderful father. He even wants to adopt her. I don't know why Ed said those things, but I have to go by what I know."

Our small wedding went ahead as planned. However, the Priest who married us was drunk. He staggered and slurred his words. Afterward, we all went to the Italian restaurant where we'd gone on our first date. Then Joe, Diane and I left for our little house. I was happy I found someone that would make a wonderful father for Diane. I looked forward to our future together.

On Monday, when I got home from work, I went to the mailbox and brought in the mail. It was junk mail, and after I opened it, I put it on the coffee table. Joe came in from work and saw the mail.

In an angry voice, he said, "Why is the mail opened? You do not open the mail! I will open it, and I'll let you know what you're allowed to see."

"It's junk mail. It's not personal mail."

Joe shouted, "Do you understand English? I open the mail. I will tell you what you can see, and what you can't see. Do you understand? Get the supper on the table."

I went into the kitchen as the tears rolled down my face. At that moment I was afraid of Joe and tried to hide my feelings so Diane wouldn't get upset.

Two days later, while we were having dinner, Diane spilled some peas from her plate onto the table. Joe reached over, grabbed her plate, and threw it across the room, hitting the wall.

As Diane wailed, I snatched her out of her chair, turned to Joe and shouted, "If you *ever* lay a hand on Diane I will kill you. I mean it! If you touch a hair on her head I will kill you."

I was shaking so hard, I could hardly hold Diane. I grabbed one of her little books, went into the bedroom and tried to calm myself and Diane as I read her a story. Joe came into the room.

"I'm sorry. I had a bad day at work," he said. "I didn't mean to take it out on Diane. It won't happen again."

Ed's warning, not to marry Joe flashed through my mind.

As I laid in bed that night, I thought, 'what should I do? I can't call anyone, we don't have a telephone yet. Where would I go, and how would I get there? Maybe it was my fault. I need to make everything run more smoothly. It's an adjustment for both of us. I just need to try harder.'

Two months later, in July, I discovered I was pregnant.

During the first months of my pregnancy I was so sick I had to quit my job. Joe was helpful during that time. When he came home from work, he entertained Diane by drawing cartoon characters for her. I was amazed at how well he could draw.

Joe also had a talent for fixing anything. Our used car had several dents in the front fenders. After work, he spent three days taking all the dents out. The following day, I had a doctor's appointment so I kept the car, and Joe got a ride to work. Leaving Diane with a friendly neighbor, I headed out. After the appointment, driving home, I made a wrong turn. When it comes to my sense of direction I'm at a loss. If I should turn right, I'm positive I need to turn left. Noticing the houses were getting scarce, and little or no traffic, I soon realized I was lost. Coming upon a car stopped in the road, and the driver standing outside his car, I pulled up behind him, got out, told him I was lost and asked directions.

He said, "I'm Bill Potter. I need a push to get my car started. If you'll push, then you can follow me to where you need to go."

"I don't know if I can. What do I have to do?"

"You line up your car with mine, then just get your car going about twenty miles an hour. With your car pushing at that speed, my car should start."

"Well," I replied, "that sounds easy enough. Twenty miles an hour?"

"Yes, that should do it."

I gave him my address and we got in the cars. It looked like I was lined up directly behind his car, so I backed up to get my car going twenty miles an hour. I put my foot to the floor on the gas pedal. Seeing Bill glance in his rear-view mirror, I'll *never* forget the look on his face. His mouth dropped open and his eyes widened. He looked frantic. Like he didn't know whether to jump out of the car or stay with it. With a loud crunching sound, I hit his car. No one could be more surprised than I was. We got out of our cars. His bumper was smashed up against the dented trunk, and one side of the bumper was almost touching the tire.

He said, "Lady! What the hell were you doing?"

We looked at my car. Both fenders were completely dented. One side of my front bumper was pointing towards the ground. He looked at me, looked at the cars, looked back at me and started to laugh. He laughed until he was bent over with tears rolling down his face.

"No one is going to believe this," he gasped between his hysterical laughing.

"My husband is going to kill me," I said.

He pulled his bumper away from the tire, and it stuck straight out at a ridiculous angle. He said, "I'll push your car back a little, and I'll try to fix your bumper so you'll be able to drive the car."

After a lot of pulling, pushing, and a few choice words, he got my bumper more or less in place. On reflection, I think it was good that cars were made of steel in 1955, or they both would have ended up in the car-graveyard.

Bill said, "I still need to get my car started. I'll get in your car and line us up. Your car will be touching mine. Put it in second gear, start *very* slow, and increase the speed *slowly* to about twenty miles an hour. My car should start. Then follow me and I'll direct you home."

After he lined up the cars, I got in. I thought, 'Joe is going to have a fit!' I put the car in second, and gently stepped on the gas. We were moving. His car kicked in and we headed toward whatever fate awaited me.

When I arrived home, I asked Bill to come in and help me explain what happened. I was afraid of what Joe would do when he saw the car. After we went into the house, Joe burst in, slamming the door and shouting, "What in the hell happened to the damn car and whose beat-up car is behind it in the driveway?"

Bill introduced himself, and said, "In a million years you'll never guess the bizarre incident that happened. Let's go look at the cars and I'll explain."

I told them I had to go next door and get Diane. I was glad of the chance to get away. When I came back, Joe was calm, and they were looking at the cars and having a deep discussion about the damages.

When Joe saw me returning from the neighbors, he said, "I can't believe you could do such a stupid thing. Honestly Margaret, where were your brains? Bill and I will have to spend the entire weekend fixing two cars."

For years afterward, when with friends, Joe made fun of me every chance he got retelling the incident.

After Bill and Joe spent several weekends together repairing the cars, they became good friends. Bill's wife, Donna, always came with him. After the cars were repaired, the four of us spent many evenings together playing cards.

It puzzled me why Joe didn't become angry at major things that happened, but became enraged at something minor, like Diane spilling peas off her plate. Not knowing what to expect, made me anxious and afraid, watched what I said to him, and how I said it.

14

SPIDERS AND BATTLES

ONE MORNING, as I walked into the kitchen, the sun shone on the small, wooden table, reflecting onto the turquoise and white linoleum floor. It was a cheerful but plain kitchen. The sunshine inspired me to make an apple pie.

Apple was my daddy's favorite pie, and when I make the pie, I always remember him saying, "Apple pie without cheese is like a kiss without a squeeze."

I got Mama's delicious pie recipe from my recipe box, rolled out the crust and eased it onto the pie pan. Then, getting the Granny green apples out of the refrigerator, I peeled them and began to slice them onto the crust.

Joe walked into the kitchen, and said, "What are you doing? You're slicing the apples all wrong."

Glancing up, I asked him, "Have you ever made an apple pie?"

"No, but my mother used a different kind of knife and

she sliced the apples thicker."

"Well, I'm making this pie, not your mother, and this is how I do it," I said.

Joe picked up the pan, apples and all, and threw them in the garbage. He pushed me into the table and put his face inches from my face.

"Don't you talk to me that way. Who do you think you are? No woman talks to me like that. You'll never do anything as well as my mother and don't you forget it."

I refused to let Joe see me cry. I wiped up the table and didn't say anything. I told myself I had to be more careful of what I said to him and how I said it.

Joe walked out of the house and I heard the car start. A while later, he came back with a six pack of beer. He drank all six cans before he went to bed. That was the start of Joe's drinking beer, every night, and heavy on the weekends.

Joe found an old clock radio in the shed, and it worked. He brought it in without checking it and placed it on the end table at my side of the bed. The next morning, he got up early to leave for work, and quietly left. Hearing the car start, I woke up, turned over, and something caught by eye. I saw a large, Black Widow spider, on a web, between the radio and the post of the bed, inches from my face. I had a terrible fear of spiders, which I have to this day. Not taking my eyes off the spider, I slowly inched down to the foot of the bed and slid out. I was frantic, not wanting to go near it.

I heard the paperboy throw the paper at the front door. In my knee length nightgown, forgetting I had a very swollen belly, I ran to the door, opened it and shouted to the paperboy, "I need you. *Please* come back."

Peddling back, dropping his bike on the lawn, he came to the door.

"There's a big spider in my bedroom," I said. "I'm afraid of spiders and don't know what to do. Please, can you come in and kill it?"

"Yah, I can do it. Show me where it is."

Taking him to the bedroom, I pointed to the spider. With a rolled-up newspaper, the boy swatted at the spider. It dropped, and I thought it had jumped on me. I panicked, screaming. I tore off my nightgown, shaking it at arm's length, as the paperboy whacked at the creature, which had dropped on the floor.

"I got it," he said. He turned, looked at me and quickly looked away. "I gotta go," he said and couldn't get out of the house fast enough.

When Joe came home, I told him what happened with the paperboy, and said, "*Please*, make sure there are no more spiders in the radio."

Knowing how afraid I was of bugs and spiders, he said, "I'll take the back off the radio and look inside. You did a striptease for a twelve-year old paperboy? I bet he got a view he wasn't expecting." He picked up the radio, shook his head, and chuckled, as he went out the door.

***

Christmas was coming. Since I wasn't working, we didn't have a lot of money to spend. Joe said, "I can make some presents out of wood for Diane. I'll go to the lumber yard and see what I can get."

He made a beautiful cradle for Diane's doll and a matching little chest for her doll's clothes. He painted them pink, and then painted white kittens on them. He also made the most amazing, large, rocking horse, that was also a toy chest. The seat of the horse lifted up to put her toys inside. He painted it bright red with black eyes, mane, tail and saddle. Joe had no pattern to go by, but every piece fit perfectly. I made clothes for Diane's doll, put the doll in the cradle and put them all under the tree from Santa.

Christmas morning, Diane, in her pajamas, just stood and looked at everything under the tree. Not saying a word, she slowly walked over to the horse, climbed up on it and started rocking. Joe was disappointed that she wasn't jumping up and down with excitement. "Well, that was a lot of work for nothing," he said.

I whispered, "Diane's a quiet child, it's not her nature to show a lot of emotion. She keeps it inside. Can't you see? She's thrilled."

He went into the kitchen and got a beer. He drank beer for the rest of the day and was in a terrible mood. I had to be careful about everything I said. Every holiday from then on, Joe would ruin in one way or another.

I realized Joe was very intelligent. He could fix anything, was artistic and had a knowledge of airplanes. If a plane would fly overhead he could tell you what it was by the shape and sound. He could build model airplanes out of anything and they would fly.

One evening, after Diane went to bed, I said, "I know you're not happy with your job at Reynolds Aluminum, so I think you should take advantage of the GI Bill. You could go to college in the fall."

"We can't afford to do that," he said. "It costs a lot of money to go to college. Four years is a long time. I never took any college prep courses in high school. I only had general math. All my classes were basic. I never took algebra, or any of the higher math that you need to get into college. They don't take just anyone."

He got up and went into the kitchen to get a beer. Coming back, he said, "My parents didn't believe in college. They wanted me to work at the mill, like my father. I didn't want to, so that's why I joined the Air Force. I always wanted to be a pilot, but because I'm deaf in one ear, I'll never be one."

"After four years of college, you would make a lot more money than you ever would without a degree," I said. "You hate your job. You need to think of the future. My cousin Helen's husband, Ken, is going to Michigan State. They have a little boy and they manage. He doesn't even have the GI Bill."

I looked in my correspondence box for Helen's address, and said, "I have her address, so I'll write and make some inquires. You're so smart Joe. I hate to think of you wasting your life on a nothing job. I only wish I was as smart as you are. Being very intelligent is a gift, and I believe you're gifted. I'm not just saying that, I really believe it." I copied the address, and added, "If you did go to college, what field would you be interested in?"

"Aeronautical Engineering would be my first choice. I doubt if they have it in Arizona. In fact, Arizona State College in Tempe isn't even a university. I know they wouldn't have any engineering classes, so it's out of the question."

"We're expecting the baby in March, and I could go to work shortly after. With the GI Bill we could manage. Please, just think about it. Four years of sacrifice for a better future is worth it."

***

Michael Joseph was born on March twenty-fourth 1956. Blonde, blue eyed with a good pair of lungs, he was a big baby, weighing nine pounds two ounces. Again, it was a long difficult birth. He had wide shoulders for a newborn. As he was being delivered, it caused the tip of my tailbone to break. They didn't do anything about the tailbone, and the doctor told me eventually it would get better. Like the doctor I had for Diane, he advised us not to have more children and suggested we use birth control. Because Joe was Catholic, it wasn't possible. I had to stay in the hospital six days.

Joe told Diane, who had turned four in February, that she had a baby brother and his name was Michael.

"Can I go and see him?"

"No, children aren't allowed in the hospital to visit, but Mom and Michael will be home soon and you'll see him then."

After I was released, Joe, Michael and I headed home. I had to kneel, facing the back of the car, because it was too painful to sit. Michael laid on the seat between Joe and me. In those days, the front seat was a bench-type seat with no console in the middle. No seatbelts and no child's seat.

When we arrived home, Diane was excited when she saw the baby. She stood watch as I laid Michael, sleeping, in the bassinet. Joe went into the kitchen to get a beer, and I laid down on the living room couch. With my tightly bound breasts, many stitches and sore tailbone, I was miserable. Diane stayed in the bedroom, next to the bassinet, watching Michael.

Michael woke up and started to cry.

"Here's your baby Mom. He's crying." There was Diane, walking toward me with Michel dangling under one arm. Like she'd carry a doll. I struggled to get up. Joe ran over to Diane, and took him from her.

He calmly said, "Sit down on the chair, and I'll show you how to hold him. Babies are not like dolls. You have to be careful and support his head. He can't hold it up yet, he's too little."

Joe put Michael in her arms, and Diane sat gazing at her little brother. Michael opened his mouth and yawned.

"Mom, what does he eat? He hasn't any teeth." she said.

"He only drinks milk now, but in two months he can have some warm cereal that's just for babies," I said.

As Joe helped me up, taking Michael from Diane, I said, "I need to change his diaper. Come with me, and see what boys looks like. Boys and girls look a lot different. You can hand me the cloth diaper and wet washcloth."

She never said a word when I took the diaper off. I didn't realize that with boys you had to cover them quickly. As I bent over him, he peed, hitting me in the face. Diane burst out laughing. Wiping my face, I laughed too.

After I changed his diaper, I sat on an inflatable-donut that Joe got for me, gave Michael a bottle of formula the hospital provided, then laid him sleeping in his bassinet.

With Michael sleeping, it was a good time to make the milk formula. My mother had made it for Diane, because I had to go to work at the Bell Telephone Company, so the process was new to me.

All the baby-bottles had to be sterilized in a special large, covered pot, filled with water, that held eight bottles. The nipples had to be boiled separately and placed in a sterile jar. The formula was, Similac Powder, Karo syrup and water, all in amounts prescribed by the doctor. In a pan, you stirred it all together until dissolved. Then you poured it into the sterile bottles, capped them with sterile caps, then stored the formula in the refrigerator. When it was time to feed your baby, you put the bottle of milk in a pan of water to heat, testing it on your inside wrist, to see if it was warm enough or too hot. If it was too hot, you ran the bottle under cold water until it was the right temperature. If the hole in the nipple was too small, you had to sterilize a needle and pierce it, being careful not to make the hole too large, or the baby would choke.

It surprised me that Joe sometimes picked Michael up and changed his diaper, offered to give him a bath and once in a while, got up at night to feed him.

When I had time, I began to research information about the GI Bill and colleges. I found the GI Bill would pay twenty dollars a week for fifty-two weeks a year to go to college. Grades would have to be passable. Student loans were available under the GI Bill and you had to start paying them back as soon as you graduated. I couldn't find any Universities that offered Aeronautical Engineering. In 1956 there were no computers to look up information, and Aeronautical was not a well-known field. My cousin, Helen, wrote to me about Michigan State University where they offered electrical engineering, which was Joe's second choice.

After a lot of persuading, Joe decided to go to college in the fall on the GI Bill at Michigan State University and take electrical engineering.

We planned to leave Phoenix the first of June. We were going to stop to see Joe's parents in Crete, Nebraska, on our way to Michigan. I would meet them for the first time. I was apprehensive, wondering what their feelings were about Joe marrying a woman with a child and what Joe had told them.

15

THE VISIT

PREPARING FOR OUR TRIP across the country to Lansing, Michigan, Joe designed a small trailer to pull behind the car. It would hold the bassinet, rocking horse, linens, clothes, dishes and our other few possessions.

Monday, May seventh, was our anniversary. After work and all evening, Joe had been drinking beer and working on the trailer. Diane and Mike were both asleep. I had just sat down after making formula and cleaning up the kitchen from dinner, when Joe came in.

"We haven't had sex since Mike was born and it's about time," he said, "our anniversary."

"I just had a baby six weeks ago. My tailbone is painful and my stitches are still healing," I argued.

Joe grabbed my arm and pulled me into the bedroom. "Quit your whining. Take your clothes off and get in bed."

As I undressed, I pleaded with him to wait a while

longer, but he pushed me onto the bed. Afterwards, I got up and went into the bathroom. I felt despair and anger. Thinking, 'was it the drinking that made Joe like this? Why does he need to be in control all the time? Is it my fault? I should leave him, but how can I leave with Diane and a baby? Where would we go? How would we get there? I have no money. Maybe he'll change when he goes to college.'

For the trip, Joe made a special cradle for the car, to hold Mike, who was now eight weeks old. It was a brilliant idea. The cradle connected from the top of the front, bench-type seat, to the top of the back seat. It hung in the middle next to Diane, who would sit behind me. It would make it easy for me to change Mike's diapers by kneeling, facing the back. Diane would be able to hand me one of the diapers, that were stacked under the cradle, then put the soiled cloth diaper in the diaper pail on the floor behind Joe. I'd be able to pick Mike up to give him a bottle. Diane could get the bottle out of the cooler, sitting on the other side of the cradle. We had a bottle warmer that plugged into the car lighter.

Diane was always a willing helper and never complained. She was always like that throughout her years.

On June first, early morning, we were ready to leave Phoenix. The distance to his parent's home would be 1,200 miles. Interstate I-17 didn't exist. The road was an undivided two-lane highway, called Black Canyon Highway which took you near the tiny town of Prescott, up steep mountains, to route sixty-six, out of Flagstaff. Our car didn't have air-conditioning, and the temperature outside was 101 degrees. We had retread tires on the car and no spare.

After the trailer was hitched to the car, Diane and Mike were settled in the back. I sat on the inflatable-donut. Joe got in the car and we were off. We had to keep the windows rolled down leaving Phoenix, because it was so hot. We were able to roll them up as soon as we got to the mountains. Driving up the winding, steep mountains, on the two-lane highway was nerve-wracking. If you got behind a semi-trailer truck, you could go only a few miles an hour and couldn't pass. We didn't have a car radio, and when I saw Joe was losing his patience, I talked to him about his family, asking questions, trying to calm him when I wasn't calm myself, afraid of what risks Joe would take trying to pass a semi. After five hours, the first place we were able to stop was in Flagstaff to use the bathrooms and eat.

Diane had her doll and books. She was a great help with Mike, and when he was awake she would talk to him. I was glad they both slept a lot. The cradle worked perfectly in the car, and we were able to take it into a motel when we stopped for the night.

The remaining trip to Crete, Nebraska, was hot and exhausting. We arrived safely at the small, farming town, in the late afternoon. When we drove up to the house, Joe blew the horn and his father, mother, two sisters, and his youngest brother came out to greet us. His father was tall, slim, and had greying dark brown hair, a man that looked like he never smiled. Joe's mother was short, plump, had dark hair and eyes, smiling, happy to see us. His sister Ann was sixteen, Margie fourteen, and Jimmy, a late life child, was six years old.

After Diane and I were introduced to everyone, I handed Mike to Joe's mother. I could see that she could hardly wait to hold him.

Their home was an older, white, two-story, house on a large property. In the back, away from the home, it looked like there was a barn and an outhouse. I hoped they had inside plumbing. Next to the house was a small square building that was one big room. That's where we were to stay, for a week, before leaving for Michigan.

When we entered their plain, well-kept home, Joe said, "Mike needs to be fed, so I'll change him while Margaret heats up his bottle."

His father said, "Why isn't that wife of yours changing him? I never changed a diaper in my life."

Joe replied, "That's too bad. You really missed out on something."

"Dinner's almost ready," his mother said. "As soon as Michael's fed, we can all sit down and eat."

The kitchen was large, square, with a long wooden table in the middle, set for dinner.

After giving Mike a bottle, I asked, "Can I use the bathroom, or should I go to an outhouse?"

His mother Agnus, laughed and said, "We have a bathroom. I just like to go to the outhouse in the morning."

We sat down to dinner and it was delicious. Agnus had prepared a beef roast, with garden vegetables, boiled potatoes and wonderful home-made rolls.

During dinner, his father asked Joe, "When did you come up with the stupid idea to go to college? Who do you think you are? Einstein? You have a family to feed. You need to get a job. You'll never make it in college, and don't expect a penny from me."

"I don't want your money. I'm going to college on the GI Bill."

There was awkward silence around the table until Joe's mother said, "Joe, you remember working the summers on Uncle Joe's farm? He has enlarged his dairy herd and just put in a milking contraption. You don't have to milk the cows by hand anymore. Isn't that amazing? He wants your family to come tomorrow and have lunch."

"That sounds great," Joe said. "Diane, do you want to see some live animals?"

"Oh yes. Do they have horses? I want to ride a horse."

The next day we went to see the farm. We were greeted warmly by Joe's uncle and aunt.

Diane asked, "Do you have horses? Can I ride one?"

"Right after we have lunch I'll give you a riding lesson," Uncle Joe said.

Their kitchen was a large, square, cheerful room that reminded me of my Grandma Gordon's kitchen. A long wooden table sat along one side, right where my grandma had her long wooden table. A rocking chair was in the corner. My grandma's rocking chair was in the middle of her kitchen. She'd put a stool for me to sit on in front of her, and that's where she taught me to churn butter, shell peas and snap beans from her garden.

After a delicious lunch of fried chicken, roasted potatoes and garden vegetables, we went to the pasture to see the horses. Uncle Joe whistled to a mare that he said was gentle. After putting a saddle on the horse, he lifted Diane up on the horse. I was terrified she would fall off, but she had no fear and was delighted as Uncle Joe led them around.

"Can he go faster?" she asked.

Uncle Joe stepped up his pace. I'm sure this was the highlight of Diane's trip. To this day, quiet Diane loves the thrill rides at an amusement park, while her lively brothers won't go near them.

Uncle Joe said, "It's milking time, and I'd like you to see the time-saving process with my new milking machines."

We went to a large barn as the cows were herded in. They stood in several rows, separated by a bar on one side and the milking machine on the other. Uncle Joe and two workers began to wash and massage their udders and teats. They did this with an individual towel for each cow, dipping it in a warm solution. They then hooked up the four teats, from back to front. The milking took four minutes. The milk was then stored in a large cooling bin to keep it fresh until the morning when they delivered it to customers.

Uncle Joe kept one cow from being milked by the machine. He wanted to show Diane and me how they milked by hand. He sat on a stool, beside the cow and her udder. Grasping a teat, with each hand, he squirted the milk into a pail. I was fascinated by both procedures and asked many questions. He told me that cows have two stomachs. After eating their fill, they belched it up and re-chewed it, which is called chewing the cud. A couple of cats came into the barn, and he squirted the milk into their open mouths. Diane stood silent as she watched all of the procedures. I could tell by the look on her face that she thought milking a cow was disgusting.

"Diane, would you like to try some warm fresh milk?" he asked.

Taking two steps back, like she was afraid he was going to squirt it in her mouth, she replied, "No thank you."

At the end of the day, when we arrived back at Joe's home, dinner was ready. We all sat down to eat. The food was delicious Czechoslovakian food. We had, goulash with dumplings and buchty, which was a sweet, yeast, dough-bun. For desert Agnus made kolaches, a round piece of leavened dough, topped with a sweet filling in the center. Poppy seed filling was my favorite. Agnus gave me the kolache recipe.

Diane, who was a lover of milk, was not drinking a drop. "May I have a glass of water?" she asked.

I said, "You have milk to drink. Why aren't you drinking it?"

"I don't like milk."

Joe's mother, sensing the problem, got up and took a milk carton from the refrigerator. "Look Diane, this milk came from the store."

Diane looked solemnly at her and said, "I don't like any milk."

To this day, Diane does not drink milk.

The next day, I was in the kitchen making formula. The girls and Jimmy were at school. Diane, Joe and his mother were outside looking at newborn kittens in the barn. Joe's father came in from work.

He put his lunch pail on the kitchen table and said, "I didn't approve of my son marrying a whore."

"What did you say?"

"You heard me."

I was shocked, hurt and boiling mad. I whipped around, marched up to him, stood toe to toe, got right in his face, and said, "How dare you. You know nothing about me. Don't you ever call me that again."

"I'll call you whatever I want."

"Let me tell you something! You have two teenage daughters, and you better hope what happened to me will not happen to them. What kind of father are you that brags about never changing his children's diapers? What kind of a father are you that doesn't want his son to go to college and improve himself? I heard that you went to a bar on payday and drank away your paycheck. You may not think much of me, but I don't think much of you either."

He looked like he wanted to hit me. I turned around and went back to the stove. I was shaking so hard I could hardly function. He went out and slammed the door. After finishing the formula, I took Mike and went to the little house.

Joe came in later and said, "Dinner's ready. Were you sleeping?"

Although I was afraid of Joe's reaction, I told him what his father said, and how I responded.

Joe said, "I can't help what my dad says. Ignore him."

"I want to pack and wash diapers tomorrow and leave the following morning. I can't stay here any longer. Please excuse me from dinner. I'm not hungry and I feel sick to my stomach. I don't want to have to look at your father. If he says anything to me, I'll probably say something back and don't want to do that in front of your sisters and brother."

The next day, when I went to wash diapers, I found a bunch of bloody rags soaking in the stationary tub. Joe's sister Ann looked at me and said, "I didn't know you wanted to wash. I'll put my rags back in my pail, and do them later."

"What happened? Are you hurt? Why are they all bloody?"

Ann's face turned red. She said, "I had my monthly."

"Ann, why don't you use Kotex pads? You get them at a drugstore. They're usually behind the counter where you can't see them and all you need to do is ask for them. I usually go to a drugstore that has a woman clerk. That way I'm not embarrassed when I ask. It doesn't cost a lot, and you just throw them away. You shouldn't have to do this. I never heard of such a thing. Can you talk to your mother about it? Would you want me to talk to her?"

"This is how my mother always does it. I didn't know there was any other way. I'll tell her about it."

"Go ahead and wash," I said. "Let me know when you finish. We're leaving tomorrow morning, and I can do some packing."

I went to pack, feeling sorry for Joe's sisters, and what they had to go through every month. 'Tomorrow's a new day,' I thought, 'a new start. Things have to be better, when we get to college.'

16

INTO THE SNOW

WHEN WE LEFT Joe's parents' home, to continue on to Michigan, I was glad Joe's father had left early for work, so I wouldn't have to speak to him. Perhaps he said goodbye to Joe while Joe was loading the car for our trip. I said goodbye to the girls and Jimmy before they left for school. His mother seemed sorry to see us go and hoped to come visit us in the future. I wondered if Joe's father had told her about our heated conversation.

The trip from Nebraska to Michigan was uneventful, except I was car sick several times and we had to stop for a short while until I felt better.

When we arrived at Michigan State University, we were amazed at the beautiful campus with the remarkable buildings. Joe, never having been to Michigan before, remarked on all the trees and greenery.

"It's green because of all the rain and snow Michigan gets," I said.

My cousin, Helen, gave us excellent directions to their married student apartment on campus, where her husband, Ken, was a student. I had been looking forward to seeing Helen, who was a few years younger than me. She had a calm, quiet nature like Diane. Ken and Helen had been high school sweethearts, and I admired them for their ambition and struggle to make a better life for themselves. They had a little boy, Butch, who was three years old.

After lunch, we were discussing Michigan State, when Ken said, "Joe, if you're going into engineering, why aren't you going to Michigan Technological University in Sault Ste Marie or Houghton Michigan? Michigan Tech is among the top engineering universities in the country."

Joe said, "Margaret, why didn't you tell me about it?"

"I knew there was a college in the Sault, but I thought it was just a small general college," I said. "I had no idea it was an engineering university."

Ken said, "You'd have to take a tough exam to get into Michigan Tech. You said you didn't take any higher math in high school, and I know engineering is all about higher math. Also, it's been six years since you were in school. It would be easier for you to go the first two years at Sault Tech, the smaller campus, and your last two years at Houghton. They have married student housing at both campuses."

I liked the idea. "Joe, this is only June. We could go to the Sault and talk to Michigan Tech. College doesn't start until September tenth, so we'll have until then to decide what we should do. I'm sure my parents will let us stay with them until we make a decision. They were so happy we were coming back to Michigan where we would be closer to them."

"We're getting low on money," Joe said.

"I can get a temporary job in the Sault, and you may be able to get something too. Just until we decide. I think my mother would watch Diane and Mike while we work. You know how good Diane is with helping, and Mike's a good baby as long as he gets his bottle and baby-food."

When my parents had returned to the Sault, after our wedding, we wrote letters a couple of times a month. Mama send me recipes and I'd write to her about Diane and Mike. I never told her about the difficulties with my marriage. When I wrote that we would be coming back to Michigan, so Joe could go to college, she was delighted that they would be able to see Mike for the first time and Diane again.

After a lot of discussion, we called my parents and decided to leave in the morning for Sault Ste. Marie.

That evening, I heard Diane coughing while she was playing with Butch. Thinking she might be coming down with something, I got out the orange flavored baby aspirin and gave her one.

A short while later, Diane came up to me and said, "Mom, you know the pill you gave me? That you said I must never touch? Well, Butch said he was going to eat some. I told him not to, but he said he already did. I didn't touch them."

I was stunned! I had left them on the bathroom counter, thinking I would give Diane another one in the morning. Diane always did as she was told, and I didn't think about Butch getting into them. Horrified, I told Helen and Ken what happened.

Helen asked Butch, "How many did you eat?"

Butch started to count, "Six, seven, eight, nine."

Ken said, "We need to go to the emergency room and have his stomach pumped."

I felt so guilty as they pumped poor little Butch's stomach. I kept telling Helen and Ken how sorry I was. They never criticized me for leaving the aspirin out. In those days they didn't have child protective caps on medicine.

Butch was exhausted from his ordeal and slept all the way home. I thought, 'maybe Mike won't be as easy as Diane, so I'll have to be careful in the future.' Little did I know that in years to come my three boys would test my patience to the limit, and the emergency room would become very familiar.

We left the next morning for the Sault. As we were driving, I remembered that when I left home to go to Phoenix, I thought I would never return to the Sault again, and here I was, on my way. My friend Joyce had written to me that Pat joined the Navy Band, then graduated from College in Detroit. I was relieved he would no longer be in the Sault.

When we arrived at Mackinac City, at the top of lower Michigan, we had to take a ferry across the Straits of Mackinac to the upper peninsula. The ferry held ninety cars and many passengers. The seven-mile ride over the usually turbulent Straits of Mackinac was smooth and interesting. They were building a bridge across the Straits. They said it would open in 1957. It's hard to imagine a bridge that long.

Driving down the main street of the picturesque, small town of Sault Ste. Marie, Joe asked, "What are all those poles all along the street? They're long and there's a lot of them."

"They're snow markers. It's to let the snowplow driver

know where the road is. They haven't taken them down yet. I've seen it snow in May, but there shouldn't be any snow now."

"Holy Cow," Joe exclaimed.

"In the winter you can't park on the street because they plow the streets almost every day, and the snowbanks are high. Being in the center of the Great Lakes, you get a lot of snow. Even though it's early June, you'll find some snow deep in the woods," I said.

When we arrived at my parent's home, they were happy to see us. Mike was awake, and when my mother held him, he gave her a toothless smile, which delighted her. Daddy lifted Diane up, holding her tight. Joe took the bassinet out of the trailer and set it up in the down-stairs bedroom where Joe and I would stay. Diane would sleep upstairs in the bedroom that had been mine.

The white, two-story home looked exactly the same as the day I left, four years ago. It seemed smaller than I remembered. The living-room and dining-room still had the green vine wallpaper, the furniture was the same, and the square kitchen, where I took turns with my sister, Virginia, washing and drying many dishes, remained as I remembered. The absence of a dog surprised me because we always had one in the years I was growing up. Dad told me that after our dog, Blondie, died they decided not to get another.

After getting settled, I called Michigan Tech and made an appointment with the Dean of students. Dr. Young listened without comment as Joe told him about his background, lack of higher math, his interest in engineering and our desire for a summer job. When Joe stopped talking, the Dean was silent for a few minutes and seemed deep in thought.

Then he said, "I'm surprised you want to go into engineering with only a general knowledge of math. I don't want to discourage you, but if you don't pass the entrance exam, you'll not be admitted. I suggest you take a summer school class in geometry that the high school offers. You should get on the list for married student housing and apply for your GI loan. It can be used at any college, so I suggest you do that today."

Joe agreed to take the summer school class.

Dr. Young added, "Joe, if you're looking for work, try the golf course, there might be something there for you. However, I don't think you should work while you're going to college." He turned to me. "With school starting in a few months, I need another girl in my office. Talk to my secretary, Doris, fill out a form, and, Margaret, I'll see you on Monday."

I was thankful to get a job immediately and work at the university for the Dean of Students. I'd start at thirty cents an hour. Joe got a job at the golf course doing ground work. They gave him flex hours so he was able to take the math class. He'd make sixty cents an hour. One of our expenses would be gasoline for the car. Gas was fifteen cents a gallon in 1956. With us both working, we would be able to cover our expenses and maybe save a little.

Daddy said, "Stay here as long as necessary. We'll look after Diane and Mike while you work. Joe, I'm glad you're going to college. I graduated from the University of Toronto, Canada. I worked my way through. It's worth the sacrifices you will make now, so you can improve your future."

I worried about staying with my parents, because of Joe's habit of yelling at me. My parents never raised their voices. When daddy said a lengthy prayer before meals, I was embarrassed, knowing Joe's family never said one. At least Daddy never pressured us to go to Meeting.

I enjoyed the campus and working with the Dean, who was a pleasant, compassionate man. I was a receptionist, scheduling appointments for the students and professors when they wanted to see him. I also did some clerical work. His secretary, Doris, was patient and helpful since I'd never done any office work before. The campus was ninety-nine percent male students because engineering was not a field that females went into.

I was again getting sick to my stomach in the mornings and I remembered Joe insisting on sex when Mike was six weeks old. I was sick to my stomach at Joe's parents and had motion sickness while traveling in the car. I hadn't had a period since Mike was born and had wondered why. I was terrified I was pregnant. I remembered the two doctors telling me I shouldn't have more children. I made an appointment with a doctor, and he confirmed, I was pregnant.

Close to tears, I said, "I can't be. My husband's going to start college. We have a four-year old daughter and a baby-boy only two months old."

Dr Mark said, "I went through medical school with four children. You can do it too. It won't be easy, but it will work-out. Whatever you do, don't let your husband give up college."

I told him what my previous doctors said about not having any more children because it was dangerous for me.

When Mike was born it broke the tip of my tailbone. "I'm terrified of having another baby. I might die and what will become of my kids?" I had a fear of dying and leaving them with Joe because of his temper, and the possibility he'd take them to his parents to raise. I didn't want them to be raised like Joe was.

The doctor said, "Your tailbone will make it uncomfortable, but I don't see any other problems you'll have with delivery. You do have a lot of scar tissue, but I will watch your weight so you won't have another large baby. I'm going to put you on diet pills, and that should help keep your weight down."

I took a diet pill each morning when I got up. Within an hour I was flying around the house like a speeding bullet, tidying up before I left for work. Nothing escaped my flying hands. After a few months, at night I'd feel depressed, and worried about everything, but as soon as I took the pill in the morning I felt better and regained my energy.

On weekends, we would go to the cabin at Lake Superior, and Diane enjoyed playing in the sand. I had learned to row boats when I was very young, and I often rowed her around the lake. In those days, life-jackets were not something people put on. We just told children to never stand up in a boat and be careful or they would never get a boat ride again. We expected them to do what they were told.

Joe aced the geometry class, and in August he passed the entrance exam. He said he just used his reasoning to figure out the difficult math. The Dean told me his score was one of the highest he'd seen in a long time. The score was so high, Joe won the United States scholarship that paid for his out-of-state tuition.

Before classes were to start, all freshmen students were given a psychological and IQ test, which was designed to see if they were in the correct engineering field, or if they should even be in engineering. Dr. Young designed the test, and it was being used in most universities. He told me about one student who was enrolled in engineering, and the test showed that engineering was the wrong field for him. The student went to a Divinity College and became a pastor.

The Dean met with each student and went over the results with them. When Joe went to see him, the Dean said, "Joe, you're in the wrong field. You should be in mechanical engineering not electrical. I now know why you passed the entrance exam with no background and got such a high score. Your IQ is 179. Very remarkable."

We were assigned a two-bedroom apartment, on campus, furnished, utilities paid, for sixty dollars a month, Joe switched to mechanical engineering, quit his job at the golf course and started college.

17

DIAPERS DIAPERS

THE SINGLE STORY student apartments were all connected, with a sidewalk in front. Our apartment was small and worn, but I was thankful it was on campus.

Walking into the apartment, you entered into a small, bright kitchen, with two windows. On one end of the kitchen was the sink and cupboards. In the middle of a long wall was a stove with a counter on each side and cupboards beneath.

Behind the wall was the small, square living-room. A table with four chairs sat in the living-room against the wall. I moved one of the chairs and put Mike's highchair by the table. A faded brown couch was against the opposite wall with a chipped, scared coffee-table in front of it.

The two bedrooms were both small. A full-sized bed and four-drawer chest were in one, and the other had bunk beds. A little closet was in each bedroom. The bathroom had a stained tub with a shower, a toilet and single sink. All the rooms had linoleum on the floors.

At an apartment nearby a couple leaving college, had a sale. We bought their used ringer-washer and put it beside the door in the kitchen. We bought a worn highchair because we would need another one when the new baby came. They gave us a bright, red-print tablecloth and some red throw pillows for the couch, which brightened up the room. We decided to purchase their seven-inch black and white television with its antenna. My mother gave us some blankets for the beds. The rest of the linens we brought from Phoenix.

In September, it started to get cold. The daytime temperature was in the low 40's and below freezing at night. The small wall heater didn't keep the apartment warm enough, especially in the kids' bedroom. I had to put them to bed with snowsuits on.

By October, my pregnancy began to show. I hoped the Dean wouldn't notice for at least another month, but one day the Dean called me into his office and said, "Margaret, I noticed you're going to have a baby. We can't have anyone working at the college that's pregnant. Mostly boys attend the college and it wouldn't be proper for them to see you in your condition. I hate to lose you, but after your baby's born, I hope you'll come back."

Years later, in 1964, they passed a Pregnancy Discrimination Act pertaining to pregnant women because of the way they were treated in the work force.

I knew that without my paycheck, I'd have to figure a way to stretch our grocery budget.

One day, six-month old Michael was crawling around on the living room floor under the watchful eye of Diane.

She was telling him the story of the Three Little Pigs, holding the book so he could see the pictures, but far enough away so he couldn't grab her precious book and tear the pages.

With Mike occupied, I decided to wash diapers, which was a time-consuming job. Dragging the wringer washing machine over to the sink, I hooked up the water fill-hose to the faucet and put the drain-hose in the sink. I filled the machine with cold water to rinse the diapers. I got the diaper pail from the bathroom and dumped the diapers into the water, then took the pail back to the bathroom to wash it out with soap in the bathtub and brought it back to the kitchen.

I had to hold the agitator handle the entire time it was agitating, because the handle wouldn't stay at the on position. Standing, holding the handle, I timed the rinse for five minutes. I then emptied the rinse water into the sink, put the diapers through the wringer into the clean diaper pail. I refilled the washer with hot water and soap, put the diapers back in the washer and held the handle in place for another five minutes.

Unfortunately, the diapers got caught in the agitator at the bottom of the washer. Bending over to get them loose, I let go of the handle. My arm bumped the wringer, the wringer whipped around hitting me in the back, and I jarred the washer. As I fell against it, the drain hose fell out of the sink, and the water emptied onto the floor.

Hearing the commotion, little Michael decided to come and investigate. He came crawling into the kitchen gleefully splashing his hands in the water that had quickly covered the kitchen floor and was going into the living room. As I called Diane to come and get Mike, the door opened, and Joe stood in the doorway.

"For God's sake, what in the hell are you doing! Did you forget to put the hose in the sink? What's it doing on the floor? Can't you do anything right? How are you going to get all of this water up? Why are you letting Mike play in it?" he yelled.

"It was an accident. It just happened. Take Mike and wash his hands and get dry clothes on him. I can't do everything. I'll deal with the water."

"Don't you talk to me in that tone of voice. Get this mess cleaned up, I have studying to do."

He picked Mike up and headed for the bathroom. I got a broom and began sweeping the water out the door. My neighbor Gracie just missed being sprayed with the water as she came by. I told her what happened.

We'd met our neighbors, Stan and Gracie who came from Ohio. Stan was a year ahead of Joe, also on the G I bill. The friendly couple had no children.

"I'll run home and get some towels," she said.

When she came back, Stan was with her. He said, "Joe, grab a book, and study at our place while Gracie and Margaret clean up."

We finally got the apartment back to normal and Gracie entertained Mike while I continued washing the diapers. I wondered if they heard Joe yelling at me through the thin walls.

***

Trying to bring down the food budget, I fixed meals with lots of potatoes and beans which were cheap. We had potato soup, bean soup, baked beans, and potato casseroles. I fixed them any way I could dream up. We caught a break when my parents had us for dinner every few weeks, and we looked forward to my mother's wonderful cooking and brought home leftovers.

One day, Gracie brought us a loaf of her homemade bread. It was delicious! She said it was cheaper to make your own bread than to buy it. That's all I needed to hear and asked her for her recipe. It was for four loaves of white bread.

I bought four bread pans, cake-yeast and flour. Mama made bread every Saturday while I was growing up, but I never paid any attention to how she did it. Little did I know that beginners should start with one loaf, not four.

When I put Mike down for an afternoon nap, and Diane was out playing with neighbor kids, I decided to bake bread.

Putting the cake-yeast in lukewarm water, I got out my biggest bowl. Following Gracie's recipe, I started putting the ingredients into the bowl. Having only a large spoon to mix with, I began to have trouble stirring in the flour. I soon realized I needed a larger bowl. Not having one, I got out my big roasting pan I cooked turkeys in and dumped my batter in. I then thought, 'hands were made before spoons' and started mixing with my hands.

It worked for a little while, but as I added more flour, I was still having difficulty mixing. I now had dough up to my elbows, down the front of my shirt, on my face and in my hair. I decided to dump the mess onto the counter and work it there. As I tried to lift and turn the dough my arms got tired. I decided to get the bathroom stool that Diane uses, and stand on it, so I'd have more leverage. The dough was covering most of the counter—not to mention down the cupboard and on the floor. Standing on the stool, I continued to mix in the flour.

Joe opened the door. I froze, worrying about his reaction. His mouth fell open. With a look of disbelief on his face, he quietly closed the door and left.

I thought for a fleeting moment, I should just throw the whole mess in the garbage, but I was determined to see it through to the end. I was now pounding the dough with my fist out of shear frustration. The instructions said the dough would spring back when it was ready. Well, my dough wasn't doing any springing, and I doubted it ever would. I covered the mess with a towel to keep it warm while I waited one to two hours the recipe said was needed for it to rise to double in bulk.

I spent the time cleaning the sticky dough off of me and the kitchen. At the end of one and a half hours the dough was larger, and I had to knead it all over again. I then shaped the dough into what I thought looked like loaves and put them into the greased, floured pans. I had to cover them and wait a half hour for them to rise before baking.

Mike woke up, and after changing him I put him on the living room floor to play with his cars.

Diane came in from playing, and said, "I learned to play hop-scotch. It's a lot of fun. Can you get some chalk for me to draw the game on the sidewalk?"

"I'll get some the next time I go to the store. I loved to play hop-scotch when I was your age. It's a game you can play by yourself or with friends. When Mike's bigger you can teach him. Can you watch him for a while, so I can finish baking? Why don't you watch Mr. Rogers on the television with Mike?"

Joe came in a while later and said, with a grin on his face, "I'm not even going to ask what you were doing standing on the stool, or what that mess was all over the counter, kitchen and you. I went to the library to study where I figured it would be safer. Something smells good."

With Joe, I never knew if he would blowup, or laugh in a stressful situation. It made me very nervous when unexpected things happened.

When I took the bread out of the oven, I was shocked that it smelled and looked good enough to eat. We ate almost a whole loaf and it went well with my potato soup. It wasn't as good as Gracie's or Mama's bread but it was alright. I never dreamed that in the future homemade bread would become my specialty.

Gregory Paul was born on February 22nd, 1957, on Diane's fifth birthday. He was nine-pounds, four-ounces with curly blonde hair and blue eyes. A pretty baby. Again, a difficult birth with a lot of stitches. The diet pills didn't keep me from having a big baby like the doctor said they would.

We had to get a GI student loan to pay for the hospital and doctor expenses. We won't have to pay it back until Joe graduates from college.

Gregory cried a lot in the nursery during the seven days we were in the hospital. The doctor thought he had colic. When we brought him home, he still cried a lot and we had to walk the floor with him. I worried about it, but it finally lessened.

In 1957, doctors didn't know that diet pills were the drugs known today as speed. They were addictive. I now believe that Gregory was addicted at birth. Later in his life, it would become a problem.

Diane was excited to see her new brother. Mike, who learned to walk at eleven months, would pat Gregory on the head or try to kiss him every time he'd walk by.

With only eleven months between the two boys, it meant a lot of diapers to wash. When they had a poopy-diaper, I'd put it in the toilet to soak, then swish it around to get most of the poop off before putting it in the diaper pail. Sometimes I'd forget I had the diaper in the toilet.

One day, Joe went into the bathroom and yelled, "Margaret, get in here and get the diaper out of the toilet. Why in the hell did you leave it in there?"

"Just swish it around to get most of the poop off and put it in the diaper pail," I said.

"I have other things to do besides your work, so get in here and take care of it."

When I went into the bathroom, frustration thoughts filled my head. 'Why must I remember everything? Washing diapers every day in that old ringer-washer was hard not to mention getting up at night every few hours to feed Gregory. Keeping Mike out of mischief all day, trying to keep the house decent, fixing meals, getting very little sleep. I have to potty-train Mike as soon as possible. Why does Joe have to get mad all the time and yell at me? It's not good for the kids. If I talk to Joe about it, when the kids are in bed, he'd get angry. I'll just have to make things run more smoothly.'

***

One afternoon, when I was in the kitchen washing dishes, Mike was playing with his cars, Greg was on a blanket on the living room floor and Diane was outside playing. Mike loved to play with cars. His favorite was a tiny, cast-iron car, that fit in his little hand, and he was showing it to four-week old Greg. All of a sudden Greg started to cry. Dropping the dishrag, I ran to see what happened. Mike tried to give the car to Greg and he wasn't able to grasp it. Mike put Greg's finger through one of the tiny windows so he could hold it. The finger swelled and was cut on both sides. I couldn't get the car off his finger. Joe was at school.

Calling to Diane to come home, I wrapped Greg's hand in a clean dishtowel. "I have to take Greg to the hospital, he's hurt. Hurry and get Mike and you in the backseat."

I laid Greg on the front seat beside me. With one hand on the steering wheel and one on Greg, we headed for the hospital. The doctor in the emergency room called in an orthopedic doctor. He used some type of bone-saw to cut through the metal. Because they had to be so careful not to further injure the little finger, it took a very long time. Both boys cried at the top of their lungs. I kept telling Mike it would be all right, but he continued to howl. Diane looked like she was ready to cry too, and the nurses tried to distract them.

When the doctor finally got the car off Greg's finger, he said, "His finger will be alright. I washed it, put in a stitch, and put some ointment on it. This is one incident the ER won't forget. It's a first. You have your hands full with two boys so close together. Worse than having twins."

When I got home, I told Joe what had happened, and that Greg's finger would be alright.

"I hope you gave Mike a good spanking," Joe said.

"Mike just turned twelve months old," I said. "He didn't mean any harm. I would never spank him for what happened."

"How is he to learn if you don't punish him?"

"Mike was trying to share his most prized car with his little brother. That's really commendable for someone his age. Greg wasn't able to hold the car, and it's amazing that Mike thought to put his finger through the window so he could hold it."

Joe picked up two of Mike's cars that were on the floor and threw them in the garbage.

I said, "I doubt he'd ever put Greg's finger in a car window again. I'll make sure that Greg isn't around when he plays with his cars."

"He doesn't deserve to have the cars after what happened. Don't you dare give them to him. Next time he does something wrong, he'll get the spanking he deserves."

I felt a chill go through me. With Joe's temper, I wondered if he would start taking it out on the kids. Diane did as she was told, never got into trouble. But the two boys? They were different.

18

THE TAR PAPER SHACK

DIANE STARTED KINDERGARTEN in September, and she loved school. I thought she would make a great teacher because she'd patiently teach Mike to talk. Every time he'd master a word, she'd be delighted, but ever since Mike started walking at eleven months, Diane kept her dolls and books out of his reach.

One of the couples at Michigan Tech gave us a small playpen they didn't need anymore. It was great to be able to put Greg in it, so Mike wouldn't be able to reach him easily.

One morning, after Diane and Joe went to school, I decided to iron some shirts for Joe. I got the ironing board out from the bedroom closet and set it up in the living room. Mike played with his toys and Greg was in the playpen. As I began to iron, I didn't notice Mike coming up behind me. Being the right height to stand under the ironing board, he spotted a round, circular object. In an instant he pulled it and collapsed the board on top of him. He was pinned, and I couldn't rescue him. He started to howl.

Out the window, I saw a professor walking by. I ran to the door, and frantically shouted, "I need your help. Something's happened to my son. Please, can you come in and help me?"

Coming to the door, he said, "I can hear him crying, what happened?"

"He collapsed the ironing board and he's under it. I can't get him out!"

When he saw the problem, he said to Mike, "Don't cry, we're going to get you out of there. Just stay still."

Mike's howl changed to a whimper. It took a while but the professor was able to bend some spokes, and the two of us were able to get Mike from underneath the ironing board. Besides being frightened, Mike only had a long scrape on his arm and a little bump on his forehead.

When I told the professor what Mike did to get himself in that predicament, he laughed and said, "It's great he has an inquisitive mind. Boys will be boys."

Afraid of Joe's reaction, not knowing if he would spank Mike, just for being curious, I decided to lie about what happened. I told him Mike fell outside and scraped his arm and bumped his head.

As I had to do in the past, I needed to lie to survive or prevent trouble.

***

Christmas was coming and we went into the woods to cut down a tree. After looking at many shapes and sizes we finally found one that would fit in our small living-room. Diane thought it was perfect. Joe made a stand to balance the tree and hold the pail of water we put the tree in. That evening we decorated it. I gave Mike some ornaments and tinsel to place on the tree and he put them all in one spot. Diane would rearrange them when he wasn't looking. Then, Joe lifted him up to the top of the tree and Mike helped put the angel on. After the angel was secured, I said, "All done, don't touch the tree Mike."

Mike looked at the tree, looked at me and said, "All done."

Each morning when he got up, he went into the living room and walked up to the tree and said, "All done."

Soon after, Diane's teacher called me and said, "I need to talk to you about Diane. We had Santa visit the children today, and he asked each child what they wanted for Christmas. When it was Diane's turn, she told him she wanted money for her mom and dad, so they could buy things. It's not a good idea to talk about money in front of Diane. She's a serious child and it must worry her."

Embarrassed, I said, "I didn't realize she paid any attention to what we were talking about. As you know, my husband is in college during the day, so we discuss things at dinner. We'll have to be more careful in the future. Thank-you for telling me."

When the kids went to bed, I told Joe what the teacher said. "I've been thinking about calling the Dean and asking him if I could work part-time in the afternoon. I'll ask Mama if she could stay with Mike and Greg until you or I get home."

Joe and my mother agreed, and I began working at the

college, one to five, every day in the Dean of Student's office.

When our neighbors, Stan and Gracie, moved to Houghton for their last two college years, our new neighbors were Sally and Jerry O'Mara from New Hampshire. Jerry was a freshman in Civil Engineering and also on the G I Bill. He was Catholic, Irish, nice looking, a quiet kind of guy. Sally was pretty and outgoing. They had a little girl, Vickie, who was Greg's age. The O'Maras would become my life-long friends. The four of us would get together often. My parents sometimes invited them to dinner with us, and we also spent time at the cabin at Lake Superior. Sally and I got together when I wasn't working and the guys were in school.

"Why does Joe yell at you and the kids all the time?" Sally asked one afternoon. "He seems to have quite a temper. I worry that he'll get physical. Should I have Jerry talk to him?"

"No, please don't. It will only make things worse. I try and keep the kids occupied and away from him when he's in a bad mood. I just have to watch what I say to him. We'll be alright."

As June approached, we were getting ready for our move to Houghton for Joe's last two years of college. On the last day of my work at Michigan Tech, Dr. Young asked me to stay for a few minutes. He wanted to talk to me.

I sat down across from his desk, and he said, "Margaret, I want to talk to you about Joe. First I want to ask if everything is alright at home."

Surprised, I said, "Yes, why?"

"There's no easy way to say this. The reason I questioned you about what was happening at home was because of the psychological test we gave Joe when he was an incoming freshman. The results indicated that Joe is capable of doing harm to himself and others."

He got up and went to the window. Looking out, he continued, "After he took the test, I went over it several times and got the same answers. I went over it just this morning to be sure, with the same conclusion."

Coming back to the desk, he said, "I feel Joe needs to see a psychiatrist. There was no-one in the Sault that I would have recommended, and there certainly will not be one in Houghton. Joe's a brilliant man. He aced all his classes, but I feel he's not capable of having social relationships."

I stared at him as he continued. "I felt obligated to say something, because I know you well, having worked with you. I wanted you to be aware because he won't be easy to live with. You have your family here, but you will not have them in Houghton. I can't give you any advice, I have none, just felt you needed to know."

I was silent for a few minutes, trying to take in what Dr. Young just said, "Yes, Joe's hard to live with at times. It's like living with two different people. I appreciate what you told me. I hope Joe can get help after he graduates. Because he's so brilliant, I want him to succeed and do something wonderful with his life."

I got up, we shook hands, then he gave me a hug, and said, "Please, take care."

As I walked out of the office, I sadly thought, 'I knew Joe had problems and this confirms it, but there's nothing I can do about it now. He has to get a degree and then we'll see if he can get help.' I felt I could tolerate things and handle him for the coming two years.

***

Three days before we left for Houghton, Diane woke me and said, "Mom I don't feel good, and my head hurts."

She had a high fever and rash on her neck. When I lifted her pajama top I discovered her stomach was covered in a red rash.

When I called the doctor, he said, "There was a measles outbreak at school. Keep her in bed in a darkened room. Give her baby aspirin every four hours and a lot of fluids."

I called my mother and said, "Diane has the measles! I don't know what to do. We have to get out of the apartment in three days and go to Houghton."

"Measles will not clear up in three days," she said. "It's more like three weeks. Since the kids sleep in the same room, the boys may come down with it too. There is nothing you can do about measles except wait it out. Why don't you leave them here, and go to Houghton and get settled? You wanted to find work in the evening when Joe will be home, so this will give you a chance to find something. We'll bring them to you when everyone is healthy."

"Won't it be too much for you? Greg just turned one in February and Mike two in March. Even though they both take afternoon naps they can be a handful."

"The boys adore their grandfather and he'll keep them occupied. As soon as you get a telephone, we can call and keep you updated. It won't be too much."

After we talked it over, we decided to go to Houghton as planned and leave the kids with my parents. We set up their down-stairs bedroom for them. I tried not to be tearful in

Mama, Greg, Diane, Daddy and Mike

1957

front of the kids, and Daddy kept the boys occupied. Saying good-bye, telling Diane to stay in bed except to use the bathroom, with kisses all around, we headed for Houghton.

It was a five-and-a-half-hour trip across the Upper Peninsula to Houghton, which is situated on Lake Superior and Portage Lake. The quaint town had densely wooded hills and bordered the waterfront of the lake. It was originally settled by the Cornish and Finnish immigrants that worked the copper mines. Along with the college and copper mine, it was a winter tourist attraction and the birthplace of professional hockey. It's said that Houghton has two seasons, winter and winter coming. Snow average is 218 inches and it can freeze 100 days per year. I call the upper peninsula of Michigan, the North Pole of the United States.

When we arrived in the pretty small town, we went to the university and checked in. Arriving at our housing, I was shocked. I had never seen such poor, dreary houses. They were individual tiny, army-green, tar-paper shacks in several rows. We later learned they were condemned in 1940, and we were living in them in 1958. Our house only had one door so that made it a fire- trap, although you could probably just push the wall out and escape.

Inside the house, the walls were a gunmetal grey with no curtains on the windows. On the left side was our bedroom with only a three-quarter bed that fit wall to wall. You could see daylight between the wall and the thin roof. A small closet and nothing else fit in the room. The tiny living room had a couch that made into a bed plus a rocking chair. Our black and white seven-inch TV fit in a corner of the room. The floor was broken through in one place, and you could see the ground. After leaving home, anything I previously lived in was a mansion compared to this.

I worried about the little gas-heating stove between the living room and kitchen. I was afraid the kids would get burned if they bumped against it. The kitchen had no cupboards or door under the sink, leaving pipes exposed. There was a small refrigerator, two-burner electric stove with a small oven. A table sat in front of the window. The narrow bathroom had a shower, sink and toilet all in a row. No tub. Next to the bath was the other bedroom with built-in bunkbeds.

I burst into tears and cried, "I can't bring my babies into this tar paper shack. Where am I going to put my dishes? There's no tub for the kids. If you pull out the couch to make a bed it will touch the other wall. The winters are cold and our heating bill will be high. I can't believe they charge forty dollars for this horrible place."

"We don't have a choice," Joe replied. "I'll go to the grocery store and see if they will give us wood fruit crates. I can make cupboards along the wall over the sink with them. I might be able to build a narrow long cupboard for canned goods. The floor I can fix. I'll go under the house and put a block of wood under the hole."

I realized he was right. We had no choice. I would try and make the place as livable as possible before the kids got there. Joe went to the grocery store and came back with several wooden crates and the promise of more. We were able to fit a cot for Diane in the bedroom that had the bunkbeds, with only a narrow path between beds.

I went to the paint store and said to the manager, "My husband is a student at Michigan Tech, and we live in student housing. The walls are gun-metal grey and I would like to paint them. Would you have any paint you can't sell that we could have at a discount?"

He said he had two gallons of pale blue paint a customer rejected after he tinted it for them. "If you can use it, you can have it. I hear they need to replace the student housing. Is it as bad as they say?"

"You can't imagine how bad it is. We're fortunate to have a place to live, though. With college expenses and three kids, we can't afford to live anywhere else."

Handing me the paint, he threw in a couple of paint brushes, masking tape and a yardstick. I thanked him over and over for his generosity.

While Joe began putting up the cupboards, I started painting the walls.

"Good God, don't you know how to paint?" Joe asked. "Quit brushing the same spot. You're putting the paint on and taking it off doing it that way."

After showing me how to do it right, we worked in silence for a while.

"Watch what you're doing," Joe yelled. "You have more paint on you than the walls. It's going to take two coats, so just cover it the first time, and quit being so particular. We'll have to go over it again anyway." And so it went through the afternoon.

The next day I got some white paint for the cupboards and bunk beds. He refused to take any money for the paint.

It took us several days to paint and put the cupboards up. Joe did a fantastic job with only the wooden crates.

The cupboards looked professional. He fastened a rod across the bottom of the sink, and I made a gathered curtain out of an old flowered skirt to cover the pipes. I made curtains for the windows out of an old white bed-sheet.

My mother taught me to mend and sew on her peddle, Singer sewing machine, and when we were married, my parents gave us a Montgomery Ward sewing machine. I don't know what we would have done without it.

The place shaped up nicely. Joe went into the woods and cut down branches and made a bench with a back. He put it outside, against the house for us to sit on in the evenings.

We heard regularly from my parents. Several days after being exposed, both boys came down with a slight case of measles. My mother said it was hard to keep the two boys in a darkened room but they managed to do it. It was thought that exposure to the light would damage eyes when you had measles. There was no vaccine in those days.

I went to the university to see if there was any part-time work. When I went to the administration office, I told them I had worked for the Dean at the Sault branch. They said their Dean was out of town. If he needed any help they would contact me. They had an opening in the cafeteria for the evening meal shift. I talked to the head of the cafeteria and he said they could pay me thirty cents an hour. I would start next Sunday from four to eight.

The job at the cafeteria was interesting and exhausting. The evening meal was the main meal, except on Sundays when it was at noon. The stoves, refrigerators and ovens were huge. Besides the chef and his assistances, there were four of us that prepped the meal and then worked the cafeteria line.

I peeled many potatoes and carrots, chopped onions, sliced tomatoes, and stirred gravy in huge vats. The meals varied, and the students were polite and friendly when they went through the line. I wiped tables, stacked dishes to be washed, and put leftovers in the refrigerators. Once in a while the chef gave me food to take home. I had to fix Joe's dinner before I left for work, so the extra food came in handy for his meal the next day.

One evening, my mother called and said, "I have good news. I think the children are over the measles and we will be bringing them to Houghton on the twenty-eighth of June. If you have room, we thought we would stay a few days since we've never been to Houghton."

I said, "Please, stay as long as you want. We have room. You'll be surprised when you see where we're living."

I was glad we'd been able to have the time to fix the place up without the kids there. It was a tense time, and with the boys underfoot I'm sure Joe's temper would have flared. Now we looked forward to having the kids home again and a new beginning.

19

THE BARGAIN SHOP

ON THE TWENTY-EIGHTH OF JUNE, my parents brought our three children to Houghton after they'd been staying with their grandparents while getting over the measles.

When Daddy saw our housing, he said, "This too shall pass."

Mama said, "How will you manage to bake bread in that little oven and cook in such a small kitchen?"

We pulled out the couch to make a bed for my parents. We couldn't give them our bed because it was only three-quarter, and Joe and I could hardly fit in it. While we were setting it up Daddy played with the boys. He enjoyed teasing and playing with them, and they loved it.

Joe shouted and spanked Greg for running around and making too much noise. When Greg began to cry, Joe yelled, "If you don't shut up, I'll give you another spanking."

My parents didn't say anything, but from the sad look

and frowns on their faces, I knew it bothered them.

When the kids went to bed I whispered, "Joe, why did you spank Greg for being rambunctious? He's only one and a half years old and was playing with his grandpa."

"I'm sick and tired of you contradicting me! I'll spank the kids when I feel like it. Get that through your head or I'll give you something to think about."

Angry, I didn't say anything more. My parents left the next day.

Shortly after, the Dean called, and said, "I understand you worked in the Dean's office at the Sault branch and you're looking for work. I need a girl and wondered if you could come in tomorrow afternoon, so we can talk about it."

I agreed to meet with him, thinking that leaving the kids with Joe for eight hours every day during the summer wouldn't be good. But we needed the money. If I worked half days in the afternoon, the boys would be taking an afternoon nap. With both boy's potty trained and Diane there to play with them, they shouldn't be too much trouble for Joe. I could ask the cafeteria manager if I could work only on Sunday night. It may work out.

When I met with the Dean, I told him I could only work half days in the summer and he said, "We can start with half days; however, after school starts in September, I'll need someone full time. I talked with Dr. Young, and he gave you an excellent recommendation. The pay will be thirty-five cents an hour. See if you can work something out, so you can work full-time in the fall." The plan worked.

***

The professor's wives held a tea for the Tech wives one Sunday afternoon. It was held at one of their homes. It was a large, beautiful, brick home on a rolling wooded hill, close to the campus and not far from our housing.

About thirty-five Tech wives attended. The professor's wives were friendly and I met and talked with the Dean's wife. They were interested in our concerns about our housing and low wages. It was a pleasant and interesting afternoon.

The other Tech wives agreed that if we worked, we couldn't afford a baby-sitter with the low wages women were paid. I said, "What we need, is to have a school for kids under kindergarten age near campus."

One of the wives said, "The problem is, we can't afford a teacher and don't have a place to hold it."

A couple of days later, I went downtown, in the morning, for groceries. With no shopping malls in that time-period, if you wanted to buy something you had to go to the downtown main street. I noticed the store next to Woolworth had been vacant for a while. Looking in the window, I spotted a man inside. I knocked on the door.

When he opened it, I said, "I'm a Tech wife, and I noticed the store has been vacant for some time. Until someone rents the space, I wondered if you could let the student's wives use it. In Phoenix, Arizona we had second-hand stores. There isn't any in Houghton. We need money to start a school for our children who are under school age, so we can work in the fall when our husbands are in school. If we could get donations of clothing and goods to sell, we may have enough money to have our school."

"I'm just an employee," the man said. "The owner is a copper mine executive and has me check on the place a couple times a week. Let me talk to the owner and have him call you."

When the owner called, he said, "Herbert told me the Tech wives wanted to use my shop as a second-hand store and why. I'm assuming you're not planning on paying me for it. When were you thinking of starting this adventure?"

"I need to talk to the other wives. It will take us several days to get organized. Can I call you back and give you the details?"

"See what you can do. I'll wait for your call and then decide."

That evening, I went door to door down the streets of our housing and told them of my idea. Everyone thought it was a great plan and volunteered to help. I called the Dean's wife and told her what we were hoping to do and asked if we could get donations from the professor's wives.

She said, "What a wonderful idea! I'm sure you can get a lot of donations. I have things you can have. I'll talk to the other women and start collecting things for you."

I called the owner and described our plans. He agreed to let us use the store until he could find a renter.

"If you have anything you can donate, we'd appreciate it," I said.

He laughed, "You want to use my store for free and now you want donations from me. You had me from the start when you said it was so little kids can go to school while their mothers worked. I'll see what I can do."

When the word got around to the other main street stores about what we were trying to do and why, one store gave us a manikin for our window and other stores gave us tables and racks to hang clothes on. Now we needed donations of second-hand items.

Ten wives could work the store on rotation. No stores were open on Sunday in Houghton back then, so Monday through Saturday our hours would to be ten to five.

Our husbands helped us set up the store. Donations flooded in from the faculty wives. Some of the dresses looked like they had never been worn. Our window display made our shop look elegant. We dressed the manikin in a bright red gown with a rhinestone necklace. Joe made a wooden sign for the window and painted TECH WIVE'S BARGAIN SHOP on it. We opened the next day and were flooded with people and sales.

When I arrived at the Dean's office on Monday afternoon, he said. "I've arranged for one of our conference rooms we don't need for your school. Mary, the wife of one of the staff, will be here in a little while to talk to you about teaching."

Mary looked like a pleasant young woman. "I'd love to teach the class for the children. I'm pregnant and pregnant women aren't allowed to work in the school district. If you don't care that I'm pregnant, I can teach them and I won't charge you for it. It will give me something to do. I'll need an assistant, and I have a friend that is able to assist. Would you be able to pay her? They could use the money."

"Yes! With the store doing well, donations coming in from church groups and others to keep it going, we can pay her thirty-five cents an hour. We'll pay for any supplies you need for the class. When you purchase them, give us the bills, so you can be reimbursed."

The boys loved going to school like their sister. There were eighteen kids in the class. Mary was a great teacher. She had a graduation for them the following June and made graduation caps for all the students. She had a little ceremony for the children that wouldn't be coming back the next year.

In August, in the middle of the night, there was a loud crash. Joe jumped out of bed, to see what happened. "Margaret, quick, come here!" he said.

When I got out of bed and went into the living room, I saw that the canned goods had all fallen out of the long cupboard on the wall in the kitchen. There was something hitting the house. We then saw a large back bear walk by the window! Behind the houses were heavy woods. We were told to be cautious of wild animals. We never thought we'd see a bear.

October, we had our first snowfall. The kids had to walk to school. There was no bus service because we lived only a few blocks from Diane's school and the pre-school at the college. The roads were plowed continuously during winter. In the sub-zero mornings the children were bundled up, so the only thing visible was their eyes. Parents did not walk or drive their children to school like everyone does today. Today, it is no longer safe because of two-legged predators.

We shoveled the snow against the sides of our shack to help insulate it. Some of the engineering students made tunnels from their front door so they wouldn't have so much to shovel.

Joe and I had a pair of snowshoes that looked like fat tennis rackets without handles. Very different from today's snowshoes. They were used in deep snow so that your weight was distributed over a large area, and you wouldn't sink up to your hips in the snow. You had to be careful when you walked, so you didn't trip yourself.

The first time I took a step, I started with picking up my right foot and putting it forward. I picked up my left foot and didn't notice I'd put part of the left snowshoe on the right. When I went to pick up my right foot, which was trapped, I fell over into the snow bank. It was quite a challenge to get up with two huge snowshoes strapped to my feet. I was bundled up from the cold and looked like a hippopotamus. Turning around was difficult. You either had to walk in a large semicircle or kick turn like you do on skis.

The professor's children came to the student housing to play with our children. There were lots of kids and Joe built an igloo big enough for five or six kids. The snowmen were gigantic and there were a lot of snowball fights. The kids made a long snow train that about twenty kids could sit on. They used their imagination and called out places they were going while making lots of whistles and train noises.

Our Christmas tree was another challenge. We went into the forest and cut down a pretty pine tree. I was sitting on the couch when Joe brought it into our tiny living-room and put it in a corner. Half of the tree sat on my lap. Joe cut all the back branches off and set the tree trunk in the corner. The tree fell over nearly knocking me out, so Joe put a hook into the wall and tied the tree to it. It worked, even though it was a strange looking tree.

One night, in the middle of the night, I heard the two

boys giggling and I thought it was coming from the kitchen. Getting up to see what was happening, peeking around the corner, I saw the two boys sitting on top of the kitchen table, eating from the can of Hersey's chocolate powder I'd put on the table for the morning. They didn't see me, so I grabbed my camera and when the flash went off, they turned their heads toward me. Their faces, from the nose down, were brown from the chocolate, not to mention their two hands which they used to dig the chocolate out of the can.

The flash woke Joe up. He got out of bed and looked over my shoulder, "What are you two doing?"

I froze.

Joe started to laugh. "You're both a mess! Don't you ever do something like this again or you'll get your butts spanked." Picking up the Hersey's can, he added, "You ate almost all of it. No chocolate milk tomorrow for you guys."

Relieved that he didn't blow up in anger, I grabbed a dish-cloth and started to wipe up the chocolate.

"What will those boys think of next," Joe said. "It was probably Greg that thought of it."

I didn't say anything but wondered why he always seemed to pick Greg out to criticize and blame.

Our first winter in Houghton was a hard winter. December was record-breaking for snow and cold. On December twentieth it was thirty-one degrees below zero. The snow was 107.8 inches. Joe's bathrobe froze to the wall in the closet. We had to wait until the spring thaw to pry it off. The winter seemed to never end. I could hardly wait for spring and seeing the O'Mara's again when they would transfer from the Sault to Houghton.

20

PIZZA

WORKING IN THE CAFETERIA at the college for the Sunday night supper was fun and interesting. The food was mostly cold cuts and leftovers from Sunday afternoon dinner. The boys knew me by name, and we had a good rapport as I served them at the food line. They complained constantly about the Sunday evening food.

One Sunday, Mark, a student from New York, said, "I hate the Sunday night dinner. I wish they had a pizza restaurant in Houghton like they do in New York. They don't even have an Italian restaurant here."

Jokingly I replied, "I make a good pizza. Too bad I can't sell you one."

The next night, I got a telephone call from someone in the dorm. "I'm a student, and I'd like to order a pizza. Do you have one with pepperoni?"

Shocked, I said, "Why on earth do you think I sell pizza? This isn't a restaurant."

"There's a poster in the dorm with your name and telephone number advertising you sell homemade pizza. There are about eight of us that want to order pizza."

"If I sold you a pizza how would it keep warm? It's still winter and a ten-minute walk from my house to the dorm in freezing weather. I was joking with Mark about my pizza. I never thought about making and selling it. Let me think about it and see if I can figure out a way to do it. I'll let you know next Sunday."

Before we left Phoenix, pizza had begun to appear on the menu at Italian restaurants. We went to our favorite restaurant where we had our first date before leaving for college. We ordered pizza for the first time and loved it. When the chef made his usual rounds talking to customers at the tables, I told him that we were leaving Phoenix and going to college in Michigan. I asked him if he could tell me how to make the pizza. He told me how to go about it and I started to experiment with it when we got to the Sault.

I baked our pizza on a large cookie sheet. Since baking my own bread, I figured out how to make the thin yeast crust, spread it on the cookie sheet, then lightly coat it with olive oil. After many attempts, I came up with a tasty sauce which I poured over the oiled dough. Then I sprinkled it with mozzarella cheese, pepperoni and topped it with parmesan cheese. It took twenty to thirty minutes to bake at a high temperature.

The small oven in my kitchen could only hold one cookie sheet at a time. If I did sell pizza to the guys in the dorm, I would have to figure out a way to package it.

I decided to use a cut-down cardboard box, lined with

aluminum foil. I'd place the pizza on it and cover it with the foil. To keep it warm, I'd cover it with newspapers. I called the newspaper office and asked if I could pick up unused papers. Then I went to the grocery store and asked if there were any boxes I could have. I figured I could store the cut-down boxes under the boys bunk beds and the newspapers under our bed. After discussing it with Joe, I decided to try selling pizza. Joe said, "I'll cut the pepperoni for you, every day, paper thin like I do for our pizza."

Figuring out the cost to make it, I decided that the price would be two-fifty for a large cookie sheet of cheese pizza and three dollars for pepperoni pizza. I would have to space the orders forty-five minutes apart.

The next Sunday, as Mark went through the food line he asked, "Are you going to sell us pizza?"

I said, "I'll give it a try. There will be two types. Cheese and pepperoni. If you want to order it again maybe you can bring the box back so I can reuse it. I can't take any orders before five o'clock in the evening."

My pizza business became such a success, I had to quit my Sunday night job at the cafeteria. I got orders almost every night. Sunday was the biggest day, and on Saturdays I got calls until midnight. With working at the Dean's office and my pizza business, I didn't worry as much about how I was going to pay our bills.

When Jerry and Sally O'Mara came to Houghton in June for their last two years, I asked Sally if she would help. I taught her how to make the pizza and told her that any she baked and sold was her money to keep. After we left Houghton, Sally continued to sell pizza.

The O'Maras were assigned student housing directly behind our place. I was so glad to see my friends again. Since both Joe and Jerry were Catholic, on Sunday we went to church together with our families. Friday nights we sometimes had dinner together. Usually we had tuna fish casseroles or fish sticks since at that time members of the Catholic church could not eat meat on Fridays.

On Saturday mornings, Sally and I took our kids to the shore of Lake Superior. The lake was too cold to swim in so we hunted for agates. Sally was not familiar with agate stones that wash up on the shore, and I showed her what to look for. Agates come from volcanic rocks or lavas. Lake Superior agates had reddish hues. They have a brilliance from glacier polish and iron oxidization. Some agates, when cut and polished, were made into jewelry, paper-weights, or a beautiful decoration on a table.

We took a picnic lunch, spread a blanket on the white sand, and watched the kids play in the lapping waves, in their bare feet. They didn't seem to mind the cold water.

We had wonderful times at the lake and I had quite a collection of agates by the time we left Houghton. I have a lot of wonderful, happy memories connected to those agates.

***

Joe forbid me to read books. He said, "It's a waste of time and you have other things you should be doing. If I come home from class and catch you reading you'll be sorry."

When I'd find a book at our bargain shop I wanted to read, I'd buy it and keep it hidden under the clothes in the dirty clothes basket, knowing Joe wouldn't find it there. I thought 'once he graduates, I'll be able to read it.'

Late one winter night, after Joe did his studying and went to bed, thinking Joe was asleep, I decided to read one of my books. He usually was a sound sleeper so I put on my nightie, curled up in a chair and began to read. While I was engrossed in the story, Joe came into the room.

Furious, he grabbed the book out of my hand, opened the door and threw it outside. He grabbed me and tossed me into the snow-bank in my bare feet and nightie. He locked the door behind me.

I tapped on the door and yelled, "Let me in."

Joe turned out the lights. Not wanting to wake the kids and frighten them, I didn't pound on the door. If they cried, Joe might take his anger out on them.

Not knowing what to do, I ran, barefoot in the snow, to Sally's house and banged on the door. Jerry came to the door. Embarrassed, upset and freezing cold, with teeth chattering, I told him what happened.

Sally got up, wrapped me in a blanket, gave me her slippers and was making a bed on the couch for me when Joe came to the door and yelled, "GET HOME."

Without saying another word, we left. I knew it would only make things worse if I tried to discuss what happened. I was so angry at Joe that I didn't even feel the freezing cold as we went home. I had to grit my teeth to keep from telling him off. Afraid of what he'd do to me, I kept quiet.

When we got to the house, Joe said, "Maybe in the future you will pay attention to what I tell you to do or not do. I don't want to hear a word out of you. Now get to bed."

Without saying a word, I got in bed, shaking both from cold and anger. Joe immediately lifted my gown, climbed on top of me, spreading my legs. I didn't move and just let him do whatever he wanted.

***

Joe was hard on the boys. I tried to keep them quiet when he was home. Sometimes he'd let the mischievous things that boys did, go without a word. He could be playful and good with the kids. Other times he became enraged at the smallest thing and spanked the kids harder than he should. If I tried to stop it, he'd start in on me. I kept hoping that once he finished his education and got a degree, we wouldn't have to struggle, not be under so much stress, things would be better.

Jerry knew Joe had a temper problem because he could hear him yelling at us. He also worried Joe was getting physical after the night he threw me in the snowbank, so Jerry went to his priest and talked to him about Joe.

When the priest talked to Joe about how he was treating his family, Joe was furious. He asked the priest if I had talked to him and the priest told him no and wouldn't reveal who it was. Maybe Joe suspected Jerry but he never said. He left the Catholic church and never returned.

Since Joe left the church, he didn't care if I used birth control. I was using over-the-counter products and the rhythm method to prevent getting pregnant. Birth control pills had not come on the market.

In February, I began to have signs that I was once again pregnant. When I went to the doctor he verified it and said I was due in November. I was frightened and concerned about bringing another child into the family because of Joe's temper and his harsh treatment of the boys.

I knew I would lose my job with the Dean since pregnant women couldn't work in public. I began to show right away and couldn't hide it. I was glad I had my pizza sales for extra income.

In a magazine at the doctor's office, I found an article about how to make monkey dolls out of men's work socks. I thought I would make the doll for the new baby. I didn't have any paper to write the instructions down, so I looked to see if anyone was looking at me and slowly tore the page out of the magazine and slipped it into my purse. I felt like a criminal and guilty of the crime of stealing monkey doll instructions from the doctor's office.

I made the monkey doll and it was adorable. I showed it to Sally and she wanted one. I made one for her and when others saw it they wanted one too. As the word got around I began to get calls from people asking me if I would make them a monkey doll. I decided to sell them for a dollar fifty. I was glad of the extra income, even though I only made thirty cents a doll.

As June and graduation approached, Joe interviewed for jobs. We hoped he could find an engineering job in Phoenix, but no company submitted a request for mechanical engineers. Joe wrote to AiResearch in Phoenix but didn't get a response from them.

He accepted a job with Whirlpool in St. Joseph in lower

Michigan. The town was on the shores of Lake Michigan. Whirlpool would pay for the move and they gave us a list of apartment and home rentals in the St Joseph area. I was glad to be leaving terrible never-ending winters. Even though Lower Michigan's winters were still cold with lots of snow, it wouldn't be as bad.

At the June graduation, I looked like I was nine months pregnant. The doctor thought I might be having multiple births even though he couldn't find any other heartbeat. There was no ultra-sound in those days to view the baby or tell if you were having multiple births or a boy or girl.

With Joe graduating and getting a good job, I was looking forward to a new beginning and hopefully being a stay-at-home mom.

21

THE STRANGE CHRISTMAS TREE

It was an eight-hour trip from Houghton to St. Joseph, Michigan. Whirlpool gave us a moving allowance, and Joe had a week before he had to report to work. Since we still had the little trailer we pulled from Phoenix, we didn't need movers, so we were able to put aside money for emergencies. The map we picked up from the gas station routed us through Wisconsin and the tip of Illinois. The trip was uneventful and the kids slept a lot.

We arrived in the evening and found a hotel for the night. We planned on looking for a place to rent the next day. With the rental list Whirlpool gave us, we hoped to find something quickly. As we looked, I worried that the two boys, tired and bored, would become a handful and Joe would become angry with them.

St. Joseph was a quaint port-town bordering Lake Michigan and the mouth of the St. Joseph River. It had dune-backed sandy beaches and two lighthouses dating back to 1834. The pretty town had brick streets and unique shops.

After seeing two places for rent that we weren't impressed with, we found an old, beautiful, furnished, two-story home. It was on a bluff, overlooking Lake Michigan. With no other homes in front, the view was magnificent. Sailboats and other crafts slid by the picture window. It was for sale and we could rent it month to month. We could store most of our meager possessions in the garage.

I begged Joe to rent it for the summer. Since it was June, we had time to find a more permanent rental near a grade school. In September, Diane would be starting third grade. Joe agreed to temporarily rent the beautiful house.

I loved the place with its panoramic view of Lake Michigan. I never tired of watching the sunsets with their red, yellow and pink colors dipping into the lake. Even though we couldn't afford to buy the house, I was happy we could spend the summer there. It was a home I'd never forget.

The day after we moved in, the next-door neighbor, April, came over to welcome us to the neighborhood. Her daughter was Diane's age and they became friends. The boys didn't have anyone in the neighborhood their age but they always played well together. They loved to race up and down the large winding staircase in the house or jump down the steps two or three at a time. I kept a large supply of Band-Aids for their scraped knees and elbows.

Joe started working for Whirlpool and seemed happy with the work. He didn't talk much about it but I could tell from the way he was at home, things were going well. It was a wonderful summer, and it seemed like we were living in a palace.

In August, we began looking for a place to rent near a school. We found a fairly new ranch style home on a corner lot with three bedrooms and a large fenced backyard. It was in a nice neighborhood within walking distance to a grade school.

Joe built a big sandbox in the backyard for the boys to play in. They made sand castles and imaginary roads for their trucks and cars. Mike was three years old and Greg two— constant companions. Mike was the stronger personality and Greg followed his lead. They were always getting into things or getting hurt.

One afternoon, I was busy dusting and picking up toys when Mike came up to me and said, "Pick, Pick."

He held out his arm toward me. On his wrists, he had put all of Diane's tiny ponytail elastic bands. The hand was beet-red and swelling.

As I managed to cut the elastic with thin, sharp embroidery scissors, I said, "Michael, how many times have I told you to leave Diane's things alone? Now, she won't be able to wear a ponytail. Your hand hurts and if I wasn't able to cut the elastics off, I'd have to take you to the emergency room. When Diane gets home from school, tell her you're sorry you were messing with her things again."

April recommended a doctor for my pregnancy. He too thought I might be having twins or triplets because my stomach was so big but he could never find another heartbeat. I had gestational diabetes and was put on a strict diet. My ankles and legs were swollen, and I couldn't get comfortable when sitting in a chair or lying in bed.

In November, when the baby was due, my mother came

to St. Joseph to take care of the kids while I'd be in the hospital. November came and went and still no baby, so she had to return home. I was so huge I had to sit spread-eagle to make room for my stomach. If I had a cup of tea, I would rest the cup on my stomach. My diet consisted of salt-less, sugarless porridge and not much else. I thought the baby would never come.

On December eighth, the doctor put me in the hospital and induced labor. Joe had to take vacation days to take care of the kids. After many hours of labor, the doctor realized I should have had a Caesarean section but it was too late. I couldn't have sedation of any kind because it was a difficult forceps delivery. I vacillated between wanting to die, and being afraid I'd die and leave the kids with Joe.

Brian Richard, was born on December 9th 1960 with curley blonde hair and blue eyes. He weighed TEN-pounds, SIX-ounces and was *only nineteen inches long*. He was as wide as he was tall. It was like giving birth to a bowling ball. They put him into an incubator due to the difficult long birth. We were in the hospital fifteen days. People came from all over the hospital to see the cute, plump baby boy.

The second day, after the birth, the nurse came in to check on my many stitches. All of a sudden, I started to hemorrhage. She quickly turned the bedside monitor light on and ran to the door to get help. It was like someone turned on a faucet and a most frightening experience. After packing me, to stop the flow, they took me to the operating room for surgery and repair the problem.

Brian was alert from day one. He was the most contented baby. When we got home, he looked around and turned over on the changing table. He never cried, even for a bottle. He would wake up, stretch and make squeaky, gurgling noises. I'd pick him up, change him and get the bottle ready. He'd drink it all with no coaxing and go back to sleep. Brian learned to sit up early. By six months he could pull himself up to a standing position by holding onto the side of the playpen. He walked at eight months. Today, he is a six-foot-two big man, with a size thirteen shoe.

One morning, I decided to sew something for Christmas. I got out my sewing machine and set it up on the table. Brian was in the playpen.

To keep an eye on them, I said, "Mike, Greg, come and watch how I sew."

I put Mike on one side and Greg on the other. As they were quietly watching, I started to sew a seam. I didn't see Mike pick up a straight pin. Aiming it exactly, he dropped it into the electric socket of the sewing machine. Sparks flew and the machine stopped working.

"Look," Mike said, "I made fireworks."

I thought, 'Mike's lucky his father isn't home. I don't think he would have let this slide.' I worried about Joe's punishment whenever these incidents happened.

Getting ready for Christmas was hectic. Diane went with Joe to pick out the tree. It would be the first time the tree came from a boy-scout lot since leaving Phoenix. We missed going to the woods to cut down our perfect tree.

After New Year's, we took the tree down and Joe put it outside by the road next to the driveway because the city was going to pick Christmas trees up early the next morning. It was also the day the garbage was being collected.

After I was released from the hospital, I had heavy blood flow. In those days they only had Kotex pads for women to use to capture it. I went through large boxes of them and put the used, folded and tied pads in the empty box.

I asked Joe, as he left for work, to put the box of used Kotex pads in the garbage and take the container out front for the garbage men.

"The garbage can is full, but I'll set it on top of the garbage with the lid over it," he said.

In those days, we didn't have the huge garbage bins they have today. They were just a large metal can with detachable lids. The garbage men had to get out of their trucks, take the lid off the cans and throw the contents into their truck.

Right after breakfast, the boys wanted to go outside and make a snowman. After I put them into their snowsuits and boots, I sent them outside.

A short while later, the doorbell rang. I still had my bathrobe and slippers on and wondered who would be coming to the door that early. Opening the door, I saw two young men from Jehovah Witnesses standing there with their leaflets. With a grin and surprised look on their faces, they were looking at something in the front yard toward the road. Sticking my head outside, I saw my two boys decorating the Christmas tree with my used Kotex pads!!

Dumbfounded, I stammered, "OH MY GOD!"

Trying not to look at the two men, I said, "I don't want anything."

I flew by them and told the two boys, "Go in the house. NOW!"

As the traffic went by, people turned their heads to see the Christmas tree with Kotex hanging on it. I grabbed the box, and as quickly as I could, began to remove the pads.

I must have been quite a sight standing at the tree in my bathrobe and slippers, in the snow, with a Kotex box in my hand. I was sure the people driving by were trying to figure out if I was putting them on or taking them off. Either way they must have thought I had a serious mental problem.

When I got in the house Mike said, "Mom, did you like the tree? We decorated it all by ourselves."

I sat down and laughed until I cried.

22

SEWERS, INCH WORMS AND TICKS

THE NORTHWEST LEATHER COMPANY, where my father was employed as a supervisor, closed in 1958. In those days, companies didn't give any benefits when they closed.

Needing to work, my father decided he would like to become a Medical Technician. One of the members of the Gospel Hall in Minneapolis, was a doctor who encouraged Daddy to go to the University of Minnesota and take courses there.

My parents sold their home in Sault Ste. Marie and their cabin at Lake Superior in order for Daddy to move to Minneapolis and go back to college. Daddy gave up the Ministry of the Gospel Hall Meeting, where he preached most of his adult life. It was not a paid position.

My sister Virginia and I were shocked. My father was fifty-nine years old and both my parents were raised in Sault Ste Marie. All their relatives lived in Michigan and Sault Ste. Marie, Ontario, Canada. They never traveled. Their home, cabin, friends and family meant a lot to them, as did the Gospel Hall.

At that time in my life, someone that was fifty-nine years old seemed elderly to me. I wondered if Daddy was too old to start a new career and leave all that he knew behind.

I hated the thought of their selling the cabin at Lake Superior. I loved it and had many happy memories. My father built it himself. I learned to swim there, row a boat, and in the evening, we had many bon-fires, cooking marshmallows and hot dogs on a stick. I picked wild blueberries at the edge of the white sandy beach for my mother to make her delicious blueberry pies and muffins.

It was their decision, so we never told them how we felt when they sold everything and moved to Minnesota. My mother got a job as a dental assistant and my father went back to college.

Virginia and her family lived in Rochester, New York. Her daughter, Linda, had bronchial asthma, and after a severe attack, their doctor advised them to move to Arizona. At that time, it was thought to be the best place to recover from lung conditions. When I lived there, I wrote her glowing reports of Phoenix. Virginia had always wanted to go west, so they decided to make the move.

When my dad got his degree, my parents decided to move to Phoenix too, since my sister was there. Daddy immediately got a job working at a hospital as the Medical Technician.

***

In January, 1962, Whirlpool transferred Joe to St. Paul, Minnesota. It was a promotion. He was going to work as the mechanical engineer for the Whirlpool dishwasher division. My parents left Minnesota for Arizona just a short time before we were to leave Michigan and go to Minnesota. We never thought we would leave St. Joseph and were surprised when Joe was transferred.

St. Paul lies on the east bank of the Mississippi River. In the beginning it was settled by the French and called "Pig's Eye". A Catholic priest from Dubuque, France, came to the settlement and they built a log chapel for the priest. It was called "The Log Chapel of Saint Paul," and later became "The Cathedral of Saint Paul." They then renamed the settlement to the current name, St. Paul. It became known as the "Twin Cities," only a twenty-minute drive to Minneapolis.

Before being transferred, we had purchased some furniture and a new turquoise and white Chevy station-wagon. Whirlpool provided for the move, and after the movers came we settled the kids in the car, got a road map from the gas station and headed for St. Paul. It would be a seven-hour trip through some of Illinois and Wisconsin. Since it was winter, I worried about the roads and snowstorms that could come up with little warning. Fortunately, it didn't happen, the boys slept a lot and were no trouble.

When we arrived in St. Paul, it was forty degrees below zero. I thought we must have made a wrong turn and we were back in Houghton or perhaps the real North Pole.

We rented a new, ranch style, three-bedroom house in Little Canada, a suburb of St. Paul. It was five miles to downtown St. Paul and eleven miles to downtown Minneapolis. Little Canada was considered rural and there were a lot of new housing developments.

When the movers arrived, it was still forty below zero, and when they began transferring the furniture, every time they opened the door, we saw a bank of fog. I soon realized the Minnesota winters were going to be very cold and damp.

Our landlord lived next door. He and his wife were our age, as were most of the people that lived on our street. We were the first tenants, and I quickly made friends with my neighbors. Our kids had a lot of children their age to play with.

We immediately enrolled Diane in school and she rode the school bus, a new experience for her. She was a good student and made friends easily.

During that very cold winter, I longed for spring. When it finally came, the weather wasn't much better. First, we had lots of rain, making it gloomy. The boys couldn't go out to play and kept begging to go outside. When the rain stopped for a while, they still couldn't go out because the yard, never having been grassed, was a sea of mud.

Then came the green inch-worms. They hung from the trees getting in your hair if you passed under them. Inch-worms covered the tires of the cars, roads, sidewalks and grass. They made the roads slick as they marched across.

If I thought spring was bad, I didn't realize that the summer could be worse. The temperature was not as high as in Phoenix but the humidity was unbearable and we had no air-conditioning. You couldn't go outside after the sun began to set because the mosquitoes were big enough to carry you off. In the dark of night, thick with insects, the weight of the Minnesota summer sat heavily. But mosquitoes were nothing compared to the people-ticks. Arizona had animal-ticks. Minnesota had people-ticks.

The neighbors told us to search the bodies of the kids when they came in from playing to see if they had any ticks. If they did, they said not to pull them off because the tick's head would be left in. We were told to hold a lighted match to the tick until it popped, releasing the head and killing it.

That day at bath time when I looked the kids over, I discovered that Greg had a large tick on his chest. I told Greg not to touch it, then called to Joe to bring a match so we could kill the tick. Greg started to cry.

I said, "It will be okay Greg, we'll remove the tick, it won't hurt. Daddy will be careful. It will just take a minute."

But he continued to cry.

Joe came in with the matches. He shouted at Greg, "Shut your fucking mouth and stand still."

Greg, terrified, cried harder. Joe hit him on the side of his head telling him, "If I tell you to shut up you better do it."

Holding the burning match to the tick, it popped. It was full of Greg's blood. I decided to learn if there was any other method of getting rid of ticks beside that disgusting one.

After I put the kids to bed, I said to Joe, "You shouldn't have yelled at Greg. He's only four. He was terrified. Yelling at him only made it worse and you shouldn't hit him for being afraid."

"He has to learn to do what I say," Joe said. "Don't you tell me what to do. Do you want him to be a sissy? Crying over nothing?"

"It wasn't nothing to him! We told him that matches

would burn and not to touch them. You can imagine how scared he was when you held a lighted match to his chest."

Joe replied, "In the future take care of ticks yourself. Don't expect any help from me. So, shut up. I don't want to hear any more about it."

From then on, I pulled ticks off with tweezers and put Peroxide on the area. I wasn't fond of bugs of any kind so it was a task I hated. I refused to ask Joe for help with the ticks ever again.

***

Although we were on the city sewer system, Sam, the neighbor across the street, was not. He had a septic tank. A very nice man, Sam loved to garden and grew a lot of vegetables. The problem was, Sam drained his septic tank onto the garden for fertilizer. It smelled up the entire street. He said they used human waste in China and they had great vegetables. He would bring me some of the vegetables he was so proud of. I would thank him, remark on what a great gardener he was, but when he left I threw them away, afraid that they would make us sick.

One day, Sam brought over some vegetables when Joe was home. Joe took the vegetables, walked over to the garbage can and threw them in. "Do you think we want your germ-infested vegetables?" Joe shouted. "If you don't stop draining your shit on the garden you'll wish you had." He threatened to pull Sam's garden up by the roots.

I was so embarrassed. I felt he could have talked to Sam in a civilized way without threatening him and hurting the man's feelings. Needless to say, the neighbor and his wife never spoke to us again and wouldn't allow their kids to play with ours. They never stopped draining the septic tank onto their vegetable garden.

In the summer, Joe helped the next-door neighbor, Henry, who owned our place, put sod on our front and back yard. It was a hard and dirty job but Joe and Henry had become friends, so Joe was glad to help him and didn't ask for anything in return. We had them for dinner often and played Monopoly afterward.

One night, Joe told me he had invited his boss and his wife for dinner the next night. I was surprised since Joe had never talked about them. I decided I would make pizza. The next day, I told the kids we were having important company. I would give them dinner early and I wanted them to remain in their room and play with their toys until bedtime.

When our guests arrived, everyone was introduced, including the kids who then went into their bedroom, and I put the pizza in the oven. After chatting for a while, the timer went off and the pizza was ready. We had a pleasant time at dinner and they asked us if we knew how to play Pinochle. We said we had the Pinochle cards and would be happy to play a game with them.

I cleared off the table so we could play cards, then I went into the kids' room and said, "You have been so good. I'm proud of you. It's eight, so it's time to go to bed."

Joe set up the cards and we started to play. After a few games, Joe got up in the middle of a game, and without saying a word, left the room.

When he didn't return, his boss asked, "Where's Joe?"

"He probably went to the bathroom," I said.

We waited a while longer. When he didn't return, I got up to look for him. *He had gone to bed.*

"What are you doing?" I asked him "We have company, why are you in bed? We are in the middle of a card game."

"Because I want to. Get out of here." He turned his face to the wall, and I went out and closed the door.

I thought, 'Joe did this because he was losing at cards. What on earth will I say to his boss? I don't want him to lose his job.'

Back at the card table, I said, "Joe's sick to his stomach. I think he may be coming down with something. He had to lie down. I guess we'll have to play cards some other night."

They got up to leave, saying, "I hope Joe will be alright and feel better soon."

I couldn't believe Joe went to bed, leaving the game and everyone just sitting there.

***

In May 1963, I received a telephone call from AiResearch in Phoenix. They wanted Joe to call them as soon as possible and left their number. Joe had applied at AiResearch before leaving college. He had hoped they would offer him a job because we wanted to return to Phoenix. He was disappointed when he didn't hear from them.

When Joe came home from work, I told him about the call. He was surprised and excited about the possibility of a job in Phoenix. Knowing it was still early in the West, he made the call.

When he got off the phone, surprised, he said,

"AiResearch is flying someone to St. Paul to interview me tomorrow evening for an engineering job!"

I danced around the kitchen with excitement. "I can't believe it," I said. "We actually have a chance to return to Phoenix. No more winters! I hope they need you right away. You probably have a good chance of getting the job or they wouldn't be sending someone to interview you."

I wanted to call my parents and sister in Phoenix right away but Joe said to wait until he was sure he got the job.

When Joe left for the interview, I was so anxious that I paced the floor the entire time he was gone. I couldn't think of anything else. I worried that in some way Joe would blow it. I thought, 'he doesn't have the necessary people skills.' My mind kept going in circles thinking of all the times he'd offended people.

When Joe came home, the first words out of his mouth were, "I got it. We're going back to Phoenix. They got a big government contract and they want me on July first. That will give me time to put in my notice at Whirlpool. AiResearch will pay for the move. The salary is only a little more, but we won't have to deal with the high winter expenses."

I was so relieved, I could hardly speak. "You *did* it," I said.

Every year Whirlpool chose one engineer for an award of three thousand dollars if they made an outstanding design or part. It was given the first of every year. When Joe gave his resignation at Whirlpool they told him he had won the award that year for his design on the dishwasher. The problem was he had to be there the first of the year to get the money. (Joe had designed a second water spray for the dishes just under the top rack of the dishwasher which is still used to this day.)

In those days, three thousand dollars was a lot of money. You could buy a Ford Mustang for less money. When Joe came home and told me about the bonus and they were going to give him a raise, we had to make the decision of whether to stay, or give up the money and take the job with AiResearch. Joe decided to forego the money and take the new job.

I was happy to be leaving the inch-worms, ticks, mosquitos, and freezing winters. I looked forward to seeing my sister and parents again. Another new beginning.

23

THE TERRIBLE MAN

WHEN JOE ACCEPTED THE JOB at AiResearch in May, we immediately told our landlord, Henry, who was also our next-door neighbor and friend, we were moving to Arizona. We would be leaving on June twenty-first, Friday, because Joe had to start his new job on July first. We paid our rent through June.

The morning before we were going to leave, I went to the bank to draw out the money from Joe's last paycheck. The teller called the bank manager over.

The manager said, "There's a hold on your money, so you can't take it out."

I was shocked. "It's our money, how can you keep us from drawing it out!"

"Your landlord gave us a legal paper that prevents you from taking the money. My advice is, see a lawyer."

Driving home in a hurry, I was so angry it's a wonder

I didn't get into an accident. I pulled into the landlord's driveway, got out of the car, slammed the car door, went up to the house and rang the doorbell with one hand and pounded on the door with the other.

Henry came to the door with a smug look on his face. Not asking me in, he said, "What?"

"Why did you put a hold on our money? The movers are coming tomorrow morning and we're leaving right after. Why would you do such a thing?"

"You didn't give us a three-month notice, so you owe us three-month's rent. July, August and September. If you don't pay us, we'll take you to court. Since you're leaving Minnesota tomorrow, it's our security to put a hold on your money."

"You, terrible man! When we told you we were leaving, you said nothing to us about an extra three-month rent. Why would you do something like this when we've been good friends? I had you and your wife to dinner many times. Joe spent an entire weekend putting sod on *your* property and never asked you for a dime. Joe fixed things that went wrong at the house and didn't bother you with it or ask for a reimbursement."

Wiping tears off my cheek with my finger, I added, "I guess you never know people's true nature and how nasty they can be. Evidently money means more to you than friendship. You'll eventually get what's coming to you. You can't treat people like this and get away with it. When I tell Joe what you've done, I don't know what he'll do. This is unreasonable and he has a temper."

"If he does anything to our property or us, he will go to jail. I will not hesitate to call the police if he steps a foot on this property." He shut the door with a slam.

Defeated, angry, I thought, 'I don't need Joe blowing up and doing something that will land him in jail and keep us from going to Phoenix.' Going into the house, I immediately picked up the telephone book and looked up the number of a lawyer. Writing the number down, I then told Joe what had happened.

At the top of his lungs, he yelled, "I'LL KILL THE BASTARD."

"Joe, do you want to go to jail? Let a lawyer handle it. I'm sure we can get our money. We have a travel credit card to get us across the country. Gas is twenty-eight cents a gallon. I have twenty dollars, and you must have a little money. We just need to get to Arizona and things will be better."

I called the lawyer, explained the situation, and said, "We have to leave tomorrow for Arizona."

He was sympathetic and thought he could resolve it to our satisfaction. He wanted us to come to his office, within the hour, to give a statement and sign some papers.

I decided to take the kids with us instead of asking my friend down the street to look after them. I thought he might try harder to solve the problem when he saw we had four kids. I said to them, "We're taking you with us to see a lawyer who we need to talk to. When you get in the office, please say hello and be on your best behavior."

We trotted into the lawyer's office. Mike walked up to him, and said, "Hi, I'm Mike."

Greg put his thumb in his mouth and looked up at him with his big blue eyes. Diane, who was holding little Brian's hand, just smiled and said, "Hello."

It was a large office and the desk was littered with papers and files. A wall had bookshelves, floor to ceiling, with overflowing books. An American flag stood in the corner of the office. The lawyer was a tall man, about sixty years old with beautiful white wavy hair. Smiling at the children, he shook hands with Joe and me.

After listening to what we had to say, he said, "It might take a month or two before I can resolve the situation. I'm confident that with Joe's statement of all the things he did without reimbursement, I can get a settlement in your favor."

I said, "What is your fee?"

"It won't break the bank. We'll just have to wait and see what it's going to entail. Do *not* have any contact with your landlord from now on. I'll need telephone and address information in Arizona so I can correspond with you."

Since we were going to stay with my parents until we found a place, I gave him their address and phone number. In those days, there were no cell phones or computers, so the only way we could communicate was by telegram, telephone or letters.

The next morning, we loaded the car and the movers came on schedule. It was especially hot for Minnesota, with a temperature of eighty-five degrees and high humidity. It was unbearable.

We put Mike and Greg in the bed of the station wagon with suitcases, pillows and somethings for them to play with. Diane and Brian were in the backseat with pillows and a small ice-chest with snacks in it. I had a large container of water at my feet. We didn't have air-conditioning or seatbelts.

We had gone only about fifteen miles when Greg threw-up. Immediately, seeing his brother throw-up, Mike threw-up too. Fortunately, there was a small shopping center a block away. We pulled in to clean-up the mess.

"Nice start to the trip. I'll clean the car and you clean up the boys," Joe said.

There was a drug store in the shopping center, so I was able to wash the boys in the bathroom. I rinsed off their shirts and put them back on thinking it was so hot the wet shirts would feel good.

I told the pharmacist what had happened and we were headed for Arizona. He said, "It's probably the heat as well as the motion of the car that made them sick. There's some Dramamine you can buy. Give the boys half a pill every morning and at lunchtime."

Joe was still cleaning the car when we got back. He had paper towels and a bucket of water from the gas station next to the shopping center. I walked Diane and the boys around outside, looking in the shop windows until Joe finished. I gave the boys Dramamine and we were off.

Fortunately, the pillows escaped the mess and the boys soon laid down and dozed off. Since we had to stop for quite a while to clean up, Diane, Joe and I ate snacks instead of stopping for lunch. We would stop early for dinner and a motel so we could leave very early the next morning. We planned to stop at Joe's parents in Nebraska, on our way to Arizona.

When we arrived at Joe's parents, we were glad to have a day of rest before continuing on. The boys needed the time to run around after sleeping in the car. It was hot, and the clouds were black with pending rain. Tornadoes were possible and it looked frightening.

Still everyone was happy to see us. I didn't know how Joe's father felt about us stopping, but he was pleasant to me. He didn't have the playfulness with the kids that my father had and pretty much ignored them. After dinner we all went to bed early, so we could get an early morning start.

Through the Pan-Handle of Texas, the road stretched in what seemed like an eternal emptiness. In Texas and New Mexico, the heat was unbearable. The windows were all rolled down but the hot breeze didn't cool us.

Fortunately, the boys slept most of the time thanks to the Dramamine. Diane slept some too, but mostly looked at her books, talked about school and how glad she would be when we got to Phoenix.

As we were driving, Joe glanced at me and said, "You'd better put some water on your face and drink some. You are beet red. I don't want you having a heat stroke. We'll be in Flagstaff soon, and it will be cooler."

I longed to breathe cool air. I picked up the water container and poured water over my head, soaking my hair, clothes and seat. "Boy, that felt good."

At last, in the late afternoon, my parents' home came into view. It had been several years since we'd seen my parents. Joe honked the horn and my mom and dad came running out to greet us.

Mama said, "I'm so relieved that you arrived safely. I wondered if you would make it today. What a long trip that must have been with four children."

When the kids hopped out of the car, there were hugs

and kisses all around. While my dad and Joe unloaded the car, my mom took the kids to the patio where she had a basketball hoop. She shot a few hoops, then handed them the basketball, told them to practice, so we could have a contest after dinner.

My mother loved sports, especially basketball, and she shot hoops until she was in her eighties.

I helped fix dinner and then we all went outside to play basketball until it was time to go to bed.

The next day, Joe went to AiResearch to let them know we were in Phoenix. He was gone for a very long time, and when he returned, I could smell beer on his breath. Staggering a little, he seemed to have had too much to drink. Joe sat on the sofa next to my dad and I worried that my dad, who was so strongly against drinking, would notice.

"How did it go at AiResearch?" I asked.

"While we were traveling across the country, the government dropped their contract with AiResearch, and I don't have a job."

I was too stunned to speak.

My dad said, "Joe, going to a bar, spending your money drinking, will not solve your problems."

Joe hit the coffee table with his fist so hard he cracked it. We all jumped. Joe said, "I gave up a 3,000-dollar bonus and a promise of a raise if I'd stay with Whirlpool. We can't get our money out of the bank in Minnesota and who knows how much the lawyer will cost."

He got up and started to pace. "I have no job, mouths to feed and no place to live. We have a month to get our furniture out of storage from the movers. The payment is due on the GI college loan we're paying off. So, I had some drinks," he said.

He couldn't keep the despair from his voice.

I said, "You can get another job. You had very high grades in college and I'm sure that will be a big plus. Motorola, Sperry, Reynolds Aluminum and others may need an engineer. Maybe you can get unemployment since they hired you and let you go. Tomorrow you can apply at other companies. In the morning you can look at employment ads in the paper. Everything will work out. I know it will."

My mother said, "You can stay here as long as necessary. Things are bound to get better, you just have to have faith."

24

CHARCOALED EYES

WITHIN A WEEK, Joe got a job with a company called The Job Shop. It contracted engineers to companies that only needed them for a specific length of time. The pay was not as good as it was with Whirlpool but we could get by.

We began to look for a place to rent. Although my parents told us to stay as long as we wanted, it was crowded in their two-bedroom home with four kids. One of Mama's neighbors, said, "Owning a home is better than renting. We have a GI loan which enabled us to buy a house, and the interest on the loan is low."

I thought we should rent until Joe finds a permanent job with benefits, then maybe we could buy a home. We found a house to rent with option to buy in Paradise Valley, a suburb of Phoenix, with a grade school within walking distance and a high school about five miles away. It was a new development in the desert, a "bedroom" community. It only had a Bayless grocery store and one gas station in the area. There were three such subdivisions in Paradise Valley. All the homes were ranch style and the one we rented had a nice, fenced backyard, and I could watch children playing outside on the street and sidewalks.

Phoenix was slightly lower in elevation, and you took a winding dirt road called Dreamy Draw to Paradise Valley. It was a thirty-minute drive from Paradise Valley to downtown Phoenix. As I'm writing this, Dreamy Draw is now a freeway and Paradise Valley is no longer a "bedroom" community. It has a large population with many apartments, schools, colleges, malls, restaurants and hospitals.

The Minnesota lawyer got our money out of the bank in just one month and only charged us fifty dollars.

Six months later, AiResearch called and wanted to talk to Joe. When he got home from work, he gave them a call and they set up an appointment.

When Joe came home from the appointment, he said, "AiResearch wants to hire me back and they're going to buy my contract with The Job Shop. I'll start next week."

I felt relief. We'd now have health insurance and other benefits.

Everything went well at AiResearch, and Joe and I started talking about buying the house we were renting. We thought we could use the GI loan Mama's neighbor talked about. When we told my parents, we were thinking of buying the home, they suggested we contact Bob Corbin, a lawyer friend of the family, to see if there would be any legal problem with our purchase of the house.

When we met with Bob, he told us he would look into the deed and see if there were any liens against it. Sure enough, there were leans and he said not to buy it, so we started looking at other houses. Diane, Mike and Greg were in school, so we wanted to stay in Paradise Valley. We liked the small community.

I drove up and down the streets looking for houses for sale. I saw a house on a street called Shangri La that had a large repossession sign in the window. The street had nice homes with well-kept landscapes. It was a large ranch style house on a big lot. We called Bob and asked him what the repossess sign meant and was it for sale?

He said, "It's for sale. Contact a realtor, and they'll tell you what to do. With a G I loan there will be no down payment and no closing costs. The interest will be low."

Joe applied for the loan and we got the house for sixteen thousand dollars. Our house payment was 160.00 dollars a month for forty years. I was excited that we would finally have our own home.

The large, three-bedroom house had only been lived in for six months. It came with a washer, dryer, stove, dishwasher and refrigerator. Joe especially liked the double garage with a workshop. The home had a refrigeration unit on the ground and a swamp cooler on the roof. At that time, Phoenix was drier, so the cooler worked great in the spring, early summer, and fall, saving a lot of money on electric bills.

The new dryer was stored in the garage and was not hooked up in the laundry room. During the entire time I lived in the house with Joe, he would *not* hook up the dryer. I had to dry my clothes on an umbrella clothes line in the back yard. I kept hoping he would connect the dryer. I didn't dare call a handyman to hook it up, or Joe would have destroyed the dryer. If I mentioned hooking it up, Joe would say, "I was just going to do that, but because you're nagging about it, I won't."

We had enough furniture for the family room, but we didn't have furniture for the living room or dining room and couldn't afford to buy any. It took three years to complete the rooms. I didn't believe in putting furniture on credit and being in debt. We were almost finished paying back Joe's GI college loan and I didn't want to stretch the budget any further.

Joe's hobby was designing, building and flying model airplanes. He spent most evenings in the workshop drinking beer and working on his models.

One evening, I put Mike and Greg together in the bathtub for their bath. Joe burst into the room and shouted, "Who took a rubber band from my workshop?"

No answer.

"I know one of you took it."

He took off his belt, yanked the boys out of the tub, belted them on their bare bottoms leaving big welts. I tried to stop him and he belted me across my stomach. He threw the two naked wailing boys into the dark front yard and told them to find the rubber band.

"I've had enough," I said, "I'm going to call the police." I ran to the wall phone to call. Joe came up behind me and yanked the phone out of the wall.

"If you ever call the police you'll be dead and so will the kids."

As terrified and angry as I was, I knew I had to get

control of the situation. "The neighbors can hear you and *they* will call the police if you don't stop. I'll get the boys in and put them to bed. I'll make sure they don't touch any of your things in the future."

Before Joe could say anything more I went out the door. The boys were standing outside the front door crying.

Putting my arms around the two boys, I whispered, "*Please,* stop crying. Daddy has a headache and didn't mean to hurt you. If you go right to bed and don't make any noise, everything will be better tomorrow. Be very quiet. Don't say a word. Go right to the bedroom and get in bed. I'll be there in a minute."

Diane had gone into her bedroom and shut the door. Brian was hiding behind the door of the boy's bedroom. Joe went back into the workshop. Putting the boys to bed, I said, "Whatever you do, don't go near your dad's workshop. He doesn't want his things touched. Okay?"

"It was only a rubber band," Mike said. "We were shooting bugs with it."

"Stay out of the garage and workshop if you want to stay out of trouble with your dad. You have lots of things to play with. When your dad is home, play across the street with your friends, in their yard, not here."

The next morning, calling the phone company, I said, "While talking on the phone, I walked too far with it and pulled it out of the wall. Can you send someone to fix it?"

I knew it was impossible to pull it out of the wall that way but embarrassed I couldn't think of anything else to say.

Bell Telephone paid for all phones, installed them, and

did any repairs or replacements free. We had very long coiled cords on the phones, enabling us to talk, walk around, and continue working with the receiver tucked under our chin. With the type of phone, we have today, you can't do that and I miss the old phones.

***

I was very concerned about whether my children would be able to get a good education in the Paradise Valley school district. When I first enrolled them, I talked to the teachers about my concerns. One question was whether they taught phonics or sight-reading in the grades. I was taught sight-reading and I'm a terrible speller because of it. The teacher said, "Unfortunately they teach sight. We need parents to get involved in order to change it."

I asked if they had a Parent Teacher Association (PTA) in the school district and she said no. When talking with the family across the street, who had three boys and a girl, my children's age, we decided to try to organize a parent teacher group. After going around many neighborhoods and discussing it, we formed a parent teacher organization (PTO). Because the PTA was a national and political organization, the majority of the parents didn't want to belong to it but would join a PTO. We got a petition circulated to change sight reading to phonics and presented it to the school board. We were able to get the change accomplished.

During the time of forming the PTO, I met Delores Bork. She was my age and had two boys, Freddie, Diane's age, and Rick, Mike's age. Although her husband wasn't interested in getting involved with the schools, Delores shared the same interest in education for her children as I did. We began to attend all of the School Board meetings. The fast-growing community needed more schools. For a couple of years they tried to get a school bond passed and it was always defeated.

The schools had to go on double sessions, which meant some students went very early in the morning and others later in the day. Another election for a school bond was coming up. Delores and I decided to make it our priority to get the bond passed.

The newly formed PTO members became involved, making signs and telephoning residents. I went to the high school and talked to the band director. He agreed to a parade on Saturday with the high school band marching down the main street of our community. I went to the police chief and asked if we could have a police escort and hold traffic on the street. The cheer leaders marched in front of the band holding large signs, the football team behind the band, in the bed of a truck—shouted "PASS THE BOND." When the word got around about the parade, the street was lined with kids and residents. The bond issue passed.

Residents, mostly retirees, who didn't want to spend the money for the bond, circulated a petition trying to recall the School Board. Again, I got my friend Delores to campaign with me to keep the board.

In that time period, a lot of people smoked. Tareyton Cigarettes had large billboards and magazine ads with a picture of someone with a black eye, smoking a cigarette and a slogan "I'd rather fight than switch." It was a popular ad.

Delores and I blackened one eye with charcoal, took a

large sign saying "We'd rather fight than switch," went to the newspaper and talked to a reporter. Our picture was on the front page of the newspaper the next day with an article about the recall.

I organized coffees to be held in homes throughout the community, talking about why we needed to keep the current school board. The recall was defeated. I received a letter signed by each school board member thanking me for my help.

***

Watching Greg throw a ball when he played with the neighbor kids, I saw that he had great coordination and could throw the ball fast and accurately. He was always coaxing the kids to play ball with him.

They had a sign-up for Little League baseball in Paradise Valley one Saturday. I told Joe I thought we should sign Greg up for Little League. Joe said, "I never got a chance to play baseball when I was young, why should he? It costs money. He'd need a glove and shoes. I'm not going to drive him to practice and go to all those damn games."

"You don't have to," I said. "They practice at the grade school and some of the games will be held there. If Mike wants to play, he could join too. I think it will be good for the boys. It will keep them busy and out of mischief."

Joe finally agreed to let Greg sign up for Little League baseball. Mike didn't join that year but joined the following year and Joe helped coach Mike's team. Brian joined Little League when he was old enough.

Greg became a marvelous ball player. He could play any position and especially loved being the catcher. He could steal bases and was a good hitter. He was fun to watch. He teased the pitcher of the other team and stole the bases. Other fathers came to see him play even though their sons were playing elsewhere.

At one baseball game, Greg slid into home plate and injured his knee. The manager said that Greg should see a doctor. When I took him home and told Joe what had happened he said Greg was just being a sissy and didn't need to go to a doctor.

The next day, Joe was going to cut the backyard grass. He always had the boys pull the weeds first. He made Greg go into the backyard and pull weeds on his hands and knees. When I saw what was happening I ran out and yelled at Joe, "*Stop*! What do you think you're doing? If you continue to treat Greg this way I will divorce you. I'll not stand for your abuse any longer."

Joe pushed me back into the house, and with an insane look in his eyes yelled, "If you think you can divorce me, think again. I will burn the house down, track you down and kill you and the kids. Don't think I won't. Till death do us part. You remember that."

Determined to rescue Greg from further knee injury I said, "I want Greg in this house. With an injured knee it will cost a great deal of money to repair it. Look what happened when your mother struck you in your ear. You're suffering to this day without being able to hear out of that ear. You are doing the same thing to your son, only it's his knee. Cut the damn grass, the weeds are green, so who cares if they're pulled." Trembling with anger, I went to the door and told Greg to come in. Mike, ever protective of his brother, ran out to pull the weeds.

25

ABUSE

ONE DAY, Joe came home from work in the middle of the day, and said, "I was fired from AiResearch."

Afraid of what the answer would be, I asked, "What happened?"

"My boss showed me a design he made for an airplane part, and I told him he was stupid and it would never work. I told him he was ridiculous to think it would. He was furious and fired me."

Thinking, 'that sounds like something Joe would say.' I said, "Couldn't you have just explained what was wrong with it?"

"His calculations were off. I'm right and he's wrong. Nothing to explain. I don't want to hear any more about it." Joe grabbed a couple of beers and went into the garage workshop.

The boys came home from school and I met them in the front yard and said, "Whatever you do, keep out of your dad's way. Don't make any noise. If you have homework, do it, or play at Robbie's house. Not here. Your dad has had a terrible day. Don't cross him in *any way*. Okay?"

Mike rolled his eyes and sighed. Greg put his thumb in his mouth and went to his room with Brian. Diane was at her friend Ann's house and wouldn't be home until dinner time.

Worried, I thought, 'Joe will be looking for something to take his anger out on. I have to be careful of what I say, remember to think before I speak and keep the kids away from him. Dinner is going to be hard. If he yells at Mike, Mike won't keep his mouth shut. He'll defend himself. That's the way Mike is. Greg is the one I worry about the most. Joe always has it out for him and picks on him every chance he gets. What did he think was going to happen when he called his boss stupid? How are we going to pay our bills? If he keeps on drinking tonight anything could happen.'

Joe came in to get more beer and said, "Did you know the Ransoms are watering their lawn and some of it's going on our lawn? Well I fixed them, I cut their hose into pieces."

He went back into his workshop slamming the door.

I was dumbfounded. I thought, 'is he drunk or losing his mind? It's great that the neighbor's water was coming onto our lawn. We wouldn't have to water and that'll save us money. What on earth will the Ransoms think? Will they call the police? If I call them, tell them I'll replace the hose and Joe comes in and hears me, all hell will break loose. All the neighbors must hear Joe yelling and cussing at us. He's never been friendly with them.' I figured I would talk to the Ransoms as soon Joe wasn't around.

Planning on what to have for dinner, I decided to fix Joe's favorite meatloaf. Afterward, if nothing happened to set him off and he calmed down, maybe he'd talk about it. I just wanted to take the kids and leave, but I knew he'd hunt us down. I had to keep control of the situation. Maybe I'd get a job and go back to work.

We ate dinner mostly in silence. Joe was drinking beer heavily, and after dinner left to get more beer.

I immediately told the boys, "As soon as you hear your dad drive up, go into your room and get in bed. I know it's very early but your dad has lost his job. You know how your dad reacts when something goes wrong. I don't want any giggling or talking in your beds after he comes home. Tomorrow is Saturday, so keep out of his way." At fourteen, Diane always seemed to sense when Joe was in a bad mood. After helping me clean up the kitchen she went to her room and quietly closed the door.

Joe came home very late that night. He must have gone to a bar to drink, and I could tell right away he was very drunk. He spent most of the night throwing up in the bathroom. I laid awake all night worrying if he would start a fight or insist on sex. What could happen tomorrow with the boys was my biggest worry.

When things went wrong, Joe took his frustration out on the kids and me. I never knew if he'd let it pass, think it funny or blow up. It was like living with a ticking time bomb, never knowing when it would explode.

He was hardest on Greg. Mike got a lot of beatings too because Mike always defended himself and his brothers by speaking up. Joe would then start hitting and yelling at Mike and ending up hitting us all. Brian learned very young that if he didn't say anything, he didn't get in as much trouble as his brothers. As a result, Brian isn't talkative and is quiet to this day. Greg, living in fear that his father would strike out at him, sucked his thumb until he was thirteen years old.

Saturday morning, Greg was lying on the family room floor, watching his favorite movie on television, "The Wizard of Oz." Joe walked into the room, kicked Greg and said, "Why are you watching this? It's for little kids, not ten-year old's. Turn it off. I don't want to listen to this racket."

Not seeing his dad come into the room, Greg jumped up in terror when he was kicked. Holding his side where his father kicked him, said, "Can I just turn the volume down?"

"You heard me, turn it off."

Greg shut the TV off and said, "I'm going to the pool to swim."

In the next block of our subdivision was a neighborhood pool called, Melrose Pool. We belonged to it and Greg was on the swim team. He swam for hours everyday when he wasn't playing baseball or football.

Greg went into his bedroom to put on his swimsuit. His dad went into the workshop and immediately came out shouting at Greg, "You've been messing with my airplanes. How many times have I told you to keep out of there?"

"I haven't been in the workshop, and I never touch your planes," Greg said.

Grabbing Greg by the arm, Joe said, "Get over here and sit in this chair. I'll teach you a lesson you won't forget."

Joe went into the bathroom and came out with the hair

clippers and started to shave all of Greg's hair off. In those days, long hair was "in". No one shaved all of their hair off unless you were in the military. Greg didn't wear his hair long, but had beautiful blonde, curly hair that people often commented on.

I begged Joe to stop and he told me to shut up or I'd be next. Greg started to sob. I wrung my hands in frustration, Mike went out the door and Brian disappeared into his bedroom. I later found him curled up in a box in the closet hiding from Joe. Diane was at her friend Ann's house and was spared another scene of Joe's rage.

After Joe finished shaving all of Greg's hair off, he went back into the workshop with a beer.

Afraid other kids would make fun of Greg, I said to him, "Your hair will grow back fast. Wear your baseball cap. Actually, you look pretty cute. This too shall pass, don't let it get the best of you."

Greg put his thumb in his mouth and went into his bedroom.

Picking up the newspaper, I looked at the employment ads. There was a Motorola ad for women to do assembly line work. The ad wanted women to solder parts to a circuit board. I had never soldered anything in my life and wasn't sure what a circuit board was. I hoped they would explain how to do it. I desperately needed the job with Motorola because they had benefits and we needed health insurance, especially with the boys and all their accidents.

I went into the workshop and told Joe about the job. "I'm going to apply on Monday. Diane's old enough to look after the kids when they get home from school. With instructions, she can start supper for me. Why don't you go to The Job Shop and see if they'll give you a job?"

"You won't be able to do that kind of work. You're too stupid. But do what you want," Joe said.

As soon as the kids left for school, I went to Motorola. In those days the only way you could apply for a job was in person.

Motorola had a large plant, about forty minutes from Paradise Valley. After filling out the application, I was interviewed by John, the man that supervised the line workers.

He said, "Do you know how to solder?"

Desperate to have the job, I decided to lie. "Yes, I do. But it's been a while since I soldered."

He said, "I'll be giving instructions. It's very important government work that we will be doing. The pay is a dollar-forty an hour, and the hours are eight to four-thirty. I'm glad you know how to solder. This is precision work. If you've never done line work before, it will take getting use to."

I was to start the following Monday.

When Diane came home from school, I told her I was going back to work. "Would you please take care of your brothers when you all get home from school? If I leave you instructions, could you start dinner? Like peel potatoes and set the table? I'll talk to your brothers and make sure they do what you tell them to do. I'll set down some rules for them. I'm hoping your dad will get a job soon."

Diane, smart, slim, pretty, with long blonde hair, and mature for her age, agreed to watch over her brothers and do what she could. The boys looked up to their big sister.

I knew I could count on her. She was always willing to help and never complained.

I had to make the job work. We had a house payment coming due. Diane was supposed to get braces on her teeth in a few weeks and that would be costly. There was no dental insurance in those days.

When I told Joe that I got the job with Motorola, he just laid in bed and stared at the ceiling. If he didn't look for work soon, I'd have to get a second job. I thought, 'I have to keep a roof over our head. I *will* get through this. *I have to.*'

26

RIGHT THING TO DO

ON MONDAY MORNING, my first day of work at Motorola, I was undecided what solder workers wear. After taking clothes out of the closet and putting them back several times, I decided on black slacks, red blouse and tennis shoes.

When I arrived at Motorola, I was directed to the area where I would take training. I tried to look confident. I told myself if others can solder so can I. It was a class of five, taught by John who interviewed me. He was tall, about thirty, dark hair and eyes. He wore dark slacks, white shirt and tie. He smiled at us, cleared his throat, and told us, "It's important government contract work, that has to be done with perfection. It's circuit boards for bombs."

We all sat at a table that had electric power next to each of us. In front of me was a tool like a thin curling iron that looked hot. Some silver metal, in strings, was in a container, and different colored wires were in another container. He handed each of us a circuit board, that was smaller than

I thought it would be, and an instruction paper that told where the colored wires went.

"I want you to solder the wires onto the circuit board. This is to be a practice exercise until you perfect it. I will demonstrate it for you. Then I want you to complete the practice board and pass it to me for inspection."

Watching him intently, I thought, 'it doesn't look too hard. I hope I can do it.'

The first two wires I soldered were not very good. The first had way too much solder and the second not enough and the wire fell off. Each wiring became better, and when I finished I was proud of the ending row. Handing the board to John he put a magnifying glass in his eye and went over it carefully. Frowning the entire time. All our boards were rejected. I worried I'd never get the entire thing right, but when I did, it was an exhilarating feeling.

In the class I met two women who would become my lifelong friends. Lois was attractive, with long blonde hair and striking, large blue eyes. Phyllis was a petite, lovely woman. They were both around my age. We had a competition among the three of us to see who could finish the circuit board first without any rejection.

When we finished the class and moved to the line, I was fortunate when seated, to have Lois on one side and Phyllis on the other. We were all at a long table. About thirty workers, fifteen on each side. There was no talking during work, and John walked back and forth behind the line. However, when he was down the line, away from us, we managed to whisper to each other.

When we finished a circuit board, it was placed it in a

numbered box beside each of us. Then John picked up the box and gave it to the inspector. The inspector sat at the end of the table. He kept a record of how many we did and if we had a rejection.

Motorola had a cafeteria with good inexpensive food. The three of us had lunch together every day. After going through the cafeteria line, we took our food into a large room with long tables. Sometimes it was hard to find three seats together.

One noon, we saw three seats vacant where the engineers always sat. We immediately ran over and grabbed the three seats next to the engineers. I sat beside a large, heavy set, arrogant looking man. He looked at us like he was too good for us to sit next to him. The engineers had finished their lunch and were deep in conversation. The man next to me took out a cigar and lit it. Taking a deep drag, he blew the ill-smelling smoke directly on my food.

Coughing, I asked him, "Would you please not smoke the cigar? We just got our food and the smoke is spoiling it."

With a smile of someone who believes he has the upper hand, he took another deep drag on the cigar and blew it directly in my face. I had a bottle of perfume in my purse that I was going to give to Lois because I didn't like the scent. I reached down into my purse, took out the perfume, looked him straight in the eye, and sprayed it on him, starting with his hair, going down his shirt and into his crotch.

"There, that smells better," I said.

Noticing that he had a wedding band on, I added, "Explain that to your wife."

"You bitch," he said. The other men at the table laughed

and said, "You had it coming. Let's get back to work and leave these ladies alone."

Phyllis, with her mouth and eyes wide open, looked shocked. Lois was doubled over in laughter. I said, "Sorry Lois, I don't have a lot of perfume left for you."

***

Joe was called back to AiResearch about a week after he was fired. Over the years he would be fired and rehired several times at AiResearch. He carpooled with a couple of engineers in our area, and one of the wives told me Joe could always solve a difficult problem. They couldn't do without him. I knew I had to stay working to keep a roof over our head when Joe wasn't working.

After school, Diane managed her brothers well. She and her friend Ann kept the boys in line. She had tremendous patience with her brothers, never raising her voice. Once in a while, when they wouldn't listen, she would chase them around the house swinging her hairbrush and threatening to clobber them if she caught them. They would promise to stop whatever mischief they were doing. Diane was very helpful. I wouldn't have been able to work if it hadn't been for her.

I remained working on the line for about six months. One day, Motorola posted an opening in the health insurance claims department. They needed someone with some medical knowledge to process health insurance claims. I wondered what kind of medical knowledge you had to have to process the claims and how you went about doing the processing. It would pay twenty-five cents more an hour than what I made on the line. I decided to check it out.

What did I have to lose? I asked John if I could take time off to interview for the job. He gave me an hour and told me how to get to the claims department.

The health insurance department was on the top floor of Motorola. Entering into a large room, I saw seven desks in a row against one wall. An office, enclosed with glass, was in the corner of the room, for the claims manager. His secretary sat at her desk outside his door. There were files covering a wall, floor to ceiling. It was a pleasant room and the women in the office looked about my age.

When the manager, John Keating, called me into his office, we shook hands and he said to call him John. He was average height, slightly overweight, fair complexion and mostly bald. I felt that he stared at my chest a little too long. I began to wish I didn't have a sweater on. I tried to figure out how I was going to convince him I could process claims. As I was sitting down, I noticed a book on his desk called, "The Merck Manual". I didn't have a clue what it was about.

"I see you have The Merck Manual," I said.

"I consider it a great reference book. It gives excellent coverage of diseases, pharmaceutical, medical and surgical procedures. Are you familiar with it?"

"Somewhat," I said. "I have always been interested in medicine. I haven't been able to pursue it. I thought this would give me an opportunity to do something in the medical field. With a little training, I'm sure I could become a claims processor."

Staring at my chest again, he said, "I haven't interviewed anyone with the slightest knowledge of the medical field, so I'm glad you have some knowledge. I see on your application you were a bookkeeper in a bank. You need to be good at math to process the claims. You will have to learn medical terminology and each processor is given a medical dictionary. I will give you a six-week trial period. The lead processor will train you. I'll put the transfer in and you can start next week."

On my way back to the line my mind was in a turmoil. I thought, 'I'll have to buy a Merck Manual. I wonder where I can get one? This is going to be a challenge. If someone else learned to process claims I can too. I don't have the faintest knowledge of the medical field. I was never interested in it, but if I can study that book, I'll know something about it. I have a week.'

I called my dad and told him I was going to work in the health insurance claims department at Motorola. I said, "I need to learn about the medical field and I have a week to do it."

He laughed.

I said, "Do you know where I can get the book called The Merck Manual?"

"You will probably have to order it," he said. "I have some medical books you can have. You should start with anatomy. Remember one of your mother's favorite sayings, 'Don't Bite Off More Than You Can Chew.' We'll drop off the books this evening."

During the week before I was to start, I studied the books in the evening, especially the one on anatomy.

On the day I started in the insurance office, I was worried that maybe I might have "Bitten Off More Than I Could Chew." After being introduced to everyone, I sat down with the lead processor, who was patient, I soon caught on.

After the six-week trial period, John gave me the Chicago Motorola Employee claims to adjudicate.

***

After working in the health insurance department of Motorola for over a year, there was an opening again in claims. I wanted my friend Phyllis to leave the production line and work with me in insurance. I told her to apply.

"What exactly do you do? I don't know anything about medical things," she said.

"Our office handles the medical claims for all of the Motorola plants, including Chicago where the CEO lives. Chicago is the group I work on. We scrutinize hospital bills for items not pertaining to the hospital stay and deny those items. We pay medical bills that employees are eligible for, read operative reports, and sometimes talk to doctors about their surgery claims if they seem too high. I love the work and I think you would too. It's more pay. What do you have to lose?"

Phyllis agreed to give it a try and I recommended her to the office manager, John. She was hired and started as a file clerk and in about six months trained to be a claims processor.

One afternoon, I received a telephone call from a man asking, "Why did you send me a letter requesting a claim-form instead of paying my claim right away? Do you know who I am? I run Motorola. Why would you need a claim-form from me?"

"I'm sorry sir, it's a rule. All employees that have a medical claim, must submit a claim-form once a year. We don't have a claim-form from you. I can't process your claim until you submit the form. Those are the rules."

"What is your name and how long have you worked in the insurance department?"

"I'm Margaret Valenta and I've worked in claims for about two years. Submitting a claim-form is one of *your* rules, and I feel that if employees have to submit a claim-form, that means *everyone*."

Laughing he said, "Well Margaret, I guess I will have to send you a form. It's refreshing to speak to someone that goes by the rules, no matter what could happen."

After I received his form, I immediately paid his claim. He called to thank me and we chatted for a few minutes. Every time he would submit a medical claim he'd phone and ask if I'd received it. We would talk about it and we developed a good rapport.

John, our manager, often came up behind me at my desk with a file and grazed my breasts with his hand as he put the file in front of me. In anger, I would deliberately roll my chair back, running over his foot with my chair. He would walk away with a smirk on his face.

One day, he came to me with a claim for a newborn baby that had muscular dystrophy. The father, African-American janitor, was the Motorola employee. John told me to deny the claim with the reason it was pre-existing.

I said, "It's not pre-existing, John. He has family coverage. We paid for his wife's maternity claim and he's worked for the company over a year. We can't deny it."

"It will cost Motorola a lot of money over the years.

He probably isn't smart enough to question it, so deny it."

"John, Chicago sends auditors periodically, and if it's caught in an audit, I will be in trouble for not paying the claim. If you want me to deny it, I'd like you to write "deny" on the claim with your signature."

Red-faced with anger, he told me to go ahead and pay it. "If you question my authority again, you won't have a job," he said.

About six months later, John called me into his office and told me to deny a maternity claim. "Why?" I asked.

"According to her insurance enrollment card, she's a Negro and she already has four children with different last names. I'm sick and tired of these nigger women having kids every year for everyone to support. She probably came to work here just to get maternity coverage. Give, "not eligible for maternity benefits" as the reason. She probably won't question it."

Going back to my desk, I felt sick at heart. I knew if I refused to deny the claim I would be fired. The rest of the day, I had a hard time concentrating on my work. Phyllis also thought I would be fired if I didn't deny the claim. At the end of the day, I didn't deny or pay the maternity claim.

That evening, I told Joe about the problem at work and that I might be fired if I refused to deny the claim. He said, "Don't ask me what to do. I don't want to be blamed if you take my suggestion and it doesn't work out. It's your problem. I have enough of my own."

I could hardly sleep that night. I tossed and turned with anxiety, as my mind went back and forth thinking about the situation and the consequence. 'Diane will be going to college soon. A big expense. Mike and Greg have braces on their teeth, that costs a lot of money. Joe's been fine at work for several years—but for how long? We just bought a second car and have car payments. I have to work. We need the money. The woman with four little kids and a baby will be desperate if we don't pay the claim. How will she pay the medical bills if Motorola doesn't pay them? It isn't fair to her, she's eligible for the benefit. What if I'm fired? Where will we get the money for Diane's college? After going over and over it in my mind, I finally decided on the action I'd take.

When I went into work the next day, I picked up the file and went into John's office and put the claim on his desk.

"John, she's the employee, she has maternity coverage, and is eligible for the benefit. I can't deny this claim."

"You're fired. Take your things and leave the office right now."

There was dead silence. Everyone stopped working and looked at me with sympathy in their eyes. I gathered my things and left.

I immediately went to the unemployment office and said, "I want to file a claim against Motorola. How would I go about it?"

The clerk took my name and gave me a number, telling me that when the number is called I would talk to someone who would explain the procedure. She directed me to a room of about fifty people waiting.

I discovered most of the people were filing for unemployment benefits, others were seeking employment and a few were filing a claim against their employer. In today's world you file for unemployment by e-mail only.

If you had a claim against the company that you worked for, you would have a three-way conference call over the telephone with the judge, employer and yourself before a formal hearing took place.

When my number was called, I went into an office and a young man asked me the reason for filing a claim against Motorola.

After telling him what happened, he said, "There will be a hearing before a judge. John Keating will get a subpoena to appear. You can bring documents and have witnesses to testify for you. Lawyers will not be permitted at the hearing. The judge can rule on the evidence or set a trial date. If it goes to trial you should have a lawyer. If you lose you will have to pay all court costs plus the lawyer fees. Do you want to file a claim?"

"Yes."

Calling Phyllis, I told her, "I filed a claim against Motorola. I need you to testify for me at the hearing. I know you still have to work with John, so I understand if you don't want to. I'm going to subpoena you to testify for me, then John will not be able to blame you for testifying under oath on my behalf. I hate to do it but I'm afraid he will lie and what proof will I have?"

I called my friend Delores and told her what happened at Motorola and about the hearing. "I have a big favor to ask of you. *Really big.* I want you to go with me to Motorola as one of my witnesses."

"WHAT! Are you crazy? How can I be a witness? I don't work at Motorola," she said.

"The way I figure it, John has probably denied claims he

shouldn't have. He won't know who you are and will worry that you are an employee that had a claim denied. I want to intimidate John. You won't have to say anything and I'll be the first person to talk. You just have to sit there. If they should ask if you have anything to add, just say, not at this time. Think of it as an adventure."

"*Margaret*! I remember when you dragged me down to the newspaper with a charcoaled black eye for one of your causes. Our picture was on the front page of the newspaper the next day. Now you want me to be a witness at a hearing, pretending I know something I don't. *Well*, I can't pass this up. If you're sure I won't get in trouble, I'll do it. What makes you think you can take on a big company like Motorola and win?"

"Because it's the right thing to do."

Delores

27

THE PROMISE

I WANTED TO ARRIVE at the hearing after everyone else, so Delores would surprise John when we went in. We sat in my car, watched for their cars, and after they arrived we went inside.

The Judge, Phyllis and John, were seated at a large conference table. John glanced up at us as we entered the room. His face and neck turned bright-red as he looked at Delores. The judge told us how the hearing would commence and I would be the first to speak. Although I was nervous because a lot was riding on the outcome of the hearing, I took a deep breath and began.

I told the judge the reason I was fired and that I wouldn't go against my principles even though I faced termination.

"I see from your claim against Motorola, you're not asking for monitory satisfaction," the Judge said.

"No, I want to be sure the woman's claim is paid and my claim against Motorola is on the record so this doesn't happen again."

John was the next to speak. Glancing at Delores, his hands were shaking as he tried to brush it off as a misunderstanding on my part. He claimed he never said the medical benefit should be denied, that I was at fault for questioning him and refusing to listen. "That's why I fired her," he said.

When Phyllis was asked what her account of the incident was, she said, "I overheard John telling Margaret to deny the claim. It was wrong to fire her because she was right, the woman was eligible for benefits."

"You didn't hear the whole conversation. You misunderstood what I was saying," John said.

"I couldn't help but hear all the conversation, because you were shouting at Margaret."

The judge turned to Delores and asked. "Mrs. Bork, do you have anything to add?"

Hesitating, glancing at John, she replied, "Not at this time."

"There will be a ten-minute break," the Judge said. He left the room, and there was dead silence.

Then Delores whispered in my ear, "What if he asks me again if I have anything to say?"

"Just say no," I whispered back.

I thought that John was going to have a stroke with his shaking hands and red face as he watched Delores and me whisper to each other.

When the judge returned, he turned to me and said, "I'm ruling in your favor. You may have your job back at Motorola. Do you want it?"

"No," I replied. "It would be impossible to work with John."

"Then you can have unemployment benefits. The claim will go against Motorola as filed. Good luck in the future." Shaking hands with me, nodding at the others, he left the room. John rushed out without saying a word. I breathed a sigh of relief as I thanked Phyllis and Delores.

When Joe got home from work, I told him what happened. He said, "You did the right thing. Why don't you wait to look for work? You'll have unemployment for a while, Greg will be graduating from eighth grade next week, and Diane will be going to college in August, so you'll be very busy."

A short while later, Phyllis told me the Motorola CEO in Chicago called, asking for me. When he was told I was fired and why, John was removed from the health insurance department.

***

My parents were invited to come for dinner before Greg's graduation. He was excited that his grandparents were going to be there. Just as my parents arrived Joe walked in the door.

I fried fish for dinner that Greg previously caught and had in the freezer. As I put the food on the table, my parents congratulated Greg, hugged him, and told him how handsome he was. As we were eating, they told him how proud they were that he was getting an award for outstanding athlete.

Joe suddenly grabbed his plate of food, shoving it across the table, spilling Mike's milk.

"I'm sick and tired of everyone making a fuss over Greg!

No one makes a fuss over me," he said. He got up, went into the bedroom and slammed the door.

Horrified that my parents had to witness Joe's outburst, I cleaned up the spilled mess. I knew better than to go and try to reason with Joe.

My dad put his arm around Greg and said, "Never mind Greg, let's eat this lovely fish you caught."

When we were going out the door, Greg asked, "Where's Dad? Isn't he going to my graduation?"

"Your dad doesn't feel well," I said. "He won't be able to make it. I'll take a lot of pictures. We're so proud of you."

Knowing how important graduating from eighth grade was for kids, I wondered why Joe would disappoint his son by not attending. Maybe he was jealous of Greg. His verbal and physical abuse toward Greg was becoming more frequent. Although he abused Mike and Brian too, Greg got the brunt of it. Joe told him over and over that he was stupid and punished him for insignificant incidents that sometimes weren't even his fault.

I thought, 'if only I could leave Joe. With no money, four kids, Diane going to college, no job, no place to go, his threats, I'm trapped. I have to keep the peace the best I can.'

When we arrived home from the graduation, Joe wasn't there. Greg said, "Dad was well enough to go out and get drunk. He went to Diane and Mike's eighth grade graduation, why didn't he want to go to mine?" With a dejected look on his face Greg went into his bedroom and closed the door.

Greg's graduation was the last time I would see my dad

alive. Daddy flew to Michigan the next day to visit his sisters for a few weeks in Sault Ste. Marie. He died of a stroke while visiting them. There was a funeral both in the Sault and Phoenix. Both funerals were large with family, friends and residents attending. During his lifetime, Daddy daily visited the hospital and jail doing charitable work. Neither my sister nor I attended the Gospel Hall in Phoenix so were not aware of all the charitable work he did not only in Phoenix but in the surrounding towns.

Joe and I took Diane to Tucson in August where she was enrolled in education at the University of Arizona. She and her friend Ann were accepted in a sorority and Joe helped them move into the sorority house. He was friendly and helpful with everyone. We took the girls to lunch and after saying our goodbyes had a pleasant trip back to Phoenix.

***

My friend Delores was divorced. Her brother Richard moved in to help support her and her two boys. Richard was my age, easy-going, and fun to be with. They sometimes came to dinner and they had us to their home.

One evening, Delores, Richard, Joe and I decided to go to Valley Luna, a Mexican Restaurant. We didn't go to restaurants very often, and I looked forward to a night-out with friends. It was Delores and Richard's favorite place to eat and they went there often. They had a waitress they liked and always waited to be seated at one of her tables. Joe drove, we picked them up and headed for the restaurant.

It was a charming place with brightly colored wall hangings. The booths had vivid pictures painted on the table tops, and the waiters and waitresses were dressed in Mexican style. The scent of the food was enticing. Their waitress spotted us, saying a table was being cleared and we would be seated in a few minutes. After we were seated, a man brought four small plates, large bowl of chips, large bowl of salsa and placed them on the table. The waitress approached to take our drink and dinner orders.

Joe said to the waitress, "Why do you have the salsa in only one bowl? I want individual ones. It's stupid to have salsa in only one bowl."

"We don't have individual bowls," she replied. "We give you plates and you put the salsa and chips on them."

Joe shouted, "Fuck you." He reached over and turned the salsa upside down on the table.

The waitress, Richard and Delores, looked shocked. I was mortified. People at other tables stared. Afraid of what Richard would do or say and Joe's reaction, I caught Richard's eye, shook my head, silently mouthing *don't*.

Trying to avoid the running salsa, Richard got up and said, "Let's go." As he passed the waitress, he quietly said, "I'm so sorry." When Joe passed the waitress, he reached behind her and patted her on her butt.

After we left, Joe acted like nothing had occurred. We got into Joe's car and he said, "Let's go eat." He drove us to a pizza place and there was very little conversation the rest of the evening. I knew better than to bring up the subject of his outburst when we got home. It would only end with his striking me. Joe always demanded sex after any hurtful episode with me or the kids. I wonder if he realized how I hated it after he'd been abusive.

Richard told me later that Delores confided some of the difficulties I had with Joe. He said, "Joe's scary. He needs to see a psychiatrist and you need to watch your back. I wanted to tell Joe off when we got outside the restaurant but for Delores and your sake I didn't."

I decided I would never go to a restaurant with Joe, *ever again.*

***

I figured if I brought in more income, it would ease the tight money situation and perhaps Joe wouldn't be so hard on us. I tried to figure out how to earn money. With teenage boys and Joe's temper, I thought it would be best to work from home. Wherever I went, I was always looking for an idea.

My friend Phyllis was a talented artist and my talent was simply art appreciation. We sometimes went to Art Galleries. One time, I was intrigued with a wooden piece of art that was three dimensional. I wondered if other types of artwork could be made dimensional.

I also loved the artwork on greeting cards and whenever I bought a card for an occasion, I spent a lot of time looking at all the cards. At that time, cards cost ten to twenty-five cents. One day, while looking for a birthday card, I thought 'if I bought three cards that were identical, cut out everything on the picture, rearranged and layered them, maybe I could make them into a dimensional picture, and I could do the work from home.' I decided to talk about it with Joe, who could solve any problem and was very artistic.

We talked about what I had in mind. He said, "You will need to go to The Scissor Store, and get a small, fine pointed, very sharp pair of scissors. You should use silicon glue between layers. It will be tedious work. For the backing, I'll cut heavy cardboard any size you want, make a dimensional frame, stain it and cut a glass to fit. How are you planning on selling them?"

"If they're good, I'll go to gift shops and see if they are interested in buying them or take them on consignment."

He made a small easel to place on the table with an attached light over it. My first attempt was a scene of an apple blossom tree with blue birds on it. It came out perfectly. Joe's wood frame was beautiful and complemented my work. I took the picture to the gift shop at Mountain Shadows Resort, and they bought it for fifteen dollars. They put a price tag on it to sell for thirty dollars. She wanted to know if I had a business card. Even though I hadn't thought of it before, I said, "They'll be ready soon."

"If it sells, which I'm sure it will, I'll place more orders, so drop off some cards when you get them." I ordered cards that said "Dimensional Art by Margaret."

My business flourished. It was the first thing Joe ever complimented me on. When I'd finish a picture he'd say, "Beautiful. You do good work."

I got a call from a doctor who was opening a new office. He saw one of my pictures at a friend's home and he wanted me to decorate the walls of his office rooms with them. I went to the get-well greeting card section of stores and was able to fill his request.

At an art gallery, I bought three identical prints of horses with riders that had headdresses of feathers that were of an Indian artist, Day.ga.Chee.

Every summer, I took the boys camping in our tent at Campland On the Bay, in San Diego. When we went to the San Diego Zoo, we collected beautiful feathers around the outside of the exotic bird cages. I put them on the headdresses of the riders in my picture.

I showed the finished picture to the artist. He told me he was going to have an art show at the Colonnade Shopping Center and asked me if I would make some dimensional pictures of his art and join him at his art show. He gave me prints, and I gladly accepted his invitation.

When I got home, I excitedly told Joe about the show. He surprised me when he said, "I have more things to do than to make frames for your damn pictures. What do I get out of it?"

"It pays some bills. Diane is transferring from the University in Tucson to Northern Arizona University in Flagstaff, which is cheaper. She needs a car because she's going to work part time. Maybe the money I get from the art show will help buy a used car for her. Besides, your frames are beautiful and no-one else could make them like you do. I get compliments on them all the time."

Joe made the frames but refused to go to the art show. I never knew why. With the money from the show, some money from Diane and Joe we were able to buy a used Toyota Corolla for Diane.

***

Some of the parents of Greg's Boy Scout troop were good friends with Joe and me. Even though Joe didn't get involved with scout activities, he didn't mind my involvement and liked the couples. We had parties in each other's homes often, with about ten couples—no kids. The scout leader played the guitar, everyone brought snacks and it was always a fun evening.

Our group decided to have an evening cook-out in the Pinnacle Peak area overlooking Phoenix. We all brought steaks with a side dish and folding chairs. One of the men brought a large grill and a folding table for the food.

It was a beautiful fall evening. The men started the grill and a small bon-fire. We sat in a semi-circle watching the Phoenix lights come on. With no streetlights or clouds, the stars were bright and beginning to fill the night sky.

The men put their steaks on the grill. Everyone sat back listening to the soft music of the guitar and watching the moon rise over the mountain.

Some of the men got up to get more beer, and Joe went to the car to get some seasoning he forgot. Someone was watching the steaks, to move them out of the flames.

When Joe went back to the grill, with his seasoning, he shouted, "Who moved my steak? No-one touches my steak. You can fuck my wife, burn my house down but *no-one* touches my food."

Bending down he picked up handfuls of dirt and threw it over all the steaks.

Horrified, I wanted the earth to open up and swallow me. No-one at the cookout knew this side of Joe. I didn't know what to do. Jim, a tall, well-built police sergeant who was sitting next to me, got up and put his hand on my shoulder. He softly said, "Stay calm." Walking over to Joe, he said something to him in a low voice I couldn't hear.

Joe came up to me, and said, "Get up, we're leaving."

The ride down the mountain was hair-raising. It seemed he took the curves on two wheels. All I could think of was, 'I can't die—what would happen to the kids?'

I wanted to get his mind off what had happened, so I casually said, "I was getting a headache so I'm glad we left. Are you going to fly model airplanes tomorrow? Maybe Brian will want to go with you."

He slowed the car down and said, "Yah, I think I will. Brian likes the two boys his age that go model flying with their dad, so maybe he'll want to go too."

The next day the policeman's wife, who was a nurse, called me. "Margaret, how long has this been going on? It can't be just a one-time thing. He needs counseling. Both Jim and I are concerned."

"He sometimes gets out of control. I know Joe needs counseling but he won't go."

She gave me the name of the head psychiatrist at St. Joseph Hospital and told me to call him. I tried to figure a way to persuade Joe to go. I remembered what the Dean of Students said about Joe needing to go to a psychiatrist. I was afraid of his reaction but I had to talk to him about it. When Joe got home from work, I told him about his need for counseling and the doctor that was recommended. "I'm going to make an appointment for you. If you don't go, I'm going to file for a divorce. I can't live with your temper and outbursts any longer. It's damaging the kids."

"If you ever divorce me, I will hunt you down. I'll burn the house down, kill you and the kids, and that's a promise."

Joe had made that threat several times before and it always sent chills through me. I believed he really would do it. Several times the kids overheard him make that threat and I tried to reassure them he didn't mean it. Before Diane left for college, I asked her what she thought her dad would do if I divorced him. She said, "He'll either do nothing, or he'll kill you."

I said to Joe, "If you don't want a divorce, then go and see the doctor. Your insurance covers some of it. You haven't anything to lose. Please, give it a try. At least go once."

After a long argument, Joe agreed to go one time to see the psychiatrist. With relief I called and made the appointment. Joe started seeing the doctor once a week.

28

THE DREAM

EVEN THOUGH JOE had been going to the psychiatrist once a week, for about six months, things got worse. His criticism of the boys, especially Greg, increased. I had to watch everything I said so Joe wouldn't start a fight. Because of the extra money we had to pay the doctor, Diane had to get student loans, even though she worked part time in order to get her degree in teaching from Northern Arizona University. During spring break, she often stayed at her grandmother's house, to avoid the turmoil in our home.

One day, the psychiatrist called and asked me to come and see him. The doctor was in his mid-fifties, soft spoken, with a very kind face and intelligent eyes. He told me that he felt it would take Joe many years of one-on-one counseling to come to terms with his problems. He said, "Group therapy will not work for Joe. When I first talked to him, I thought Joe was either very stupid or extremely brilliant the way he hedged around my questions. He is a very smart man. His anger issues are troublesome. He's like a bomb waiting to go off."

The doctor paused, taking a drink of water. "I'm concerned for you and your children because Joe told me he no longer wanted to continue seeing me. He doesn't think he has a problem. I felt I should inform you, so you will be prepared when he tells you. There's nothing you can say to persuade him to continue, so, don't go there. It will only cause trouble for you."

I tried to hold back the tears as I told him of Joe's threats if I left him and my growing fear of him. He said, "I understand your concern, but I'm unable legally to do anything more if Joe is unwilling to get help."

"Can he be admitted to a hospital? Isn't there anything available to change his way of thinking? His anger?"

"Joe is smart enough to get around questions if you tried to admit him to the psych ward of the hospital. It's difficult to admit someone with the new laws. You have to realize you can't change him, he has to want to change. You need to think about yourself and do what is best for you."

As I left, I felt I was trapped. In a pit. There was another pit I could go into—the unknown—but I knew this one and didn't know if the other would be worse. I couldn't turn in a direction I couldn't see.

**

My friend Phyllis took oil painting lessons in the evening once a week, from Adrian Hanson, a famous artist in the Phoenix area. Knowing Joe was very artistic, I thought it might be good for him to take art lessons and have another outlet besides model airplanes. Joe was so brilliant it was hard to give up on him. It was such a waste to be that smart and not do something great with your life. I kept hoping he would change.

I went to the studio with Phyllis and watched the class.

I asked Adrian if Joe could take lessons from him. "He's very artistic," I said.

"What does he do for a living?" Adrian asked.

"He's an engineer."

"*No*. It wouldn't work. An engineer does things to perfection. That's their nature. Everything has to be exact. A line can't be crooked, it has to be straight. I find engineers make better photographers than artists."

"Leonardo da Vinci was a brilliant engineer and one of the world's greatest artists."

"Ok. You have a point. I'll take Joe on a temporary basis. I want him to observe the first time and then he'll know what to bring to the next lesson. I'll give him two months."

I told Joe about the art class and I thought that he would be good at it. Joe said, "It sounds interesting but we can't afford it."

"There's an ad in the newspaper for temporary help during tax time in a CPA office. I do our taxes, so I thought I might apply. If I get the job, we can afford the art class. I'll apply tomorrow. With my dimensional pictures and the temporary job, we'll have enough money."

I got the job. It was just the CPA and me. I did the simple returns. Without computers it was a little more involved than in today's world.

Joe began his art lessons and not only enjoyed it but was good at it. When the art class had a showing, he sold a few of his paintings. He continued with the art class and did beautiful work.

For one of my dimensional pictures, I bought greeting cards by artist Ted De Grazia. When Joe finished putting the frame together he said, "I could make a nice wooden plaque out of De Grazia's art. I really like his work. I think I'll design something and see how it looks. Find me several individual greeting cards of his you like."

While Joe was in the garage workshop, working on the plaques, a neighbor down the street, Rick Brown, stopped by and looked at what Joe was doing. Joe had completed some plaques that were beautiful. Rick was impressed.

They talked for a long time and decided to go into business together doing plaques of Ted De Grazia's art. Rick would be the business end, selling and advertising the work, and Joe would do the engineering and art. De Grazia was contacted and he agreed to the business. Joe kept his job with AiResearch and worked on the art business evenings and weekends. He taught our son Brian how to work a table-saw and a lot of the work that went into the plaques. Brian had a knack for working with the wood as well as being artistic. Then some neighbor reported us to the authorities for having a business in the garage and a son underage working a table-saw. Joe had to stop work in the garage.

Rick found a place to rent in Scottsdale for the business, and Joe came up with the idea of making bell-shaped wind-chimes that could be painted with De Grazia's designs.

Joe designed the bells, Alex hired artists to paint the bells, copying De Grazia's work. Joe designed the necessary equipment and made racks to dry the artwork.

The business was very successful. After about a year, Joe went into the business one day and got into an argument with one of the men. In a fury, Joe smashed all the racks and equipment then stormed out.

When he came home, ranting and raving about what the man did and Joe said he smashed the equipment, my heart sank. In an instant all of his wonderful ideas, designs and work came to an end. Even though I wanted to scream at him, I could say nothing.

Of course, that was the end of the partnership. To this day you can see the Ted De Grazia bell wind-chimes, plaques and other artwork for sale. The business flourished without Joe and is in operation to this day.

***

Diane graduated from Northern Arizona University in 1974 with a teaching degree majoring in Special Education. We all went to the graduation ceremony. I was extremely nervous, fearing Joe would do something to spoil the activities but everything went well. Diane accepted a job in Winslow, Arizona, teaching Special Education in Middle School.

When Michael turned eighteen, he joined the Air Force. Greg was still in high school and playing football. One night, Joe came home from work late. He'd been drinking heavily. Greg was home from football practice and was in his room studying. I had gone to bed when Joe came into the room. Turning out the light he got into bed.

"Why is a damn light shining through the air-conditioning vent near the ceiling?" he shouted.

"Greg is home from football practice and studying. You can barely see the faint glow from the front bedroom," I said.

Joe kicked me out of bed onto the floor. Grabbing me by my nightgown, he ripped it off, dragged me naked into the middle of the family room and told me to stand there.

He said, "If you move, you'll be sorry."

He unscrewed all of the light bulbs in the house and smashed them on the family room floor all around me and made me stand there naked all night. Every now and then he would look into the room to make sure I was still there. I prayed that Greg and Brian wouldn't come out of their rooms and see me naked. When there was turmoil the boys usually hid away.

Towards morning, when I was sure that Joe was finally asleep, I carefully pushed the glass aside with my foot and tiptoed into the bedroom and put on a robe. I was cold, because it was late fall, and Joe had turned off the heat. I stayed in the bathroom for the remainder of the night trying to figure out what to do. I knew I couldn't fight back because I had learned it only made it worse for everyone. Joe will act like nothing happened after his abuse as he usually does. I felt like I was in jail and couldn't get out.

***

My great-uncle Peter and great-aunt Elizabeth were an influence in my life when I was young. Aunt Elizabeth was my mother's aunt. I want to give you the background of Uncle Peter and how he affected my future.

Uncle Peter wasn't a tall man. He stood about five-foot, five-inches. He was a little stout, bald, always wore a hat, dress pants, shirt and tie, as the men did in the 1940's. A quiet, stern man, I don't ever remember him smiling. He practiced the same religion as my mother and father and built the Gospel Hall where my father had preached.

Uncle Peter, made a fortune in precious metals. He went to the gold rush in California and found silver in Canada. They lived in Sault Ste. Marie, Ontario, Canada, across the St. Mary's river from Sault Ste. Marie, Michigan, where I lived. They had no children.

He had a cabin, built in the 1920's, on the American side of the St. Mary's river, at Dunbar, about thirty miles from our house. When they would go to the cabin in the 1930 and 40s, they took my sister and me with them.

He had a black, 1932 deluxe Packard automobile. I loved to ride in it. It had shades on the back windows, velvet with fringe on them, that pulled up and down like you would find in a house. Beautiful upholstered seats. Between the front and back seat were two seats, folded, that pulled down and we loved to sit in them.

Uncle Peter drove about twenty miles an hour under the watchful eyes of Aunt Elizabeth. She would always spell, *every* time they came to a stop sign, "S-T-O-P Peter dear." I can hear her spelling it to this day. She would say, "Peter dear," whenever she warned him of the danger of a man walking alongside the road, car pulling out or a bicycle. When we came close to the cabin, Uncle Peter allowed my sister and me to ride on the outside of the car, standing on the running board, holding onto the window. I thought it was thrilling. Aunt Elizabeth protested all the way.

My uncle had a room in the cabin and at his home, where he had gold and silver ore samples. I loved to look at them and he let me hold the rocks, pointing out the veins of the precious metals. It was a ritual with my uncle and me every time we visited his home or the cabin. One of my regrets to this day is that I never had him tell me the stories of going to the gold and silver mines in the olden days.

He had a large scrapbook at his home with post cards from all over the world. As I looked at the book, he would sit beside me and explain where they had traveled. I longed to travel to those places and told him someday I would go there too.

At ninety-eight years old, Uncle Peter died when I was fourteen.

***

One night I had an unusual dream about my uncle Peter. In my dream he said that I would be offered a job in rare metals and I *must* take that job, because "*your future would depend on it.*" I never dreamt of my uncle Peter before, and when I woke, I remembered every detail of the dream, his voice and how he looked in the 1940's. How determined he was that I should take the job and how important it would be.

That morning, I received a telephone call from a woman who said, "My name is Florence Johns. I have a rare metal business." My heart began to pound. "My husband just passed away and I need someone to work in the office. It's a small office with only my husband's partner. A friend of mine recommended you to me. He said you worked for him during tax season and gave me your phone number. Would you be able to meet with me today and consider the offer?"

The hair stood up on my arm. I couldn't believe what I had just heard. I remembered my uncle's stern words in my dream and made arrangements to meet with her that day.

As I drove to her office, I thought it would be a good time to go back to work at a regular job and not just do my dimensional pictures. Maybe I will make my fortune in rare metals, just like Uncle Peter. Perhaps I would make so much money I could leave Joe and disappear with Greg and Brian.

We purchased a second car, a Dodge Dart, and had car payments. Finances were tight even though we didn't have to worry about Diane since she'd graduated, and Mike was in the Air Force. The money just didn't seem to stretch far enough to save for the future. Living paycheck to paycheck bothered me, so I felt the job offer in rare metals came at a good time.

When I arrived at the office, Florence Johns and her partner, Tim McCarthy, were waiting for me. The pleasant, bright office had two rooms with a bathroom down the hall. Florence was an attractive woman in her late fifties. Tim was average height, about the same age as Florence, with sad, kind eyes.

She said, "My husband passed away two weeks ago, and I inherited his portion of the business. I've never worked before, so I'm not familiar with office work. Tim said we need someone to answer the phone, check the stock market every day, do the bookwork and anything else he needs you to do. We can pay you three-fifty an hour and you will get paid every two weeks."

Tim added, "We buy and sell gold and silver bars. It's important to get the price of gold and silver every day. It's an investment into the future. Right now, the gold market is down but we feel it will be strong again."

"I don't know anything about the stock market but if I can be of help with office work, I would like to take the job," I said.

When Joe got home from work, I told him about the dream I had the night before of Uncle Peter and the telephone call in the morning with the job offer.

He said, "If you want to take the job, do it. We can use the money." Turning away, shaking his head in disbelief, he sarcastically said, "Now I've heard everything. You are really dumb."

My first day on the job was interesting and different from anything I'd done before. They had a strange way of doing the bookwork. I asked Tim if they used a CPA. "No," he replied. "My partner did the books. Why?"

"Well, it's a little different than what I'm used to but I'll figure it out."

It didn't take long to realize that the business was in trouble. When Florence came into the office, she and Tim would go behind closed doors and I'd catch a few worried words. Sometimes I could tell she'd been crying. One day I heard her say, "Tim, if you don't stop stressing over the business, you are going to have a heart attack like my husband."

When it came time for my first paycheck, Florence was there and called me into Tim's office. With a troubled voice, Tim said, "Margaret, you know from handling the books we are having some financial trouble. The gold market has been down. The stock market is way down but sometimes it brings the gold price up. Would it be alright if we delayed your pay until the end of the month?"

"Yes, of course," I said.

Driving home that day, I wondered why Uncle Peter said in my dream I should take the job. Things didn't look very good. I wondered if the business would be able to survive. They were such nice people, and so worried. I felt sorry for them because I didn't think they were going to make it.

When I explained to Joe that the gold market was down at the moment and I wouldn't be paid until the end of the month he laughed and sarcastically said, "You're such a patsy. What makes you think they will pay you? They are using you. If I were you I'd quit. But do what you want. You'll hang in there because dead Uncle Peter said to. You are so stupid."

At the end of the month, they gave me half the pay due me. Tim explained that it would be only temporary and things were bound to pick up. The following payday, Tim called me into his office again. He explained that they had to delay paying me because the business couldn't continue after November, four months from then, if things didn't turn around.

"There is something in the works that might pull us out. At this time, we can't pay you. If you continue with us, I promise, you will get your money. Is it possible you can continue working even though we can't pay you right now?"

I felt Florence and Tim were honest people. I could see the stress and despair in their faces. Florence had just lost her husband, and I knew they hated to ask me to continue without pay.

"Yes, I can continue working for you," I said. "I know you need help in the office. I trust you will pay me when you can."

Again, thinking of the dream, I wondered why the job was supposed to be important to my future if it was going to fail. I continued working without pay and the business closed at the end of the year.

Tim said, "I promise, if it the last thing I do, I will pay you. I will also pay interest on the money I owe you. You have my word that I will not forget this debt."

With tears in his eyes, he held out his hand. I shook his hand and said, "I know you will."

29

THE WEDDING

My daughter, Diane, and Steve Koch lived a few blocks from each other and were the same age. Diane's first date with Steve was the high school tenth-grade Valentine dance. Steve was shy, of average height, with brown hair and green eyes. A nice-looking boy.

I was glad Joe approved of Diane going to the dance. When she was thirteen, my friend Delores's son, Freddy, asked her to go to the movies and Joe wouldn't let her go.

Diane and Steve continued to see each other off and on through high school.

I felt Diane's transfer to the university in Flagstaff, from the university in Tucson, was because Steve was in Flagstaff, enrolled in Forestry. Of course, she said it was because it was cheaper and had more to offer in the teaching field.

During college, Diane and Steve dated exclusively. Their dorms weren't far from each other and they walked to classes together.

Diane Grace

1970

I worried about Steve being accident prone. When he tried to fix his car and bent over the engine, it caught fire and burned Steve's hands severely. When he came to Christmas dinner he looked like a mummy.

Then he decided to go hunting with his friends where they killed a bobcat. Taking the bobcat back to the dorm, after examining it they believed the bobcat was sick, so they threw the carcass in the woods behind the dorm. On Monday, when Diane went to the dorm to meet Steve to go to their classes, he had a high fever. She was concerned and told him she would check on him at noontime. At noon, when she went to see how he was, his fever was higher and he was delirious.

She immediately contacted the college health department. When Diane told them he had been hunting, and killed a bobcat, they put him in quarantine. None of his hunting buddies were sick. At first they thought he might have rabies. Then after tests, they determined it wasn't that. Steve's lymph nodes were swelling, so he could hardly lift his arms. Not knowing what was wrong with him, the University decided it was best to keep his condition quiet.

Steve's fever continued to rage for days and he as very sick. After the fever broke, and many blood tests it was determined that Steve had the Bubonic Plague. A flea from the bobcat had bitten him.

In the meantime, neither Verna, Steve's Mom, or I could get in contact with them. When Verna found out what had happened she was furious they never told her he was so sick and could have died.

The university said, "If the news got around, there

would have been panic at the college, so we did what we thought best."

The bubonic plague research center, in Germany, requested vials of Steve's blood sent to them. They wanted to know why he survived without treatment. Several times, at their request, he sent his blood to them until Steve decided he wasn't going to do it anymore.

After Diane graduated, she took a teaching job in the small town of Winslow, Arizona, even though she was offered a job in Phoenix, where she did her student teaching and was offered more pay. I knew it was because Steve took a job in forestry at Chevlon Ranger Station, in the Apache Sitgrave forest, about sixty miles from Winslow.

At the first of the year, it was no surprise when Diane and Steve announced they were going to get married. They set March 22nd as the date of their wedding—before the summer fire season.

Diane came to Phoenix one Saturday to shop for the gowns. She said, "Because of my teaching schedule, I can't come to Phoenix and plan the wedding, so I'll leave it up to you. You'll have three months before we get married. We'll be down for the rehearsal the day before the wedding. I'll stay with Grandma that night so it won't be too crowded since Mike and your friend Diane are flying in for it."

I'd never met Steve's parents, even though they lived close by. I called his mother and took her to lunch. Verna, three years older than me, was an attractive woman, slim, blonde, long legged, with pretty green eyes.

During lunch, I learned that Verna and I had a lot in common. We instantly became friends. We both liked the same

Verna, Steve's Mother

1975

things and we felt comfortable talking about our problems.

Because of what happened just a few hours before the wedding took place, I want to give you some of Verna's background.

She had a troubled past and a lot of heartache the same as me. Verna was married to Gordon Koch, who was a musician. They had a daughter, Pamela, who was a year old when Steve was born. When Verna was in the hospital having Steve, her husband ran off with the babysitter. Her mother then moved in to take care of the babies while Verna worked. She divorced her husband and never received any support from him. He never saw his children. Verna married Bob Killbarger and they moved from Ohio to Phoenix when Pam and Steve were young.

***

After going to many churches in the neighborhood to try to book the wedding, I found either they were booked or they didn't want to marry someone outside their church. I finally booked the Mormon Church, not far from the house. Without a lot of money to work with, I decided to have the reception at our home. We had a large house and big backyard, so we had plenty of room for the guests.

Verna and I decided on the flowers, white carnations and pink roses for Diane's bouquet, and white carnations for the men's boutonnieres. We picked out the wedding invitations, ordered them and sent them out.

Joe didn't want to get involved in the details of the wedding, but got the backyard ready for the reception and helped with picking up the rental items.

I was worried that Joe would do something to spoil the wedding or the reception. Throughout the years he made most special occasions a nightmare, ending up striking the kids and me. I was anxious about what he might do with a lot of people coming to the reception.

Then my brother-in-law called and said, "I called Mike and we talked about his father. We decided that if he causes a disturbance at the wedding or reception, my son Joey, your three sons and I will quietly remove him. I know you're probably worried about it and I wanted to reassure you that everything will be alright." I was relieved!

My childhood friend Diane, who I named my daughter after, came from Michigan several days before the wedding. I hadn't seen her since 1962. I was thrilled that she could come. Even though we corresponded regularly, we had a lot of catching up to do. She was also in an abusive marriage and she knew I was too. Verna, Diane and I talked about our situations. The three of us had gone through so much heartache.

The morning of the wedding, I stressed over the last-minute details. My friend Diane was a big help and tried to keep me calm. Joe went to pick up the cake, beer and some soda. The flowers were delivered and I headed for the bedroom to put on my dress for the wedding.

The doorbell rang. I answered the door. Standing there, was a man I'd never seen before.

He said, "I'm Gordon, *Steve's father.* A family member in Ohio said that Steve was getting married today and gave me your address. I drove all night to be here for the wedding. I know Steve doesn't know me, but I would like to see him get married."

In a state of shock, never thinking to ask him in, the only thing I could think of to say was, "I don't have a boutonnière for you and it's too late to get one."

"That's okay. I only want to be in the background. I thought you could give me directions to the church."

Flashing through my mind was Verna, in shock at the wedding when she saw him. Not knowing what her husband Bob's reaction would be, I quickly decided on the only solution I could think of.

"Verna only lives a few blocks from here," I said. "I think it would be best if you go to her house before the wedding and you can all go together. That way she won't be surprised when she sees you. Come in and I'll give you her address and how to get there. It'll be ok with her. I'm sure of it."

He stepped in. I gave him the information and he left.

Running to the phone in a panic, I dialed Verna's number.

When she finally answered I gasped, "Verna, there's a big problem."

"Don't tell me the kids canceled the wedding?"

"No, the problem is, Steve's father, Gordon, was at my door just now and he plans on going to the wedding. I sent him to your house because I didn't want it to be a shock when you would see him at the wedding."

Silence.

"*What!*"

Hearing her doorbell ring, I said, "That's him. I'll see you at the wedding." I hung up.

My friend Diane had been standing close by and burst out laughing. "Margaret, this could only happen to you. Nothing has changed over the years. I've never seen anyone have so many unbelievable things happen to her as you've had. A greeting of 'I don't have an extra boutonnière.' Where did that come from? I had to bite my lip to keep from laughing."

I said, "It really is unbelievable that he never supported or saw his kids, and here he is, on my doorstep after all those years, the morning of the wedding! I wonder if Verna is taking this all right. I hope she won't be mad at me for sending him to her house. What a jolt it must be for her. It was for me."

I saw Verna just before the wedding and she told me it was a shock but it was all right.

It was a lovely wedding with no problems. Joe proudly walked Diane down the aisle and she was beautiful in her wedding gown. Steve, with a big smile on his face, looked very handsome. Joe, dressed in his best suit, dark hair slightly greying at the temples, still handsome, smiled to be the father of the bride.

After pictures were taken of the wedding party, we left for the reception at our house. Everyone seemed to have a good time. Joe was friendly and cordial the entire day and evening. Gordon came to the reception, and his daughter Pam talked to him for a while. Steve spoke to him briefly and didn't seem to care that he was there.

I was so happy Diane could have a lovely wedding surrounded by her family and friends. With relief, I was thankful that Joe was helpful and pleasant throughout the preparations, wedding and reception.

Diane and Steve were going to live at Chevlon ranger

station in a little log house, sixty miles, on a dirt road—far from the nearest store. Diane never wanted to go camping in my tent with her brothers and me. She preferred the conveniences she had at home. I wondered how living in the middle of nowhere was going to work for her. She was going to drive the school bus, picking up Native American students on her way to Winslow, to teach school. It certainly would be an adventure for her.

30

THE FLOWERS

JOE DRANK CONSIDERABLY MORE in the spring of 1975. He always had a beer in his hand when he was home and sometimes went to the bar until late at night. I would detect perfume on him when he returned. Sometimes he had lipstick on the collar of his shirt, but I didn't care. I hoped he would find a woman that he'd be attracted to. Maybe then he'd want a divorce and I could escape the nightmare I was living in.

He often went to a bar that people a lot younger than Joe attended. They got together on weekends to go tubing down the Verde River. Joe had a couple of huge tubes in the garage for the river ride.

That spring, his mother came to visit for a week and Joe was on his best behavior. I'd never said anything to his family about the difficulties with our marriage. It was hard not to say something, but I thought it wouldn't do any good and it would make things worse.

When Joe got home from work, and we all sat down to dinner, Greg, Brian and Joe's mother had long conversations about what the boys were doing. After dinner, Joe went into the garage for something and came out yelling, "Greg, you've been messing with my river tubes. They're my tubes not yours and don't you ever touch them."

"I had to move them a little to get my bicycle into the garage," Greg said. "They're fine, so you can still tube down the river with them."

Joe's mother said, "Joe, what's your problem? Are you in your second childhood?"

Joe whipped around, glaring at his mother, and in an angry voice said, "I never had my first!"

He went out, slamming the door. Joe's mother looked like she'd been slapped. I immediately began asking what her family was doing back in Nebraska, trying to take her mind off Joe and his outburst. The rest of the visit went well and the incident seemed forgotten.

***

Greg and Brian hated their father's drinking. Alcohol made the boys nervous because they never knew when he'd suddenly turn on them. Joe would pick a fight even when he wasn't drinking but alcohol made it worse.

One afternoon, Greg and I were seated in the family room talking, when Joe came home from work. Throwing his lunch sack on the counter, he yelled, "You fucking cunt, I told you never to put ketchup on my sandwich. You stupid bitch, you can't even remember a simple thing like that."

Greg, jumped to his feet and said, "Don't you call my mother filthy names like that."

Joe's face went red with rage. He went into the garage and came back with a baseball bat and headed for Greg. Greg, six feet three, took his father by the throat and pushed him up against the wall. Twisting the bat out of Joe's hand, he said, "Don't you ever hurt my mother again."

"*Please, stop!*" I begged, heart pounding. I was afraid of a terrible fight and someone getting badly hurt or killed.

Greg let go of his father but still held the bat. I could tell at that moment, Joe was afraid of Greg. Not saying a word, Joe left. We heard the car tires squeal as he peeled out of the driveway in anger.

The rest of the evening, I worried about what he'd do when he came back. I knew Joe had a gun in his car. I'd refused to let the gun in the house because of his temper. I imagined Greg couldn't sleep that night, wondering what was going to happen when his father returned. Joe came home drunk and went to bed. The incident wasn't mentioned again.

***

Very early on Christmas morning, I woke with anticipation of having a pleasant family dinner even though Joe was usually difficult on Christmas. I always had Christmas dinner around five for all our family, my sister and Verna's family, about twenty-five people. I put the twenty-five-pound turkey in the oven and started to peel the potatoes to keep in cold water until it was time to turn them on.

Joe came up behind me, grabbing my breasts.

"Joe, I've so much to do today, I don't have a moment to spare. I need to concentrate on what I have to do, so please let me be."

Giving me a slap on the butt, he went into the garage. Joe always pressured me to be affectionate when I was the busiest. When he knew I didn't have the time or desire.

Greg had taken out the vacuum-cleaner and was vacuuming the living-room couch. He had a long-haired white cat, Snow, and Mike left us with his German Shepherd dog, Smokey Bear, when he went into the Air Force. Greg knew I'd want the dark-green couch clean of cat and dog hair. While he vacuumed, Greg loudly sang a Christmas carol, "Silent Night."

Joe went into the living-room with a broom and came up behind Greg. With the noise of the vacuum and his singing Greg didn't know Joe was there. Joe hit Greg over his back with the handle of the broom hard enough to knock him into the couch. Greg, taken by surprise, screamed in pain.

"Shut your mouth," Joe said. "I don't want to hear any more of your racket." He then went out the door to pick Mike up at the airport.

Running to Greg, I was afraid he was seriously hurt. "I'm ok Mom," he said and continued to vacuum, but I could see he was in pain.

When Joe came back with Mike, he was in a better mood. Everyone arrived and the rest of the day was pleasant and fun even though I was on edge the entire time, wondering if Joe would spoil the day. My sister, Virginia, later told me her husband was afraid of Joe and what he might do, but wanted to spend Christmas with all the family despite his fears.

***

I did two things to keep my sanity and ease the tension of living with Joe.

In the evening, when things were calm at home, I went alone to a resort to listen to live music in the lounge. I'd say I was going to visit a friend, then I'd go to the resort and spend a couple of hours relaxing and escaping to the wonderful sound of the music I loved.

My other escape came unexpectantly when I took Brian to the County Fair. We passed by a display of dolls, made by an elderly woman. Her work had won first-place. I told her how much I admired the workmanship in her dolls. She told me her name was Sarah. She was a pleasant, friendly, tiny little woman. She said she had a lot of dolls at her home and invited me to come and see them, giving me her address and phone number.

When I went to see Sarah, I was surprised to find she had a daughter, in her forties, who was totally paralyzed from a difficult birth. Her daughter's name was Mazie. She was of sound mind but wasn't able to even brush a fly off her nose. Sarah had to turn Mazie several times a day to prevent bedsores. Mazie was in a hospital bed in a bedroom connected to the living room where she could see and hear everything that was going on.

At that moment, I knew I had no problems compared to Sarah, whose husband had passed away not long after Mazie was born, she had no way out. Whenever I felt sorry for myself, or if Joe would be especially demanding and cruel, I went to see Mazie. She always greeted me with a big smile, asking me how I was and saying how glad she was to see me. I'd spend several hours talking or reading to her. It lifted my spirits, made me thankful and gave her mother time to run errands. Sarah, Mazie and I remained friends until Mazie passed away at the age of sixty her mother, close to a hundred.

***

Joe began to stay out all night on several occasions. On March 31st 1976, my birthday, Joe hadn't been home for three days. My son, Mike, sent me a large bouquet of flowers with a card that said, "I wish I was there. Love Mike".

My friend Lois, with whom I'd worked on the line at Motorola, called and said, "Happy birthday. I baked a cake today. If you don't have any other plans, why don't you, Joe and the boys come over for cake and ice cream tonight about six o 'clock?"

"Joe isn't home but I'd love to come. Greg is staying at a friend's tonight and Brian probably will just want to watch television."

I had a good time with Lois and her husband, and returned home about eight-thirty that night. When I came in the front door, Joe had come home and was tearing my flowers apart, throwing them around the room.

"What are you doing to my beautiful flowers?" I asked as I came in the door.

In a rage, Joe crossed the room in a flash, hit me in the eyes and face with his fists. Shouting obscenities, he struck me on the side of my head. Screaming in pain, stunned, I fell to the floor. He kicked me repeatedly and I passed out. The last thing I heard was, "I'm going to shoot you, you fucking bitch."

Brian, who was in his bedroom, escaped out the window and ran into the neighbor's house across the street.

At that moment, Joe went out to the car to get the gun. In his rage, he saw the door across the street close and thought it was me running into their home, even though he had left me unconscious in the house.

To tell you how great the strength of someone of average height and weight is in a rage, Joe ran across the street and smashed the heavy oak door off its hinges. You can only imagine the shock of our neighbor, Tom.

Tom later told me Brian ran into the house, terrified, crying, "My dad is killing my mom."

Tom said, "Brian ran into the bathroom and hid in the shower just as Joe broke the door down and screamed your name. I told Joe you weren't here and my wife was calling the police."

Fortunately, I came-to before Joe got back. I ran to the back door. I could hardly see as I fumbled for the door handle. I ran across the backyard and out the back-gate. My neighbor, a few houses down the street, was in the alley taking out her garbage. I stumbled to her and said, "*Please,* I need help."

She didn't recognize me at first, I was so badly beaten. Helping me into her house, she said, "What on earth happened? You need to go to the hospital. Let me take you."

Not knowing Brian had gone across the street, I said, "Brian is in the house. I'm afraid of what Joe will do to him," At that moment she saw Joe's car roar past her house.

"Joe just left," she said, "you really should go to the hospital."

Terrified that Joe would come back and kill Brian, the dog and cat, I wanted to get them out of there. "If you would call my friend Delores, I know she will come and take Brian, my dog and cat. They can't stay at home in case Joe comes back. I have to wait until Delores comes," I said.

When the neighbor called her, Delores and her brother Richard came immediately.

When he saw me, Richard said, "Oh my god! Get in the car. We're taking you to the hospital. Of course, we'll take Brian, the dog and cat. We'll get in touch with Greg to warn him not to come home. Don't worry about them. You need to get to the hospital!"

I was in and out of consciousness going to the hospital. I kept saying, "Don't tell Mike. He'll come home from the Air Force and go after his father. I don't want Mike in trouble."

When we arrived at the hospital, I was put in intensive care.

The Red Cross immediately notified Mike, my mother and sister. When Mike flew to Phoenix, arriving at the intensive care unit, he asked where I was. The nurse told him what bed I was in, but Mike didn't recognize me. He went back to the nurse and asked again and when she took him over to my bed, he turned and headed for the door.

The nurse stopped Mike and told him if he cared about his mother, he should not go looking for his father. I remained in intensive care for four days and then went to a regular hospital room where I stayed for two more days.

I called Vi, a neighbor and good friend who lived on the street behind me. Vi was the mother of Brian's best friend. She was separated from her husband and we had talked about our problems in the past. She worked for the government at a real-estate office. I told her I was in the hospital and what Joe had done, and I didn't know what to do. I was afraid to go home.

She came up to the hospital and said, "I found out where Joe is. He's at a woman's house, probably a woman he'd been seeing. I called him and told him he had a choice of one of two things: jail or divorce."

Pulling her chair closer to my bed, she said, "I told him to sign the house over to you immediately and agree to a divorce, or charges would be filed against him. He thinks you're faking it, making a big deal out of nothing, so he's coming to the hospital with me tomorrow. I'm a Notary Public and I will bring papers for him to sign. It's a quick deed to sign the house over to you."

When Joe arrived with Vi, he had a shocked look on his face when he saw me. My face and neck were still black and blue with black swollen eyes. Not saying a word, he signed the quick deed, looked at me with tears in his eyes, and left.

I said, "You know Vi, I think he thought those flowers were from another man named Mike, not his son Mike. He was probably with that woman for the three days he was gone before my birthday. It was ok for him to be with someone else but not me. How ironic is that!"

"As soon as you're released from the hospital you should file for divorce. You can get legal divorce papers to submit to the court at a stationary or drug store. It will save you lawyer fees."

"I'm going to be released from the hospital tomorrow. Mike will be home for another day and Brian and Greg will be there. I can't live with Joe's threats and abuse anymore.

For years I thought I could fix him. Or he would change. I now know he will never change. For some reason, I'm not afraid of Joe anymore. Maybe because he tried to kill me and I survived. Maybe because he has a girlfriend, or he knows others will help me. Whatever it is, I finally feel safe."

When I arrived home, I wondered how I'd pay for a mortgage, car payment, insurance, clothes, food and utilities. I had no money and no job. Even though I owned the house I had to pay the mortgage. I couldn't apply for a job with swollen black eyes and my face and neck covered with bruises.

Mike said, "After Dad attacked you, he must have come back into the house with a shotgun. I found the gun on Greg's bed. At night, while you were in the hospital, I slept with the loaded gun beside my bed in case Dad came back."

I paid for Tom's door with the homeowners' insurance. He told about the time Greg was at the Melrose pool and Joe was there. Joe had challenged Greg to dive with him for pennies. Greg, being an excellent swimmer, came up with the pennies. Joe in a fury, held Greg under the water and several men at the pool had to pull him off before Greg drowned.

"All the neighbors were afraid of Joe," Tom added.

Two days later, I got a call from Tim McCarthy of the Rare Metals Company I'd worked for without pay before it closed. He said, "I bet you never thought you'd hear from me again. I know it's been several years but I have your money. With interest. I promised I'd pay you and I always keep my promises. Can I bring it by this evening?"

Putting the phone down, I immediately thought of my dream about Uncle Peter telling me to take the Rare Metals job and my future would depend on it.

Happiness comes through doors you didn't even know you left open.

Now, with myself, I will begin.

31

THE BLIND DATE

I HAD TO DISGUISE my bruises, so I could leave the house and get a do-your-own divorce packet and groceries. I never wore make-up, except lipstick, so I asked Vi if she could bring her make-up and help me apply it. The foundation didn't quite cover my black eyes and bruised cheeks, so she applied some rouge over the cheek area. The foundation over my eyes looked like heavy blue mascara. When we finished, I said, "I either look like a hooker or a clown. Maybe I can get a job in a circus."

When I purchased the divorce packet from the stationery store, I had to decide what I would ask for. After much thought, I decided I wanted no support for myself. I thought if I went after his retirement benefit or spousal support, Joe would change his mind about agreeing to a divorce. I *had* to get the divorce, I *just had to*!

I decided to ask for seventy-five dollars a month for each of the two boys. With two big teen-age boys, Greg, six-three, and Brian, six-two, I felt I would need the $150.00 a month. Greg could go to the refrigerator and down a quart of milk without taking a breath, and the two of them always seemed to be raiding the refrigerator. Joe's money would almost cover the house payment.

I also asked that Joe be responsible for their health and dental care until the legal age of eighteen. I wanted the 1974 Dodge Dart, even though I had to make the car payments. Joe could have the 1964 Chevy station wagon, his only car to this day. He'd also have whatever else he wanted in the garage, except the dryer that had never been hooked up. We had no savings.

When I told Vi what I was asking for, she said, "You should at least ask something for yourself. You don't have a job yet. How are you going to manage? Keeping a house is expensive. The money you have from Rare Metals will go fast."

"I'll get a job. The boys are good about helping with the house and yard. When Mike comes home on leave, he'll make sure my car is in top shape. Greg doesn't have the mechanical ability that Mike has, but he's a great help around the house, and so is Brian. Greg has a busing job at Pinnacle Peak Restaurant in the evening and Brian is working with the Brown De Grazia Art Company, so they'll have spending money."

"Greg and Brian don't drive. How are they going to get back and forth to work? You can't afford to get them a car and pay car insurance."

"Greg has a friend that drives and also works at the restaurant. They'll ride together. Rick Brown picks up Brian when he goes to work at his art company. Vi, I need to get the divorce. I don't care if I get nothing. I'll be all right. I have to be, for the boy's sake as well as mine."

Vi advised me to tell the judge I had a job even though I didn't have one, or it might delay the divorce proceedings.

On May twelfth I called Joe and asked him to come to the house and sign the papers. At first, he thought $150.00 a month for the two boys was too much. I told him if I had to get a lawyer it would cost him a lot more. Joe finally agreed to everything, and Vi was there to notarize the papers. On May thirteenth I submitted the papers to the court. Joe and I were scheduled to appear on June ninth, 1976.

On the morning of the court date, I wondered if the papers I submitted were correct and if the judge would grant the divorce. Would Joe come to court? Too nervous to eat anything, I put on a white blouse, navy-blue skirt, panty hose and heels and left for the courthouse. Sitting in the courtroom, waiting for my case to be called, I kept glancing at the door to see if Joe would come. I was relieved when he didn't show up.

When my name was called, I walked up to the Judge. After reviewing the papers, the Judge asked, "Are you working?"

"Yes," I lied, "I'm working for Motorola."

Holding up the papers, he asked, "Are you sure you can manage on this? You have two minors at home. Are you sure you don't want legal counsel?"

"I'm sure, your Honor. I'll be alright."

My heart started to pound. I thought, 'why doesn't he give me the divorce and quit asking questions?'

After looking at the papers again, the judge said, "I declare the marriage irretrievably broken. The care and custody of the minor children is hereby granted to the wife. The monthly childcare payment will be paid to the court and will then be sent to you. Divorce granted as filed."

I was so relieved, I wanted to shout, "I'm *free*. At last, I'm free."

***

After a few months, with the bruising gone and the divorce settled, I needed to look for a job. The newspaper didn't have much to offer in the want-ads. I could no longer make the dimensional pictures because I couldn't buy dimensional frames. Having someone make them would make my pictures too costly. I tried to think of what I would like to do. Not having higher education, I'd be limited on the choices. Diane thought I should take night classes at the community college. I thought at forty-three I was too old. Looking back, I realize I felt old because I'd had responsibilities from the age of eighteen, making me think my life had passed me by.

Vi called and said, "A friend of mine told me about a small landscape company that needs someone to run their office. It's a company that designs, installs and maintains landscapes for homes and businesses. It has two partners. One does the designs and the other handles the maintenance end of the business. The wife of one of the partners does the office work. She has no experience doing bookwork and wants to quit."

I immediately went to the landscape company to apply, and got the job. I would finally be earning some money!

I'd make two-fifty an hour. Not knowing anything about a landscape business, I was willing to learn.

The two partners were pleasant and easy to work for. Ralph submitted landscape designs to customers and bid on the installation. Bud bid on maintaining resident and commercial landscapes and had a crew of men that did the work.

After several months, I found Ralph was underbidding and was losing money on the jobs. I found the maintenance end of the business was also underbidding. They weren't taking into account the cost of the supplies needed for each job. They had no method in place to track it.

After thinking about it, I suggested each job be given a number. When a supply was purchased, they would put the number of the job on the receipt. That way we could keep a record and we'd know just how much the job cost to implement. It would give the partners a better idea of how to bid. They liked the idea. I hoped it wouldn't be another business that was going to fail.

***

Things at home were going well. One Saturday morning, Brian and his friend Robbie were lighting off firecrackers in our back yard while I was at the grocery store. Firecrackers were illegal at that time. I arrived home just as they lit the last one. Going into the back yard to see what was going on, I asked, "What was that loud bang I heard? What are you boys doing?"

Looking sheepishly innocent, Brian said, "Nothing."

"Brian, I heard the loud bang. Were you lighting off

firecrackers? You can get hurt doing that, not to mention they're illegal. Where did you get them?"

"Our friend, Billy, was in Mexico with his family and bought them. He let me have some. We just wanted to see how they worked."

"We would get in trouble if you got caught. I'd probably be fined. Don't do it again," I said.

That same Saturday, Greg was about to leave for work at the cowboy restaurant. The employees had to wear a white shirt, jeans, and a red scarf around their neck. As he was going out the door, he told me he was out of clean white shirts and would I please wash one so he could have it the next day.

Late that evening, Brian was in bed and I had my nylon nightie on ready to go to bed too, when I suddenly remembered the white shirt. I threw Greg's shirt and some other whites into the washing machine. I still didn't have my dryer hooked up and had to use the umbrella clothesline in the backyard to dry clothes. When I took the laundry outside to hang, I noticed a strange glow out of the corner of my eye and a crackling sound. Turning around, I saw my wood fence, next to the house, on fire. In a panic, I ran and grabbed the hose and turned the faucet on full force. The hose had the sprinkler head on it, and I was immediately drenched from head to foot. The fire was getting close to the roof, so I dropped the hose and ran into the house and called the fire department.

I put the dog and cat into Greg's bedroom, then ran into Brian's bedroom and yelled, "Get up, the house is on fire."

The fire station was only a block away and they came right

away. The firemen quickly put out the fire. One fireman went into the backyard with me to look at the fence and make sure the fire was completely out. "What is that stuff on the ground against the fence? It looks like wood shavings," he said.

"My husband had been making mulch for several years to put a garden there, which he never did."

"Someone must have flicked a cigarette butt and it landed in the mulch," he said. "It can smolder for hours before it catches. I suggest you get rid of the mulch if you're not going to have a garden."

The fireman went back through the house to leave, when Brian, half asleep, came out of his room. "What's going on? Did Dad try to burn the house down? Why are you all wet?"

Looking down at myself, I had forgotten that I only had my nylon nightie on and was soaking wet. Embarrassed, I clutched at my gown. The fireman smiled and said, "Fires out. Everything is alright," and went out the door.

"Brian, your dad did not try to burn the house down. It was your firecracker that landed in the mulch, smoldered and caught on fire. That's why they're illegal. I'll call the insurance in the morning about the fence. That's the only thing that burned. Now go back to bed and please remember not to light any more firecrackers in the future."

As I laid in bed I thought about what had happened. 'If I had washed the shirt immediately, instead of late in the evening, I wouldn't have known the fence was on fire. It could have been a disaster. The many times Joe threatened to burn the house down if I left him, must be what made Brian say what he did. The kids had been hurt in many ways. I can't change the past. No sense wishing things were otherwise.'

***

One Friday afternoon, driving home from work, I noticed the sky had a yellow-red hue to it, blotting out the sun. Dust hung thick in the air. The wind started to blow. A dust storm was imminent. I pulled into my driveway, jumped out of the car and ran to pull up the garage door. I drove into the garage and rushed to pull the door down before the sandy dirt blew in.

Over the excited greeting barks of Smokey Bear, the German Shepard, I heard the telephone ringing. Not having answering machines in those days, I hurried into the kitchen to answer, almost stepping on the cat, Snow, who yowled in protest. Grabbing the receiver off the wall phone, out of breath, I gasped, "Hello."

"You must have been running. You sound out of breath," Lois said.

"I was in a hurry to answer the phone. Did you get hit with the dust storm in Scottsdale?"

"Yes, we did. My patio is covered with dirt. It blew so hard I thought it would blow the shingles off the roof. It's headed in your direction. What I'm calling about is, my husband's friend Wally is in town from Florida and we're going to the VFW dinner-dance tomorrow night. We wondered if you could go with us."

"I don't know. I haven't danced since high school but it does sound like fun. What's Wally like?"

"Wally's a nice guy, divorced, your age, nice looking. You need to get out, so I won't take *no* for an answer. He'll pick you up at five o'clock. It'll be fun."

Hanging up the phone, I wondered what the kids would think of their mother going out on a blind-date. Greg, now worked at Walgreens, about a block away, wouldn't be home that evening. Brian was going to a movie. Mike was home on leave before being deployed to Germany, and I knew overprotective Mike would stay home. I thought, I'd better tell them tonight.

When the boys got home, I told them I was going to a dinner-dance tomorrow night at the VFW with a man named Wally. He was going to pick me up at five o'clock. They stared at me in astonishment. Getting no response, I said, "Lois and her husband are going too."

After a few seconds of silence, Mike asked, "What does he do for a living? How old is he?"

Mike, maybe thinking people my age didn't date and Wally would be his age, I said, "He's my age. He's here visiting from Florida and I don't know anything about him, but Lois said he was nice."

Saturday morning, I wondered if I'd made a mistake. I didn't have any nice evening clothes because I never went anywhere, and I didn't have the money to go out and get something.

I bought false eyelashes because most of my eyelashes had been pulled out in the hospital from nurses prying my eyes open in intensive care. After reading the instructions over and over I finally glued them on. They felt weird, but seemed to look ok. I had sensitive eyes and hoped I wouldn't have a reaction to the glue.

I decided to wear a red plaid skirt, white blouse, panty-hose and one-inch heels. Since I was five foot five-inches,

I didn't want to tower over Wally with higher heels.

Greg called in sick at Walgreens. Mike and Brian decided to stay home and the three of them paced back and forth, keeping an eye on me as the time drew closer to Wally's appearance.

Just before five o'clock, I was in the guest bathroom spraying my hair. Mike came in the doorway and said, "Mom, men don't like hairspray."

The doorbell rang. Mike ran to the door. Opening it, with arms crossed, he asked, "What time are you bringing my mother home tonight?"

Before I could get to the door all three boys were standing in the doorway staring at Wally. I grabbed my purse and went to the door. "Wally, these are my boys, Mike, Greg, and Brian."

He smiled and shook their hands. "We'll probably be back about eleven," Wally said.

The three boys stood in the doorway watching us as we walked away. Getting into his car, Wally laughed and asked, "Do your boys always try to intimidate your male friends?"

"Sorry, this is the first time I've gone out since my divorce, so the boys aren't use to it,"

"They're only trying to protect you. I think it's cute."

I was glad I didn't wear higher heels because Wally was just a little taller than me. Nice looking, with wavy light brown hair, brown eyes, he had on a black sport jacket, grey stripped shirt, black tie and grey pants. I felt self-conscious in my skirt and blouse.

When the four of us got to the VFW we were seated

close to the band. Wally asked me what I wanted to drink and I said a Grasshopper. I always felt uncomfortable when I ordered drinks. Since my parents never drank alcohol, and Joe mostly drank beer, I never knew what to order. Someone had told me a Grasshopper tasted good so that's what I got, taking the whole evening to drink it.

We had a nice dinner and Wally was easy to talk to. The band started to play and Wally asked me to dance. It was a slow number and he was a good dancer. As we were walking off the dance floor, I noticed one of my false eyelashes was stuck on his jacket. Horrified, I brushed at it but it didn't come off, so I brushed more forcefully and it flew off onto the floor. When I saw the surprised look on Wally's face, I said, "There was a bug on your jacket."

Going back to the table I immediately excused myself to the lady's restroom. In the mirror I looked ridiculous with one eye bare and the other with *really* long lashes. I tried to pull the false eyelash off to make my eyes the same but it wouldn't budge. Turning the cold water on—there was no hot water—I wet a paper-towel and soaked my eye. It still didn't come off. Now I had one bare eye, one with extra-long lashes beet-red from trying to remove the fake lash. I thought, I can't put my hand over my eye or keep my head turned away from Wally all evening, so I'll just have to say what happened. Feeling even more self-conscious, I went back to the table.

When I sat down, I told them what happened to my false eyelash. They all laughed and Wally said, "Was that the bug you brushed off my jacket? You hit me so hard I thought you had killed whatever it was."

Lois told me to use make-up remover to get it off. I told her I didn't wear make-up so I didn't have any. She said, "We should all go to my place, so you can remove it. We stayed for a few more dances and then headed for Lois's house. Applying the remover worked and it was a relief. Lois put a pot of coffee on and we had a good time laughing and talking.

Suddenly, Wally said, "It's almost midnight and I told your boys you'd be home by eleven. I'd better get you home."

When we arrived at my house, Wally walked me to the door. I noticed the large picture window curtains were open. They were usually closed at night. Most of the lights were on. Stuck on the screen door was a white paper plate that said, "Mom, where are you? It's eleven o'clock and you are not home. Greg."

Just then the door opened and Greg stood in the doorway, towering over Wally, "You said eleven o'clock. Where have you been? It's late."

I said, "We decided to go to Lois's house after the dance and lost track of time."

With a grin, Wally said, "I guess I'll be going. It was a fun evening." Getting into his car, he gave a wave of his hand and drove away.

I thought, 'this is a blind date I won't forget. I bet Wally won't either.'

32

DIVORCE-A-MOON

Since I never had a honeymoon, never been to Las Vegas, I thought, 'to celebrate my divorce, it would be fun to drive to Vegas on the Labor Day weekend for a 'Divorce-A-Moon.' I called my friend Verna and asked her if she could to go with me. Her husband, Bob, agreed we should go.

I called my sister, Virginia, who went to Vegas often with her husband, and asked her where we should stay. She said, "We always stay at the Sands, but Motel 6 would be cheaper and they probably have a hotel there."

Getting out the telephone book, I called. With no computers you had to make reservations either by phoning the hotel or a travel agent. They had a motel in Vegas near the strip, so I made the reservations. It cost ten dollars a night for two beds on the Labor Day weekend.

My mother agreed to stay with my boys, dog and cat. Greg and Brian loved having their Grandmother stay with them. She was a wonderful cook and made their favorite dishes. She loved sports, especially basketball. They would discuss the players and who had the best team. Mama got the daily newspaper and always read the sports page first. She didn't have a television in her house because it was against her religion, but when she visited, and we had the television on she would watch it.

The Vegas trip was the first of many trips Verna and I would take together. I'm terrible with directions, so Verna was always the navigator and I drove. We both liked the same things, enjoyed the outdoors, loved animals and nature, so we made good traveling companions.

Early Saturday morning, armed with an Arizona and Nevada map, (no GPS in the seventies,) I picked her up at five-am, hoping to avoid the extreme heat of the day and traffic. We both had large, hard cover, Samsonite luggage. We struggled to carry the heavy suitcases and lift them into the trunk of my Dodge Dart along with accessory cases. Not having traveled before, we took more things than we needed for just a weekend trip.

We stopped for breakfast and gas fill-up in the small town of Wickenburg. I paid the bills, and Verna kept track of the expenses so we could divide them up at the end of the day. As we were driving along, chatting and looking at the scenery, I wasn't watching the speedometer. Cars didn't have speed control, and I tended to be a fast driver. All of a sudden, going down a hill, flashing lights came on behind me. I pulled over.

When the police officer came to the window, I innocently asked, "Was I speeding?"

"You were going seventy-five in a fifty-mile-an hour

zone. I'd say that was speeding," the officer said as he wrote me a ticket.

Taking the ticket, I headed down the highway. "I'm not going to let it spoil our trip," I said. "You'd think they would make this a divided highway. They have so much traffic between Phoenix and Las Vegas. Fifty miles an hour is *so slow*."

We were getting close to Vegas and going down another hill when I spotted a police car at the bottom of the hill. "*Oh no!*" I cried, "I'm going too fast again."

The police car took off toward me, and making a U-turn, pulled up behind me with flashing lights. "Darn," I said, "this trip is going to cost me more than I thought."

Laughing, Verna said, "You're probably the first person to get two tickets within an hour, driving to Vegas for the first time."

We stopped at Hoover Dam to see the amazing structure. I had never seen a Dam before and was mesmerized as we listened to the lecture on the guided tour.

When we arrived at Motel 6, we struggled to drag our heavy suitcases up a flight of stairs to our room. It was a plain room, but very clean. We changed into cocktail type dresses, panty hose and heels. In the seventies everyone dressed up in Vegas. Today, no-one dresses up and anything goes.

Driving down the strip, we decided to go into the Riviera casino. The casino was noisy, bells and whistles going off, shouting, and *very* smoky. Neither of us were gamblers. We had decided that twenty dollars each would be as much as we'd spend gambling on the weekend.

We turned ten-dollars into quarters and they gave us a

white plastic bucket to put our money in. We looked around at the different machines. Most were quarter machines or higher. We found two quarter machines, side by side that had some cherries in the betting, and we decided to give that type a try. Verna put a quarter in and pulled the long handle at the side of the machine. She got a nickel back because she had a cherry. I put a coin in, pulled the handle on my machine and got nothing.

A young woman came by in a very skimpy costume holding a tray in front of her with cigarettes and cigars on it.

"Cigarettes, or could I get you a drink?" she asked.

"How much are the drinks?"

Looking at us, as if we just came out from under a rock, she said, "They're free as long as you're gambling."

We each ordered a Pepsi. Neither of us realized we could have had a cocktail or should have given the girl a tip. After an hour or two, I'd lost five dollars and Verna only a couple of dollars. Taking the money out of the tray and putting it in our buckets, we decided to look around the casino. First, we had to find a restroom to wash our filthy hands which were black from handling the money.

Leaving the restroom, we passed a lounge area where there was a free show going on. We took a seat and listened to wonderful music. During our two days in Vegas, we spent a lot of time in the lounges at different casinos, carrying our free Pepsi and watching talented free shows which they no longer have.

That first night we stayed up until six o'clock in the morning, going to different casinos to see what they were like and putting a few quarters in the machines. Exhausted, we fell in bed, but only slept a few hours because we wanted to go to the buffet at the Sands casino.

The buffet was three dollars, and it was wonderful. It had everything you could imagine to eat and included champagne. Never having been to a buffet before, I had to try almost every dish. It was all delicious. We ate so much I wondered if we'd be able to stand.

On Sunday, we decided to go to the Wayne Newton evening show. It was twenty dollars and included two drinks and gratuities. We thought that was high but never having been to a show before, decided to go.

While we were standing in line, waiting to get into the show, the couple next to us, said, "You have to tip the usher to get good seats."

Verna and I each had a dollar. I folded the money to make it look like more and we got terrific seats.

Trying to decide what drink to have, I finally chose a grasshopper and Verna a class of wine. When the waiter brought us our drinks he said, "*You're sisters!*"

Verna and I looked at him in amazement because we didn't look alike at all. "No, we're mothers-in-law," I said.

We didn't realize at that time, on every trip we would *ever* take, and we took a lot of them, someone would say, "You're sisters!" When we took a trip to London, walking down a street, a young boy stopped, turned to his mother and said, "Mam, twins!" We didn't know why people did this. As if sisters are something unusual. My sister Virginia and I look somewhat alike but no one ever said that to us.

The show was wonderful. Wayne Newton played many

instruments and sang way past the time the show was supposed to end. I enjoyed every minute.

Early Monday morning, we checked out of Motel 6, went to another wonderful buffet at a different casino, then headed back to Phoenix. We didn't win any money and didn't lose all of the twenty dollars we had set aside to gamble with. I had never felt so relaxed, happy and free. I didn't have to ask anyone if I could go on the trip, how much money I could spend, how long I could stay. All decisions were mine and mine alone. Freedom I hadn't felt in a very long time. I realized just how precious it was.

As we drove home, I remembered a quote I liked, "Life may not be the party we hoped for, but while we are here we might as well dance."

33

THE TREE BROKER

THE LANDSCAPE COMPANY I worked for was in trouble. Now that the two partners had a better knowledge of how to bid on jobs, they had to bid higher to make a profit. Ralph, the partner that had the custom design part of the business was a gentle, quiet man, but not aggressive enough to compete in bidding. You had to convince your customer that your design was the best. You had to be assertive; therefore, Ralph was not getting many jobs.

Bud, the partner that had the maintenance end of the business wasn't taking into consideration the cost of maintaining the machines used on the jobs.

They finally came to the decision to end the design part of the business and only do landscape maintenance. I knew there wasn't an opportunity for me to make more money or have any benefits like paid vacation or health care, so I thought about looking for another job. Going without health insurance was a worry for me. A paid vacation to visit my daughter or take a short trip was important too.

One day, a man who brokered big trees from California to Arizona, came into the office. At that time, no one grew landscape material in Arizona to supply developments with mature trees. He handed me his card and asked to speak to Ralph. When he left, he said, "I'm sorry to hear Ralph isn't bidding on jobs anymore. I need an office girl, and if you ever want to change jobs, give me a call."

I called him and set up an appointment. Barry was a big man, tall, well dressed, about sixty, divorced, brashly confident and self-assertive. His office included two rooms, a large office and a small kitchen. A bathroom was down the hall. His lovely office had a mahogany desk, plush chairs, beautiful landscape paintings and a large window behind his desk making the room bright and cheerful. Another desk, which would be mine, was just inside the door. He appeared to be successful, and after talking with him for a while, he offered me a little more than I'd been getting. After six months a one-week vacation. I took the job.

It was easy work, the books well kept. Besides the usual office work, it was my job to call the landscape groves in California to place the big tree orders. I also spent time calling nurseries and landscape contractors to see if they needed any big trees in the future.

It was only a few months before I suspected Barry had a drinking problem. He not only drank in the office when he was alone, but when friends came in they would drink and get loud, telling off-color jokes. Barry would nearly fall out of his chair with laughter. He came into work late and hung-over many times. He sometimes asked me to join him for a drink after work, but I always refused. I wasn't interested, and I wanted to get home to make dinner for my boys.

One afternoon, after a three-hour lunch, he came into the office slurring his words so badly that when a client called and asked for him, I said he was out of the office and would return his call tomorrow.

Then, a near catastrophe. An order of big trees arrived at its destination, a million-dollar home in Paradise Valley. Barry always met the semi-truck at the jobsite with paperwork to ensure what he ordered was correct and that the trees were placed in the right spot and in excellent condition.

I got a call from the customer who said, "Barry isn't here and the semi needs to be unloaded. The back-hoe and crane company charges by the hour."

I said, "I'm sure Barry's on his way. If he's not there in twenty minutes call me back."

Worried that he'd been drinking, I called his house and got no answer. I thought he might be in the shower and again called every few minutes. Twenty minutes later the customer called me and said, 'Barry didn't show up."

Making an excuse for him, I said, "He called me just now and told me he was sick. I'll be right there."

Quickly finding a copy of the order and address, I hurried to the construction site. I didn't know anything about trees except they had a trunk, branches, leaves or needles. I wondered how I'd be able to tell if the order was correct and if they sent the right trees. Their botanical names on the order gave me no clue.

Arriving, I tried not to show my ignorance. The owner

said, "I don't want any trees that shed badly placed near the pool. The holes are already dug."

Two problems: where was each tree supposed to go? The order sheet made no mention of placement. What trees didn't shed a lot? My sister had a pine tree and she complained that it always shed and she was tired of sweeping up after it, so I told the crane operator to put the pine furthest from the pool area.

The owner was standing beside me, and, to give him the impression that I knew what I was doing, I took a leaf off a tree, crushed it in my fingers, smelled it and told him it should go by the pool. A *Big Mistake*. Much later I found out that particular tree, called Chilopsis, was the worst tree to go near a pool. It would have blossoms from early spring to late fall that dropped cheerfully to the ground—or pool.

When all the trees were placed, I had another problem to deal with. The truck driver needed to be paid. Drawing him aside, I said, "My boss isn't feeling well and was unable to come today. He's the only one that signs the checks. I'm sorry there is nothing I can do. He'll be in the office as soon as he feels better, probably tomorrow, and will mail you a check immediately. Would that be alright?"

"Since I've driven for him before, I guess I'll have to trust him." Handing me the bill, he said, "However, tell him this is the one and only time I'll do it. I've a return load to pick up and this has taken more time than usual. I'm charging him extra for the delay."

On the way back to the office, I thought, 'Why can't I find a normal job with normal people? Either the company is ready to fold, or the boss has a problem.'

When I arrived at the office, Barry was there with a girl about twenty years old.

"Where have you been?" he asked.

"You were supposed to be at the Paradise Valley job-site this morning. I couldn't get in touch with you so I had to go. I told everyone you were sick. Not knowing anything about trees, I placed them the best I could. The count was correct and the trees looked good. I promised the truck driver you would send him a check immediately. He charged extra for the delay. I hope that's ok."

Giving no explanation as to where he was and grinning at the girl, he said, "Great, I'm sure you did a good job."

Lighting a cigarette, he introduced his friend. "Milly is a beautician and I'm going to set her up with a little business." He ran his hand through his hair and smirked, "She cut my hair last night. Didn't she do a wonderful job? I thought I'd turn the kitchen into a little salon. The plumber and contractor are coming tomorrow morning to make the changes."

I was stunned. "Would this mean I'd do Milly's bookwork too? Will she be considered part of this business for tax purposes or will it be separate?"

"We haven't worked out all the details yet but I'll let you know. I'm going to put another phone in the kitchen area with a different number for Milly to take her calls."

I thought, 'What is he thinking? About forty years difference in their age, doesn't he realize she's only after his money? If she's a beautician, she should do something about the bleach job she did on her hair and the heavy makeup. I hope he doesn't expect me to go to Milly to have my hair cut. A tree brokerage with a beauty salon in the kitchen. *What's next?*'

34

THE FABULOUS DANCER

There was a club called Caliente that held ballroom dances for singles Wednesday nights. They had a large dance-band and I thought it would be a fun place to go. I called my friend Verna and asked her to go with me.

She said, "How can I go to a singles dance when I'm married?"

"They won't ask for proof at the door, besides, Bob goes out on Wednesday night and he won't care if you accompany me. Maybe we won't be asked to dance. We can just sit and listen to the music. I heard it's a wonderful band. I don't want to go alone. We don't need to stay more than a couple of hours. Think of it as an adventure."

Verna agreed to go. When Wednesday night came, I picked her up and we headed for the Caliente.

A woman sat at a small table inside the door to take the two dollars to get in. The huge ballroom was an impressive room. It had a large wooden dance floor. On one end of the room, imitation leather topped-tables with matching chairs were placed close together. The other end had a stage for the many piece dance band. On the left side of the ballroom was a partially enclosed room with tables, chairs and a bar that sold drinks and hors d'oeuvres.

Verna and I took a table near the dance floor. The band was playing a foxtrot and we were both asked to dance. The man I danced with had two left feet and stepped on my toes several times. I thought the dance would never end. Returning to the table, he thanked me for the dance. Verna came back, and we chatted while the band began to play again.

Watching the dancers, I noticed a tall, thin man who was a *fabulous* dancer. I pointed him out to Verna and said, "I would love to dance with that man; he's such a good dancer."

We both danced quite a few numbers and after a few hours we headed for home. We both had a good time. The band was wonderful and we met several nice people. We decided to go again the next Wednesday evening.

The following week, we returned to the Caliente and were hardly seated when I was asked to dance. The floor was crowded. As we danced to a swing number, my partner and I bumped into the fabulous dancer. I smiled at him as we danced away. Going back to the table, the band started to play "The Tennessee Waltz." It was my favorite song to waltz to and the waltz was my favorite dance. I felt a tap on my shoulder. Holding out his hand to me was the *fabulous* dancer!

We glided across the floor and it was like dancing on a cloud. We didn't speak until the dance ended. Still holding my hand, we stayed on the dance floor and waited for the next number. "I'm Larry," he said. "Margaret," I replied.

The band began to play. After dancing several numbers, we left the floor. Still holding my hand, he returned me to my table. I introduced Larry to Verna, and he asked if he could get us a drink. We both said we'd love a Pepsi. He went to the bar to get the drinks and when he came back to the table, he sat down and asked me where I worked. I told him I worked for a tree broker, and he said he was an engineer at Motorola. Larry was fifty-four, ten years older than me, about six feet two, very thin, with short, straight light brown hair and large blue eyes. We chatted for a few minutes then got up to dance again. "You're a good dancer," he said, "I enjoy dancing with you."

"Thank you. I love to dance and you're a fabulous dancer."

When it was time for us to leave, Larry asked, "Would you like to go to the Bobby McGee restaurant Friday night for dinner? They have a band and small dance floor in the bar area."

"I'd love to," I said.

"I'll pick you up at six."

Bobby McGee restaurant was a popular place for young adults to go. It was crowded on Friday night, and while we waited to be seated for dinner, we went to the bar to dance. The band was good. They were playing a Cha-Cha and even though I never danced to it before, Larry was a good leader and I quickly caught on. We were the only couple on the dance floor, and I could tell Larry loved the spotlight, but I felt self-conscious with no one else dancing.

We were called to dinner, and Larry held my hand as we went into the dining room. Still holding my hand when the waiter came to take our order, Larry ordered a steak with vegetables and I ordered a steak, baked potato with sour cream, butter and an extra sour cream and butter. Larry looked at me with a frown and said, "That's a lot of butter."

"Lots of butter and sour cream makes baked potatoes delicious," I said.

"My father died in his sixties of a heart attack so I watch what I eat. All that butter and sour cream is not good for you," he said.

Larry held my hand all through dinner. When he wanted to cut his steak, he would squeeze my hand, let go of it, cut the steak and resume holding my hand. I was a little self-conscious about it, but I let him keep holding my hand. I didn't know at that time it would be an obsession with Larry to continuously hold my hand. I became more uncomfortable with it as time went on.

When the evening ended, Larry asked me to go to the Moose Lodge the next evening, Saturday, where they had a large dance floor and live band. Happy to go dancing again, I agreed to go. For about a month we went dancing at the Caliente on Wednesday, Bobby McGee on Friday and the Moose on Saturday. He telephoned me every night in-between our dates.

One Friday evening, Larry asked, "Do you like to go camping?"

"Yes," I said. "I took my boys camping when they were young. Every summer we went to Camp Land in San Diego and we camped with my large tent. The boys were in Boy Scouts so they knew how to pitch the tent and light the camp-stove while I read a book."

"Do you know how to scuba dive?"

"No, but I love to swim."

"I'm a certified scuba diver and I go to Rocky Point, Mexico, to scuba dive. Would you like to go with me? We'd camp at a nice campground on the shore of the Sea of Cortez, leaving on Friday afternoon and returning on Monday night. I'd like to go next weekend."

"Let me think about it. I'll let you know tomorrow night when we go to the Moose."

Rocky Point, was where my daughter Diane and Steve went camping several times a year. I thought, 'there life at Chevlon Ranger Station in the middle of the woods, was just like camping. When it came time for their vacation, I figured they would come to the city, to movies, plays, but no, they went camping.' They always said how beautiful Rocky Point was and what a fun time they had. I wanted to go and never thought I'd get the opportunity.

In bed that night, I thought about whether I should go with Larry for the weekend. I liked him and loved dancing with him. When he'd kiss me goodnight I enjoyed that too. If I went away for a weekend, my mother will have to stay with my teenage boys. She knows I'm dating Larry. As religious as she is, what will she think about me going away on a weekend with him? Maybe she won't think I'll be sleeping with him. She's probably pretty naive. The only place she's ever been is church.'

Tossing and turning, I pondered, 'What will my kids think? Greg and Brian met Larry and they both liked him. He always makes a point of interacting with the boys when he comes to pick me up. Greg, who loves the outdoors, would probably think it was great I went to Rocky Point.

Quiet Brian probably wouldn't care. Diane knows I'm dating Larry but I wouldn't tell her I'd be going off on a weekend with him. I know I can get the time off work on Friday afternoon and Monday.'

The next morning, I called my mother, "I have a chance to go to Rocky Point, Mexico, camping with Larry while he scuba dives. We'll go next Friday, coming back on Monday. Would you be able to come and stay with the boys?"

"Certainly, I can do that. I'll come Friday morning. Is there anything you want me to do while I'm there?"

"No, I don't think so. I know the boys will be happy to see you and I'm anxious to see Rocky Point. Diane says it's a pretty place, and they've been going there for years. We'll be back by Monday night."

Friday came, and I felt a mixture of excitement and anxiety. Larry said he would bring everything we needed. All I had to do was to be ready at one o'clock. Larry never said what we were going to camp in, so I didn't know if it would be a tent or travel trailer. When he came to the house to get me, he met my mother and they chatted for a few minutes before we left.

Larry had a large, older model station wagon, no travel trailer, so I assumed he had a tent. He said we were going to stop at a hotel in Ajo, Arizona, for the night, which was about half-way to Rocky Point.

We talked about ourselves while driving. He said he was an electrical engineer, taught a photography class at Arizona State University, and was on the repelling Mountain Rescue team. He told me he had two daughters, both married. He'd talked one of his daughters, Ginny, into keeping her maiden name. Any children she'd have she'd give them her last name so his name would continue on. I thought that was oddly egotistical but didn't say anything. In those days it was seldom done.

Larry's grandparents came from Germany and some of his values disturbed me. He believed if you were intelligent you should marry someone as intelligent or more intelligent than you, so it would improve the human race. He also believed that any mother who had a retarded baby should be sterilized immediately.

"If that were the case," I said, "we wouldn't have the wonderful music of Beethoven. Before he was born, his eight siblings were handicapped."

"We could do without the music for the better good," he said.

Ajo, Arizona, was a small, desolate town. We had dinner at an A&W hamburger drive-in and then stopped at a small hotel on the highway. As we entered the bedroom that had a full-size bed, I felt self-conscious. I could feel my heart in my throat. Larry put his arms around me, looked into my eyes and gently kissed me as he lifted me onto the bed. My apprehension disappeared. He was a caring thoughtful man. As I was drifting off to sleep, I thought, 'Larry's as good a lover as he is a dancer.' A strange thing happened after Larry thought I had fallen asleep. He picked up his underwear and put it over his face, even though the room was pitch black. That's how he slept all night, whisking it off as soon as he woke up. That's how Larry always slept every night.

Arriving at the campground on late Saturday morning, I was surprised that we were going to sleep in the back of the station wagon. The back seat was folded down, and after he unloaded the back of the car, he unrolled a one-inch foam mattress and placed it on the floor of the car. He put sheets on the mattress and pillows. He covered the station wagon with a tarp and put a suitcase on the top of the car to hold the tarp down. He hooked it onto the bottom of the car with bungee cords.

Our camping spot had a small picnic table next to the car. Larry brought a folding table, some campstools, a camp-stove, ice chest, a pot and skillet, large container of water and a box of food. He put some of the items on the hood of the car. The toilet area was not far away. I wondered how we were going to undress and dress, but I was glad to be at Rocky Point and I was game for anything.

Rocky Point was a colorful pretty place, not like some poor Mexican towns that bordered Arizona. It had a small local hotel and a lot of fishing boats along the docks. The Sea of Cortez was beautiful, with both rocky and sandy beaches. Mexican men, women and young children walked up and down the beach selling Mexican food, sea shells and handmade items.

After a lunch of peanut butter sandwiches, we went swimming and walked on the beach looking for seashells. It was a beautiful day, with a slight breeze off the water. Larry bought some tamales for supper from an elderly woman who peddled them on the beach. He assured me they were alright to eat, not like the local water, which would give you dysentery. In the evening, we took some towels to lay on the beach, listening to the lapping of the waves and looking at the beautiful starry sky as he pointed out the constellations.

The next morning, I woke up to hear some whispering

next to the station wagon. I could see through a small slit in the tarp at the bottom of the window the feet of a large black dog! He lowered his head to smell something on the ground and I recognized him immediately. Shaking Larry, I frantically whispered, "Larry, wake up! Diane, Steve and their black lab, Bo, are outside the car. What are we going to do?"

Grabbing clothes, we had thrown in the front seat, he whispered, "Invite them to breakfast."

Feeling like I was caught with my hand in the cookie jar, we struggled to get clothes on in the close confines of the car. Getting out of the car, embarrassed, I asked, "What are you guys doing in Rocky Point? How did you know we were here? How did you find us?"

"We decided to come to Rocky Point for the week-end," Diane said. "We called to tell you, as we usually do when we go to Mexico, and Grandma answered the phone. She said you and Larry went to Rocky Point doing some kind of diving and you were staying at a campground. We figured this was the campground and asked at the office where Mr. Stubbe was camping and they gave us the number of your spot."

"We were just going to have breakfast, why don't you join us," Larry said, "I have a pancake mix I was going to fix, instant coffee and orange juice."

"That sounds good," Steve said.

After breakfast, they left to go to their camp spot. Diane and Steve always camped with a small travel trailer at the estuary of Rocky Point. Steve loved to fish and the fishing was good there. It was also more isolated, and that's what they liked.

After I cleaned up and put things away, Larry put on his diver suit and I got into my blue, one-piece swimsuit. I had fun swimming and hunting for seashells while Larry went scuba diving.

We became friends with a man who sold seashells at the beach and were invited to his home. It was one large room, dirt floor, drying laundry on the bushes and spotlessly clean.

I was impressed with the warmth and charm of the people. The Mexican men wore colored or white shirts and pants rather than jeans. The Mexican women wore colorful skirts and blouses or dresses rather than slacks. I was very fortunate to see Rocky Point, a small fishing village, as it was before it became a popular tourist attraction, built up with hotels and condos.

It was a wonderful trip and Larry and I went to Rocky Point many times in the years to come.

35

THE STRAWBERRY PLANT

NEVER SUGGEST to your teenage boys that they should plant a garden. When Greg came in the back gate, carrying a tall, green, pointed leaf plant, I asked him. "What have you got Greg?"

"A strawberry plant, I'm going to start a garden."

Having lived in Upper Michigan, where they had abundant wild strawberries, I knew this was no strawberry plant. They grew close to the ground, not tall.

"Greg, that's not a strawberry plant so take it back where you got it. I suggest you grow carrots or peas, not marijuana. Do you want me to be arrested for growing marijuana on my property? Lose the house? I worry about you and your friends. I heard you can be addicted to that stuff, or it will lead to harder drugs. I hope you guys aren't smoking, drinking, or using marijuana. If the police catch you with it, you can go to jail, then you'll have a record. Don't ruin your life by making bad choices."

Surprised, Greg sheepishly said, "I didn't know what it was. A friend gave it to me. He said it was a strawberry plant. I'll give it back to him."

I thought, 'I'll bet he knew what it was. He just didn't think I would. I can't keep Greg and Brian under lock and key. I have no control about what they're doing when out with their friends. I can only hope they do the right thing. I've warned them enough about it.'

Worried about Greg, I asked him, "Why don't you go into the service like Mike when you graduate? You can learn a trade or get more schooling. Mike often goes to school in the Air Force. You'll have a chance to see the world."

"It's not for me," Greg said.

"Your friend Dennis went into the army. He likes it. I talked to him about the service when I occasionally gave him a ride to work. You know he wrote to me and thanked me for talking to him about it. At least think about it."

When Greg turned 18, he quit school in his senior year and joined the army. I was upset that he quit school without getting his diploma. He said, "The army is going to send me to high school as soon as I finish basic training. I'll get a high school diploma not a GED." When Greg finished basic training, he got his high school diploma and was sent to Korea.

I called Diane to tell her about her brother. She told me she was going to have a baby about the middle of June! I was excited. My first grandchild. Diane planned on teaching special education until the end of the school year. I'd stay with her at their ranger station home for a few days after the birth. June was fire season and Steve would be busy.

***

Barry seemed to have lost interest in his tree broker business. We hadn't brought the big trees in from California to Arizona construction sites or nurseries for some time. Milly's beauty salon, in the office kitchen, wasn't doing much business either. Barry and one of Milly's girlfriends were the only customers I knew of. When she was going to cut Barry's hair, the two of them would drink margaritas for several hours before they went into the kitchen-salon to have his hair shampooed. I wondered what kind of haircut he'd get with the two of them more than a little tipsy.

When Larry called me that evening, I said to him, "Boy, do I need a vacation to get away from the office."

"Why do you continue to work there? It doesn't sound like you're having much fun."

"When you have children and are a single parent, fun isn't part of the equation."

"How about taking a vacation in Mazatlan, Mexico?"

I had a week vacation coming, so we made our plans. We'd take the train out of Tucson in the late afternoon, getting into Mazatlan the next morning. Larry booked our stay at the Playa Del Ray beach hotel. We had gone to San Carlos, Mexico, camping in the station wagon several times, as well as Rocky Point, so I was looking forward to staying in a hotel. Larry taught me to scuba dive in my neighbor's pool and I enjoyed exploring the bottom of the ocean when we went to Mexico. I was excited about the adventure and seeing a new place.

I told Diane I was going to Mazatlan, with Larry, on

May 22nd, returning on Memorial Day, Monday the 30th, and my mother was going to stay with Brian and the pets. Diane said, "It sounds like a fun vacation and I'm glad you're taking it before the baby's due."

Arriving at the train station in Tucson, we boarded the train, and went to our sleeping compartment. The seats folded down to make a bed. The motion of the train put me quickly to sleep. It seemed like no time before the announcement came that we'd be coming into Mazatlan.

The hotel car picked us up at the train station. The lobby in the resort hotel was beautiful with striking tiled floors and stonework. Exotic plants were everywhere with a canopy of palms and other tropical trees. It was open to the outside. The smell of the ocean and a warm breeze flowed through. The swimming pool was on the ocean side of the hotel at the edge of the beach and our room faced the ocean and pool, with a small private balcony.

I'd heard so much about the town of Mazatlan, I was anxious to see it. Larry was only interested in the beach, renting scuba gear, and hiking around the area. I finally talked him into taking the bus into town.

It was a fascinating bus ride. People were bringing their wares to the town market so the bus was extremely crowded. There were chickens and brightly colored birds in cages, a parrot on a man's shoulder, a man in a military uniform holding a rifle and a young girl with what looked like a homemade, three-layer cake on her lap. The cake wasn't covered. The bus was extremely noisy with the chickens clucking and the birds squawking but it was fun to watch and listen to the passengers. Not being able to speak Spanish, except a few words and numbers, I didn't know what they were saying but enjoyed listening to their laughter and chatter.

Getting off the bus at the town square, we went to the market in a large building. It was amazing. Every fruit and vegetable you could think of was beautifully displayed on slanted tables. Young children, of five or six, as well as adults, were selling their wares. They had a section that sold live chickens. Large slabs of beef and sausages hung from hooks in the open air.

I said, "Larry, let's buy some of the delicious looking pastry. We could sit on the balcony tomorrow morning and have it with our coffee."

"You don't need any sweets. If you gain any more weight you won't be able to get into your swimsuit."

Turning away, so he couldn't see how hurt I was, I puzzled as to why Larry often referred to my weight and what I was eating. I was five feet five, weighed 107 and wore size nine clothes. I didn't think I was overweight. It made me self-conscious and unsure of myself when he made that kind of remark.

In the center of the town square was a beautiful old Spanish style church. Across from the church, we saw a restaurant that had outdoor seating under brightly colored umbrellas. We decided to have lunch there and dined on freshly caught shrimp. We ordered wine to go with our lunch, not knowing what was safe to drink.

Next morning, while walking on the beach, a man came up to us and said he had a boat and could take us to a small island for a few dollars. He pointed to the island, *way* in the distance. We thought it would be fun to go, so we arranged to meet him in an hour. We bought some tamales from the peddlers on the beach for a picnic lunch and went back to the hotel for bottled water.

It was a pontoon boat and the ride fun. It never occurred to either of us that we'd be stranded on the island if he didn't come back for us.

The small island was rocky, uninhabited, with lots of birds and sea lions for us to watch. We enjoyed swimming, hunting for seashells and watching the hermit crabs scurry with the tide. Sitting on a rock, at the edge of the Sea of Cortez, we ate our picnic lunch, saving a few crumbs for the noisy seagull who pleaded with us to give him some.

As the sun was starting to slide toward the horizon, we began to worry. Looking into the distance we tried to see if there was a sign of a boat. Not seeing one, we wondered if we were going to have to sleep on the beach. It would be a rocky bed. The boat finally came to take us back to Mazatlan as the sun was almost to the water edge.

On the way back to Tucson on the train, I thought about our vacation. I wasn't happy to be going back to the office but I had the birth of my grandchild to look forward to.

When I walked into the house, my mother said, "Call Diane right away. She had a premature baby girl on the 25th. They're both doing fine although the baby is very tiny."

I was shocked and disappointed that I wasn't there when the baby was born but glad they were okay. As I dialed the telephone, Larry said, "Tell Diane I'm going to take you to Chevlon as soon as you hang up."

Arriving at Diane's, I was so glad to see that she was all right and in good spirits while coping with a premature newborn. The baby, Stephanie Ann, was like the tiny doll I used to play with when I was a child. Not like the nine and ten-pound babies I had. No hair to speak of, just blonde fuzz.

When I picked her up, she opened her eyes, gave me a quizzical look, opened her rosebud mouth and let out a wail. "For such a tiny baby, I'm glad she has good lungs," I said.

Larry was busy taking lots of pictures of Stephanie with Diane and me. Steve came in from work, and the proud Dad got into the pictures too, including their black lab that came in with Steve.

That evening, driving back to Phoenix, I told Larry about Greg and the strawberry plant. He laughed and said, "It's a good thing you saw him coming in the gate or Greg would have planted it."

"Thanks for taking me to see the baby," I said. "Steve adores that little girl. They are going to make wonderful parents. I never realized grandchildren could be so special until I held Stephanie in my arms. She's perfect. It's going to be so much fun to watch her grow-up."

Lying in bed that night, thinking about my little grandbaby, I thought of how much Diane's biological father, Pat, has missed out on. Then I remembered something I had read, but couldn't remember who wrote it, "He is a wise man who does not grieve for those he has not, but rejoices for those he has."

36

THE DESERT SHADE COMPANY

Waking up Monday morning, I realized I would be late for work. The battery had died in my alarm clock during the night. It read four-am but when I woke up, the sun was shining brightly. I hate to be late for anything, especially work. Barry didn't usually get to the office before ten. If I hurried I'd get there before him.

Arriving at the office, I noticed the lights were on. Opening the door, I entered and saw a man in a business suit sitting at *my* desk, at work with my ledger. Another man sat at Barry's desk, with a large pile of paperwork in front of him. I didn't know who these men were. I'd never seen them before. I didn't see Barry anywhere and wondered how they had got in and why they were there.

Standing in the doorway, surprised and alarmed, I asked, "Who are you and what are you doing? Where's Barry?"

The man at Barry's desk got up, came toward me and said, "You must be Margaret. I'm Barry's lawyer. I'm very sorry to tell you, he had a heart attack Saturday night and passed away."

I was so shocked I just stood there with my mouth open.

"We're doing the legal work necessary to close the office and business. I'll send you a check for your money that's due plus pay through the end of the week. We haven't got the details of the funeral arrangements at this time but it will be published in the newspaper. We put your personal things in a box on the kitchen counter. Just leave the keys on the desk."

He turned around and walked back. The man at my desk, looked up and said, "Sorry. I know this is a shock."

I couldn't think of anything to say, and feeling they wanted to get back to work without any more conversation, I walked into the kitchen to get my things. I wondered what Milly was going to do without her "sugar daddy" and the kitchen beauty salon.

Dropping the keys on the desk, I asked, "Is there anything I can do to help?"

"No thanks. If you need a recommendation, I'd be happy to give you one."

He handed me his card and went back to his paperwork.

Driving home, I worried about how I was going to make the house payment next month. I'd have to get a job right away. I didn't have a savings account. I never had any money left over from my paychecks. After the house payment, I had the utilities and insurance. In the summer the electric bills were high with the air-conditioning running day and night. It was May and would soon be very hot. After Greg turned eighteen, I was only getting seventy-five dollars a month from Joe for Brian.

In the late afternoon, I sat by the window looking out at my willow tree, as I often did when I was trying to solve a problem. I loved sitting, quietly looking at trees as they gently swayed in the breeze. From childhood on, looking at them gives me comfort and peace.

As I thought about the tree broker job that ended, I wondered if I could do it on my own. If Barry can broker trees, why can't I? I remembered the names of the groves in California but didn't know their addresses or telephone numbers. If I called the 800-directory service, I could get their free long-distance telephone numbers and that would be a big help in locating them. Without cell phones and computers in those days, that was the only way to get a telephone number for a business in another state.

I sat at the kitchen table with pen and paper to make a list of what was needed to start a business and how I would go about it. Number one on my list was to purchase the "Sunset Western Garden Book." It was like a dictionary for horticulture of which I had little knowledge. I decided I shouldn't limit my business to just big trees.

Second, I'd need to go to nurseries, landscape contractors, city and state, to see what construction projects were coming up and what landscape was needed. I'd take the information to the groves in California and talk to them about the Arizona projects. After I read over my list, I remembered I would have to hire big-wheel transport trucks to bring the landscape material from California to Arizona.

I'd need a name for my company and business cards.

After much thought I decided to call it Desert Shade Company. I made a drawing of what I wanted on the business cards: a tree trunk at the side of the card with the leaves of the tree going across the top, the company name in the middle in bold letters under the leaves. I'd use my maiden name, Margaret Gordon, for the business. I had no money, but maybe I could get a loan from the bank with my house as collateral.

When Larry called that evening, I told him what had happened and I was thinking about starting my own broker business. I told him how I planned to do it.

Larry was silent for a moment, then said. "If you get the information you need by this weekend when we go dancing, I'll drive you to California next Monday. If you make appointments with the groves then you can see if it's doable."

The first thing I did the next morning was to have cards printed. As soon as I got them, I went to the businesses on my list and told them I was a botanical buyer and wondered if they had any jobs coming up that required landscape material. Three landscape companies and one nursery needed material by the first of June.

I said, "I'm going to California next Monday and if you give me a list of what you need, I can get prices for you, find what's available, see the condition of the material, and get back to you with the information by the end of the week."

They all gave me a list of what they needed.

Larry and I headed out very early Monday morning with a California map, instructions from the groves and a lot of anticipation and hope.

Arriving at my first appointment with a botanical grower, I was directed to the owner's office. He was a Japanese man who appeared to be in his early fifties. He was dressed in business attire and had a slight accent. The office was immaculate with magazines and books in neat piles on his desk.

I introduced myself and handed him my card. He looked at it in silence for a few seconds. He looked out the window then back at my card as if in deep thought.

"Tell me about yourself, why you're in this business and what you are looking for," he said.

I briefly told him about my previous job and the death of the owner, that I had a grown daughter, who was a teacher for special education students, two sons in the military and a son at home. I told him of my determination to make the business work.

Handing him the lists from the potential customers, I said, "The city and state also have projects in a year or two. The Phoenix area is growing and we get most of our landscape material from California, so I could give you a lot of business. I will be up front with you. I'm not wealthy like my former boss. I need the money and will work hard to make my business a success. I need you to give me your lowest prices on your landscape material. I will have to add a percentage for my pay."

Leaning back in his chair he listened intently to what I was saying. He didn't say anything for a few moments. "Let me take you around the grounds so you can see what we have here."

Larry, the owner and I got in something that looked like

a golf cart. Riding around, I could see it was a huge operation. Acres of horticulture. Everything from full-grown trees to greenhouse plants. It was very impressive. The many workers were either Oriental or Mexican. The smell from the fragrant flowers took me back to my father's garden.

Back in the office he stated, "When an order is placed, I always get the money up front for a truckload of landscape material. In your case I will fill your customers' orders, *on your word*, that we will be paid by your customer upon delivery. If you were a man I wouldn't be saying this to you. A truckload of landscape material costs a lot of money, and you must be able to trust that your customer has the means to pay it or you will have to."

He paused as he lit a cigarette, then added, "You understand that you hire the trucker, and I suggest you ask him to be paid by the customer also. I'm willing to trust your judgment. I'm looking forward to doing business with you in the future. Keep in mind we can also grow specific plant material for any future project for your city or state. Give me a few minutes to price the items on these invoices."

I was thankful that I didn't have to use my money up front in the transactions, even though I would be ultimately responsible. This was completely unexpected! I wouldn't have to get a loan from the bank to start my business. I wondered why he would trust a woman and not a man but was afraid to ask in case he changed his mind.

After going to the other nurseries on my list, I found they were all run by Asian men, except one. That owner was Caucasian and had an English accent. After talking to him for a while he agreed to wait to be paid by my customers also. The others did not. I was glad I would have two growers to compare prices with.

When we were driving back to Phoenix, Larry said, "It looks like your business will get a start if the customers agree to the prices. If they are pleased with the merchandise, you can count on them for future business."

"Metro Center Mall is starting to build other stores around its perimeter. I'm sure the stores will need to be landscaped. I'll have to find out who the developers are," I said.

"If you work for a company like Motorola, you would have steady income and benefits," Larry said. "You don't know that much about horticulture. Are you sure you want to do this? It could be a struggle."

Thinking about it for a few moments, I said, "If there's no struggle there's no progress. What would my life be like if I didn't have the courage to attempt anything? It seems to me that everything in life is a gamble. I know it's going to be a challenge but I'm going to take the chance and do it."

The three landscape companies and Berridge Nursery in Phoenix, agreed to the prices from the California Oriental nursery.

For tax purposes—and in case my telephone number was busy when customers called—I decided to put in an extra telephone line. Back then, Bell Telephone Company put extra lines in free and gave you a free phone. You just had to pay for the two telephone lines each month.

I found a trucking company in Tucson that would wait for their payment from my customers upon delivery. I was happy that my money would not be involved and scheduled the transactions. When I placed the orders, I told the Oriental nursery that I was relying on them to send their best material so I could retain the customers for future business and get referrals.

For the first delivery of landscape material to the construction site, I was anxious for everything to go smoothly. When the truck arrived at the Arizona border inspection station, the driver telephoned me, about three-am, to tell me what time he'd get to the jobsite. I then telephoned the landscape company with the arrival time, so they could rent the backhoe and crane to be there when the truck arrived and start work immediately.

I got to the construction site a little before the truck was due. My customer had the equipment in place and I chatted with him when the truck pulled up. The crew of workers immediately started to unload. I referred to my clipboard, with the botanical order, checking that the count was correct and the material in good shape.

While they finished unloading, I asked the truck driver, "How do they load your truck at the California nursery, and what do you do?"

He said, "I know the clearance between the road and the overpasses on the freeways in California and I-17 in Arizona. If it's an open truck with big trees like this one, I relate the information to the loader at the nursery and they load the big trees accordingly. I never handle the material at the nursery or jobsite. I watch the loading to make sure it has proper clearance. I just drive the truck."

I-17 was the first freeway in Arizona, constructed in 1958. I-10 didn't become an interstate connection from

California to central Phoenix until 1990. The editorials in the newspaper were against it, the residents, including myself, voted down the connection for many years. We didn't want Phoenix to become a mass of freeways like California. At that time, I didn't know I would be going into a business that needed the freeway connection between the two states. Without the connection it made the driving to Phoenix longer and more dangerous. Vehicles had to go through the two-lane streets of the small towns bordering Arizona and California. As I'm writing this, we now have nine freeways in the Phoenix area.

All three deliveries went very well. When the horticulture material was delivered to the Berridge Nursery, the owner said, "Phoenix is having a Home and Garden show at the Coliseum next weekend. We have a booth at the show and we can set up a table for you in our location. We've already paid our fee, you won't have to pay anything. By being at the show, you may get some contacts and business."

I quickly said, "Yes, thank you so much! I'd love to be in the show with you. Is there anything I can do to help set up?"

"No, we have workers that will set up our booth and a table for you. We'll put you at the end of our display." He gave me instructions, the time and where they were going to be located. "I'll see you on the weekend," he said.

When I arrived at the Coliseum, never having been to a Home and Garden show before, I was amazed at how many booths there were and the variety of displays: lawnmower equipment, fountains, fertilizer, seeds, barbeque grills, and horticulture to name a few.

I easily found the Berridge Nursery booth. They had a

card table and folding chair set up for me. They had placed a large sign across the front of the table that said, "Desert Shade Company." I set out a stack of my business cards, pen and tablet, asking him, "What is the procedure? I've never been to a show before, so you'll have to fill me in."

"People will file past the booth and you have an opportunity to introduce yourself, tell them what you do and find out what business they're in. Landscape contractors, nurseries, architects, builders and the general public attend. When you need a break for lunch let me know and I'll have my son sit at your table and hand out your cards to anyone interested."

Several nurseries and landscape contractors took my card and talked to me about my service. The contractor who was handling the building at Metro Center Mall made an appointment for me to meet with him.

A landscape contractor, who lived and worked in Tucson, stopped at my table. He was young, probably in his early thirties, so handsome he could have been in the movies. He had curly blonde hair, big blue eyes, tall, very well built and a smile that lit up his face.

"Well hello there," he said. "I'm Ben Underwood. How about going to lunch with me and tell me about the Desert Shade Company. They have some food vendors toward the back of the coliseum. I hope you haven't had lunch yet."

"I'd be glad to join you. I just have to go and get the young man that will take over for me."

As we headed toward the food area, he told me about himself. "My brother and I own the landscape business," he said. "We have several landscape contracts coming up in Tucson, so I'm interested in what you can do for me."

We had a pleasant lunch and he was easy to talk to. He wanted to know how I got into the botanical business, and I told him the background. Taking me back to my table, we shook hands, he gave me his card and said he would call me on Monday with a list of what he needed for a job that was coming up.

Monday, he called with the list and set the time of delivery for Thursday. I called the California Grove, then the trucker, scheduling the transaction. I planned to drive to Tucson to make sure everything was handled correctly.

At two am on Thursday morning my telephone rang. The person on the other end said, "This is the Arizona border inspection station. We can't let your truck into Arizona because it has red ants. The driver wants to know what you want him to do."

"*What?* Are you kidding? Red ants? What about them? Why are you keeping my truck from entering Arizona because of red ants? Can't they just crawl across the border anyway?"

He said, "Arizona doesn't have red ants. We do not want them and that's why we inspect all horticulture material at the border."

Nearly in tears, I said, "*Oh my gawd!* The contractor has equipment and crew ready to go. He *has* to have the material delivered today according to his contract. Let me think."

After a pause, I said, "I need this load. Everything is riding on it. Is there any way we can get a second opinion? The capitol in Phoenix must have an inspection department. It's not an open truck, can you seal it and let the driver take it to the capitol building in downtown Phoenix to be inspected again? If there are red ants, the driver will return to California with the load. Would that be possible?"

"Yes, we can do that. I will call the inspection office at the capitol when they open. If he confirms my opinion, the truck must return to California sealed."

"Tell the driver to call me when he gets to Phoenix. I'll meet him at the capitol."

Hanging up the phone, alarmed, I wondered what would happen if the red ants were confirmed? It would be impossible to get another load today. There wasn't enough time. Who'd pay to rent the equipment for an extra day in Tucson? Me? The California grove? Ben at the landscape company? It's costly to rent backhoes and equipment. Who would pay the trucker for the ant load? It wouldn't be his fault there were red ants in it. He wouldn't drive for free. If I had to pay any of the additional expenses, I'd have to borrow money. I wouldn't get paid by the landscape company. They would probably never use my business again.

I got dressed, put on a pot of coffee, waiting for the call from the trucker. I knew it would be hours before he got to Phoenix but I wouldn't be able to go back to sleep.

Brian got up and said, "What's going on? Why are you up so early and who was calling in the middle of the night?"

I told him what happened and he said, "Wow. You sure have bad luck sometimes. Hope it turns out alright," and went back to bed.

When I got the call from the trucker, I rushed to the capitol building even though they wouldn't be open for another half hour. Seeing how upset I was, the truck driver tried to be positive. He said, "I didn't see what the border inspector thinks he saw. There were a couple of ants but they were just the large black ones. Let's hope I'm right. Did you call the company in Tucson?"

"No, I thought I would wait until we get the final word from the inspection office. No sense worrying them. If the load's okay, I'll call and tell him we'll be late. Because of the heat in Arizona, I know they like to start early but the delay can't be helped."

Security came out and wanted to know why the big wheel truck was parked in front of the Capitol Building. We explained the situation, and he said he would alert the inspector as soon as he arrived.

When the inspection office opened, two men came out, unsealed the back of the truck and after looking for quite a while, said there was no evidence of red ants.

Relieved, I asked him, "How can you tell, and why did the border inspector think there were red ants?"

He said, "I can tell red ants by the way they mound the earth and there would be some activity. They're aggressive ants. I don't know what the other inspector thought he saw. I'll give him a call. You're free to go."

The trucker moved out, and I went home to make the call to Ben in Tucson. I explained the situation and told him the truck was on its way.

Ben said, "We've been busy preparing the ground and digging holes so the time wasn't wasted. I'm glad everything turned out alright. I'll see you soon."

Leaving a note for Brian, and grabbing a sandwich, I headed to Tucson. I thought about the nerve-racking night and morning. Everything previously had worked so well. I never realized that my business might not go as easily as it did and how many things could affect it. I needed to remind myself that in all things it's better to hope than to despair when things go wrong.

37

CAMPING WITH LARRY

LARRY TAUGHT ME how to shoot a rifle, scuba dive and take a good photograph. He took me camping to Canyon Lake, Arizona, San Carlos, Mexico, San Diego, Bryce Canyon, Utah, to name a few places. We always slept in the back of his station wagon.

Having my own business, I was able to schedule deliveries before and between trips. One of my most memorable trips was to Baja, Mexico. Our plan was to leave at five am, drive across the Arizona border at Nogales, proceed to Hermosillo and then to Guaymas which is about a six-hour drive. Then we'd take the Guaymas ferry across the Sea of Cortez to Santa Rosalie on the Baja Peninsula. To go to Mexico, passports were not needed in 1978, you just acknowledged you were born in the United States.

Arriving in Guaymas around two-pm, we went to the Guaymas Ferry office. No one spoke English and Larry and I spoke very little Spanish. The words we knew, such as *lights*, *good-bye*, *thank-you*, and *milk*, were not useful to hold a conversation or understand what was said. We did a lot of hand gestures, pointed to advertisements and managed to make them understand we wanted a stateroom for the ten to twelve-hour trip across the Sea of Cortez. Larry offered more money than the price of the tickets and they gave us a stateroom.

The large ferry had three levels with the vehicles on the bottom. We waited in the vehicle line several hours and at five-pm they started to load the cars and trucks into the ship. When it was our time to board, Larry drove down a ramp, and parked, putting the emergency brake on. Then we had to exit the ship. We went up about twenty steps across a long plank and stood in line, with the passengers, to get back on. I thought that was a strange way of doing things.

The tiny stateroom had bunk beds, sink, shelf and a porthole low enough to look out. The toilets were at the middle of the ship's deck and there were no showers. I think we were the only Americans on the ship. Crossing the Sea of Cortez on the Guaymas Ferry would be an adventure. It certainly was not like a cruise ship with luxurious staterooms, lounge chairs and martinis.

There had been a hurricane, so the sea was rough. As the ship got on its way, passengers got sick. Neither Larry nor I were affected by the storm. We stood at the rail and watched the waves churn below us as passengers heaved over the side.

We didn't know we had to take what was needed from the car for the long journey across the sea. We had no water or food with us. All the entrances to the car-deck were blocked. We tried to communicate with one of the ship's sailors that we needed to go down below to our car. Shaking his head, he took us each by the arm and steered us up to the navigation room to see the captain. He talked to the captain in rapid Spanish and we had no idea what he said.

The 360-degree view from the top of the ship's navigation room was spectacular. The captain spoke some English and told us about the storm. They had to cancel two previous sailing dates because of the hurricane and that was why the ship was so full. We were fortunate that we got in the car line as early as we did because they had to turn cars and trucks away.

Larry told him we wanted to go down to the car deck and the reason why.

The captain said, "Usually no one is allowed down on that deck with the ferry moving, even in calm weather. Because you have no water, I'll let you go down, but my man has to accompany you. The cars may shift in the turbulent sea so you have to be very careful."

On leaving the navigation room with the sailor, we had to hang on to each other to keep upright. When we were going down the stairs to the car deck, Larry went first, I second. The sailor was behind me holding onto my waist. We were tossed back and forth as we proceeded downward. The waves, would crash over the partially open hull all the way up to the second story. Fortunately, we were parked in the middle of the deck but we still got wet from the spray. As we passed by several beat-up trucks, they were piled very high with furniture, boxes and even live squawking chickens. I became terrified that the boat, which dipped up and down with the waves, would dip too far and send us flying into the sea. Larry threw a change of clothes, water, and a couple of peanut butter sandwiches into a sack and we struggled back up the stairs.

We headed for our stateroom hanging on to each other to keep from falling. Larry secured our bundle and we went back on deck to see if we could spot any whales or sea life.

Larry remarked, "Rough sea. I feel sorry for the people that have motion sickness."

"This reminds me of when I was in grade school and played on the see-saw which I loved to do."

As night fell and turned the sea into a black abyss, we went back to our stateroom. We were lucky to have it because most of the passengers just curled up on the deck for the night. We ate our sandwiches and drank some water. Larry took the upper bunk and the rolling of the ship soon rocked us to sleep. It seemed like no time elapsed when we heard the call that we were approaching Santa Rosalie.

It was five-am when the ferry docked and we drove off. Larry didn't want to drive in the dark on unfamiliar roads in a foreign country, so when he saw an old hotel we decided to spend the rest of the night there. The hotel was hidden behind palm and banana trees. We got a clean room with a tiny shower, toilet and sink. After showering we set our alarm clock to ten-am and slept soundly until it woke us.

Santa Rosalie was surrounded by hills that reminded me of the Phoenix terrain. The Baja Peninsula had separated from the mainland, Mexico, due to the San Andreas Fault. Most of the peninsula was mountainous and had a rocky, desert landscape, although Santa Rosalie felt humid and had a lot of vegetation.

We walked to the town square, a few blocks away, and found a little restaurant where we had a breakfast of sausage, eggs and a coke. Not being able to drink the water in Mexico, we didn't want to order coffee. The town square was close to the water, and under a huge tree were benches where old men sat and talked.

After we filled the car with gasoline, we drove on a one-lane road along the coast to Muleya. Larry said, "I hope we won't see another car coming toward us, because there aren't many places to pull over."

"Larry, I wonder who would have to back up, I hope it won't be us."

At Conception Bay, we found what looked like a campground. Pulling in, we saw four very primitive structures, in a row, on the sand. They had roofs made of palm fronds. A woven mat of fronds sat on the ground, and one side had a wind barrier made of the woven fronds. The rest of it was open. The only other structure was an outhouse which looked like the others except smaller, and the four sides were enclosed with wooden slats.

No one was there, so we pulled next to one of the structures and set up camp. Larry put his long folding table inside and I covered it with a plastic tablecloth and then set the package of dishes and utensils on it. Larry brought his card table to set up the ice chest, large water container and camp stove. He arranged the two folding chairs so we would have a view of the sea. After he finished unloading the back of the station wagon, he unrolled the foam mat we slept on. I made it up with sheets, and pillows. He blew up his large Zodiac inflatable boat with a pump and, with no one there, we changed into our wet-suits, took the boat out, dropped anchor and went scuba diving.

The next morning, after a pancake breakfast and instant coffee, we started to take turns rowing the Zodiac along the shore to see what was in the area. After Larry had gone a short way, a young man on the shore waved to us to come in. As we came to the shore, he pointed to the boat and said something in Spanish. I said, "No Hablo Espanol." He nodded and pointed to himself and then to the boat.

I said to Larry, "I think he wants a ride in the Zodiac."

He then pointed to me and to a structure on the beach where a young woman and two little kids were standing watching us.

"Larry, why don't you row him around and I'll go and see the woman and her children."

"For heaven's sake why?" Larry asked.

"Because it would be a nice thing to do," I said as I got out of the boat.

Grinning from ear to ear the young man got in saying, "Gracias, gracias."

Giving me an, 'I can't believe you're having me do this' look, Larry rowed away from the shore.

The family was obviously living on the beach. Their large round structure had a heavy palm frond roof which tall tree trunks supported. Flat stones were arranged together for the floor. Woven fronds that rolled up and down went all the way around it and gave them privacy. They were pulled up and I could see that the family was very poor. I thought, 'what an ingenious home.'

She was a pretty young woman, about twenty, and she had two boys, about five and seven, plus a baby that was only a few months old.

"Hablo Ingles," I asked? She shook her head. I pointed to myself and said, "Margaret." She did the same. We managed to silent talk with gestures and pointing. We laughed a lot and I had a good time. In a little while Larry came back, pulled the boat up, then walked over to greet the family. Everyone said, "Adios," as we left.

Larry said, "I thought you were taking a risk but it turned out alright. They seemed nice. I don't think he ever saw a Zodiac boat before. He kept patting it with a look of wonder on his face and hanging his head over the edge trying to see underneath. I rowed him by our camp but not speaking his language made it awkward."

Early that evening, the young man appeared at our camp and had a bucket with him. It was full of live clams. Handing it to Larry, with a grin on his face, he licked his lips and rubbed his stomach. We thanked him for the clams as he left.

When he was out of sight, I said, "I can't kill these clams in boiling water or eat them while they are alive. We have to throw them back in the sea." So, Larry and I walked along the beach throwing the clams back into the water.

We stayed for four days at Conception Bay and saw the little Mexican family often. She made fish tacos for us, rolling out the shell on a flat rock that had a fire under it. I never had such delicious tacos before or since.

A strange thing happened after Larry loaded up the car and we drove off: he didn't speak to me for three hours.

I finally asked, "Are you going to remain silent for the rest of our trip around the Baja or are you going to tell me what's the matter?"

"You didn't put your suitcase in the back of the station wagon. You expected me to do it."

"*You're kidding*! You have everything packed tight in the back, so I figured you would want to do it. You've been putting it in and out on all our camping trips and never said anything."

As Larry drove, he was silent for a while and so was I, as I fumed at his pettiness. In a while he started remarking on the landscape, and we stopped to take a few pictures. We arrived in La Paz and found a camping spot. We stayed for a couple of days scuba diving, sightseeing and discovering little seafood eating places. Then we headed for Cabo San Lucas at the tip of the Baja. When Larry was packing to leave, he went to grab my suitcase and I said, "*Don't* you touch my suitcase. I'll do it."

Larry raised his eyebrows at me but didn't say anything.

Back then, Cabo San Lucas was a little fishing village that had beautiful white sand beaches, only one small hotel and a little store that also served food. They had sausages hanging above a counter where you ordered your food. We bought some pastry and a coke, then took it to a little table under a shade tree and watched the few customers come and go. Today Cabo San Lucas is a huge tourist site that caters to Americans. It has big hotels, condos, cruise ships that stop, and many activities. I'm so glad I had the chance to see it in its original beauty.

Leaving Cabo, we went up the Pacific side of the Baja stopping now and then for a night. We crossed the border at Tijuana and traveled to Mexicali and on to Phoenix. It was a wonderful adventurous camping trip, and I'm grateful that I had the opportunity to see the Baja when almost no one spoke English and you didn't see Americans; you only saw the friendly Mexican people in their native land.

38

THE LAST STRAW

ON FRIDAY MORNING, Larry called and said, "I'll have to cancel our usual dinner and dancing at Bobbie McGee's tonight. It's my daughter Ginny's birthday today, and I'm going to take her to dinner. I'll see you tomorrow when we go dancing at the Moose."

"That's fine," I said, "have a good time."

That afternoon, my friend Verna and I decided to go to Mountain Shadows Resort for dinner and listen to their band. Her husband Bob was in Ohio, so Verna was glad to have the night out. When we arrived and pulled into a parking spot, I thought I saw Larry's station wagon a couple of rows ahead of us.

"Verna, that looks like Larry's car. I wonder if this is where he's taking his daughter to dinner?"

We saw Larry step out of the car, go around to the passenger side and open the door. Out stepped a woman his age. Larry held her hand as they walked toward the resort.

Shocked and angry, I said to Verna, "I *don't believe it*! Larry lied to me. He isn't taking his daughter to dinner, *he has a date.*"

"I told you, I don't like Larry. Are we going to go in, or what?"

"I really don't want to go in. I need to think about this. Let's go eat somewhere else."

During dinner, I talked about Larry. "We've been going out for four years or more, three times a week. We took many trips together. He calls me every day and has said, 'I know you aren't ready for marriage yet, but I'm not like your ex-husband,' which indicates to me he's serious about our relationship. I wouldn't have been intimate with him if I thought he was dating other women. I don't want to get some horrible disease."

Verna laughed and said, "Larry's controlling and critical. I don't know why you can't see it. He wants you to himself and is not friendly to people around you." Verna took a bite of her hamburger. "If he caught *you* dating someone else, he'd drop you like a hot potato. I always thought he was a womanizer. The way I see it, you have two choices. Call him on it or ignore it."

In bed that night, thinking about the situation with Larry, I felt betrayed. As tears fell, I knew I could never trust him again. Any serious thoughts about marriage were over. Should I continue with him? He took me out to dinner and dancing every Wednesday, Friday and Saturday. I loved to dance and he was a fabulous dancer. We traveled to places I'd never been before. If he didn't take me, I couldn't afford to go. I love to travel.

I thought about my mother's favorite saying, "don't cut off your nose to spite your face." Should I swallow my pride and not say anything? Continue as if nothing happened? I know he will expect sex as usual but now I won't feel the same about him. When I'm in a relationship, I'm fully committed to that person and I expect the other person to be committed to me too. I guess I'm just a hopeless romantic, always looking for my knight in shining armor, someone who will put me first. My knight must have got lost along the way.

When I finally fell asleep, I hadn't come to a decision. Next morning, when Larry called to confirm the time he would pick me up, I said, "I'll see you tonight," and hung up before he could say anything else.

After struggling with how I was going to handle the situation, I decided not to say anything. When Larry arrived on Saturday, I asked him, "How did last night go with your daughter?"

"Great, I don't see her that often, so it's special when I do."

"Where did you go to eat?"

"Little Italy, she likes Italian food."

I had to suppress the desire to call him a few choice words for lying to me. Instead I let him kiss me hello. Grabbing my purse, we went out the door. As the evening progressed, Larry said, "You're awfully quiet tonight. Is something wrong?"

"No, should there be? It's getting late, so maybe you should take me home."

Larry was quiet for a minute, and I could see by the look on his face he wondered if I knew what he had been up to last night. As we were driving home, he said, "I'd like to go to Puerto Vallarta, Mexico. Should I schedule a trip?"

I always wanted to go to Puerto Vallarta, so I said, "How about going next month. I'll have vacation time then."

"We'll have to fly to Puerto Vallarta. I know you hate to fly, but it should be a fun trip. We can rent scuba gear when we get there. Can you stay a week?"

"Yes, I can stay a week. Since I've never been, I'll have something to look forward to."

Monday, I decided to call my State Farm agent and go over my automobile policy with him. He made the appointment to come to my home the next evening.

When the agent arrived, we went into the family room. I saw him staring at the wall of family photos. He walked up to the eight-by-ten photo of Larry and me.

In a surprised voice, he asked, "*Is that Larry Stubbe?*"

"Yes, do you know him?

"I live next door to him. Larry and his *wife* play cards with my wife and me every Sunday night when he isn't on a business trip."

I was speechless, staring at him in disbelief.

I finally asked, "*Larry?* Who works for Motorola and has two daughters?"

"Yes, Larry is an engineer at Motorola, but has three daughters."

When he named the three girls, I recognized two names, so I knew without a doubt it was the Larry I was dating.

He had lied about how many daughters he had too and that was strange.

I was overwhelmed. The agent could see I was shocked. "Let's go over your policy," he said.

As he talked, I hardly heard a word. When he finished, he said, "I think you're sufficiently covered," and stood up to leave. When he left, I thought, 'tomorrow when Larry comes to take me to the Caliente nightclub, I'm going to have it out with him.' I was furious.

When Larry arrived, I hadn't dressed to go dancing. Surprised, he said, "I'll go out back and throw the ball for the dog while you finish getting ready."

I could hardly get the words out as I took the picture off the wall. "Sit down, I have a few things to say to you."

With a surprised look on his face, Larry sat down on the couch. "What?"

Slamming the picture down on the coffee table in front of him, I said. "I had my State Farm agent over last night. He looked at our picture and told me he was your next-door neighbor and *you are married.* What in the hell do you think you're doing! How dare you pretend you're single. Dating me for years, sleeping with me, acting like you care about me and all the time *you're married!*"

"I never said I was single, and you never asked. My wife and I are only together because of money. I own a lot of land, houses, even a forest that I log every few years. If I divorced her, I would have to give her half of everything I worked for. It's convenient for us to stay together, but go our separate ways. I do care about you. You must know that," he said, as he looked into my eyes with his large blue eyes, and put his long thin fingers over my hand.

"I met you at a singles dance. Why would I ask you if you were married? What does your wife think you're doing going out three nights a week and going on trips often?"

"Well, for her sake, I don't go into details about what I'm doing and she doesn't ask questions when I leave."

"My agent also said you have three daughters and you told me you have two. Why?"

"My eldest daughter, Susan, married a man that I forbid her to marry, so I've disowned her."

"That's harsh. You can't choose who your daughters will marry. For heaven's sake, Larry, it's your *daughter*. I bet no one could tell you what to do when you were young. If you don't contact her you will live to regret it."

He stood up and put his arms around me and said, "I'll get a divorce if you'll promised to marry me."

"Larry, you should get a divorce because you want to and think it's the right thing to do. Not because I say I'll marry you."

We talked for quite a while that evening. I decided to continue seeing him while thinking things over. I'd never marry him because I could never trust him. I also thought less of him because of his values. I began to wonder if it was his wife who he took to dinner at Mountain Shadows or another woman. I got a good look at the woman and it definitely wasn't his daughter. To find out, I'd have to see what his wife looked like.

I called my friend Delores and told her about my situation with Larry. She said, "When it comes to your love life I think you're doomed. If I had to walk a week in your shoes, I think I'd kill myself. First Pat abandoned you when you were pregnant, then Joe deceived you. He wasn't what he appeared to be when you dated him, and his true self appeared the day after you married him. Now Larry." She paused, "Just a minute, I have to let the cat in. He's at the patio door yowling to come in—So, what are you going to do now? I know you well enough that you won't let *this* go. You aren't going to involve me in one of your escapades, are you? I remember us going down to the newspaper when the school board was being recalled with a black eye and a sign, 'I'd rather fight than switch.' It was on the front page of the newspaper the next day. Then there's your suit with Motorola. Whatever it is, the answer is NO!"

I said, "I bet you always wanted to be a detective and now it's your chance! You know how everyone has Tupperware parties? I thought we could go to Larry's house and pretend we are there for a party, then act surprised that we have the wrong address. That way I could see what his wife looks like when she answers the door."

"Are you crazy? Don't you feel guilty that he's married and you are the other woman?"

"That's between him and his wife. It's not up to me to keep him faithful. He probably has always screwed around. I figure we could go next Monday and be there about two o'clock. I'll take the day off. Look at it as an adventure."

Delores was silent for a minute, then said, "Okay, I'm curious about how you're going to carry *this* off. But I'm *not* getting out of the car."

On Monday, after looking up his address in the telephone

directory, Delores and I set out. On the way, I told her she had to go to the door with me because it would look strange with her sitting in the car if we're supposed to be going to a Tupperware party.

Reluctantly she got out of the car and we went up to the house. It wasn't a big house, old, plain, very ordinary, on a small lot. I expected it to be quite fine since Larry had lots of money.

Ringing the doorbell, I became anxious as I heard footsteps coming to the door. Delores glanced at me with a 'what now' look, and rolled her eyes.

In the doorway stood a woman of average height and weight. She had no make-up on, medium length grey hair, and looked older than me. She appeared surprised and not too friendly.

"Can I help you?" she asked.

Looking at a piece of paper with the address, I said, "Oh my gosh, we must have the wrong address. We're supposed to be going to a Tupperware party." Turning to Delores I said, "Delores, you must have copied the address wrong. I bet we should be on the west side instead of the east." Glancing back at Larry's wife, I said, "I'm sorry we bothered you."

"Would you like to use the phone to call someone?"

'No, thank you, that's okay. I'm sure it's on the west side." We turned to leave as she shut the door.

Quickly driving away, I said to Delores, "His wife is not the woman Larry took to Mountain Shadows. I think his wife knows I'm the woman he's fooling around with. I could tell by the look on her face. Maybe she looked me up too.

I don't believe she thought we were going to a Tupperware party." Delores laughed and said, "I wonder if she'll say something to Larry."

"She has to know he's fooling around," I said. "I could see through the screen door that the ironing board was up and Larry's ironed shirts hung on something. If they were each going their separate ways, why would she iron his shirts? I wouldn't. So, not only is Larry cheating on his wife, he's cheating on me too."

At home that night I pondered about what direction I was going to take. If I told Larry what I thought of him, I needed to remember that a word once spoken can't be caught. I have the chance to go to Puerto Vallarta. I always wanted to see it, so I need to take advantage of the opportunity and go. I'll use him like he's used me.

Puerto Vallarta was a small village on the Pacific Ocean. Today it's a bustling tourist attraction. Our pretty hotel was on the oceanside. We took the bus to town or hiked around the area. We took photos of women with dresses on, standing in water in a creek washing clothes on rocks and putting them to dry on bushes. It made me thankful for my automatic washer. An old man, with wild white hair, naked from the waist up, sitting beside an old building, was making shoes by hand from rubber tires and various other things. They were beautiful. I had him make a pair of sandals for my son Mike while Larry and I walked around.

We took a canoe to Yelapa, Mexico, where the movie, "Night of the Iguana" was filmed. It was a very quaint fishing village with little population. I ate a fish-on-a-stick from a man who was grilling them on the beach. It was delicious.

Old man making Mike's shoe

One terrifying thing happened when we went scuba diving in Puerto Vallarta. Larry and a couple that we dived with, went into the water as I was still slowly backing in. Because I had a buoyancy problem, I was adjusting the weights on the waist of my wet suit. As I was backing into the water, I didn't hear the shout, "SHARK, *get out!*" Larry and the couple scrambled out and up a rocky cliff when they heard the warning. I continued backing in and diving down, turning around, I came face to face with the shark. I froze in terror while the shark circled around me twice, then came within inches of my face. We looked at each other, eye to eye. I could not move, in fear that I would be dragged away and eaten. Then the shark turned and swam away. I never went scuba diving again.

Larry and I continued to see each other for several more years. He sometimes joined my family at my home on Christmas day. We always spent New Year's Eve together. We took many trips.

One evening, there was a special fundraising dinner at the prestigious Biltmore Hotel, put on by the Phoenix chefs. A friend gave me two tickets for the event, so Larry and I were able to go. We were seated at one of the large round tables, thirty at each table. A Mountain Shadow Resort chef was seated beside me. I told him how much we enjoyed dinner at Mountain Shadows. We chatted and I tried to bring Larry into our conversation but he wasn't very responsive. It was a wonderful many-course dinner. When the server came by with a huge dessert tray, pointing to me, Larry said in a loud voice, "Put it down in front of her, she'll probably eat the whole thing."

Conversation stopped as everyone looked at Larry and

me. I was humiliated, but I smiled. I turned away from Larry engaging the chef in conversation. When we got home, he assumed we would go to the bedroom. Instead I sat on the couch, and he sat down beside me.

"Larry, why did you make that remark about dessert in front of all those people?"

"Well, I can see you're putting on weight. I thought I would take you to Hawaii, but I'd be embarrassed for anyone to see you in a swimsuit."

It was the last straw.

"Larry, you may want me to look like a skinny model, and I would only need to lose one or two pounds to do so. I'd like you to look like muscular Charles Atlas; let me tell you, it would take years and you'd never accomplish it. Do you think it's fun to go to bed with a pile of bones? Well it isn't. Furthermore, you are a liar and a cheat. Cheating on your wife as well as me. I want you to leave and *never* come back."

"No woman has ever talked to me like that."

"Well, I like to be the first in everything." Larry got up and left.

I didn't hear from him again except once, when he sent me a card on my birthday. Then about two years after I told him to leave, the doorbell rang and Larry stood there. "Can we talk?" He told me how much he missed me, how much fun we had together and how he wanted to see me again. Putting his arms around me, he said, "I miss making love to you. Can we get together next Wednesday night and go dancing?"

I thought, why not, maybe one last time to go dancing, but no sex. A day later, I was talking to my friend Phyllis, who still worked in insurance at Motorola. I told her about Larry coming to my house and what he said.

She said, "I *don't believe it*! Margaret! Two weeks ago, Larry submitted a new insurance card that landed on my desk because he's in my alphabet. He changed his beneficiary to his *new wife*. He divorced and remarried about three weeks ago."

Furious, I could hardly wait for Wednesday night to come. When Larry stepped in the door, I sat down in a chair, pointed to the opposite chair and asked him to sit down. I said, "I understand you were married about three weeks ago. What are you doing here? Why aren't you home with your new wife? You should still be on your honeymoon!"

"I miss you. I miss being with you. I just wanted to hold you in my arms one more time. You are a fun person and we had good times together."

"I'm so glad I never married you. I feel sorry for both your wives that have had to put up with you and your womanizing. For all your brains and money, you are a worthless piece of shit. *Get out*. I never want to see or hear from you again." He paused and seemed about to speak. Then with tears in his eyes, he left.

As the door closed I thought of the saying, "What tangled webs our lives we weave when we first practice to deceive."

39

THE IMPERSONATORS

W<small>HEN</small> G<small>REG WAS DEPLOYED</small> to the South Korea DMZ Zone with the army, I told him the same thing I told his brother Mike when he was deployed to Germany with the Air Force, "Remember, you are not in the United States, don't expect things to be the same as it is in this country. Every country has its own culture and you must embrace the difference. Be adventuresome. Get out and see the country where you're stationed. It's a chance in a lifetime to see things you never saw before. Every country has its own beauty."

Mike and Greg had very different personalities. Mike was a serious person but adventurous. Greg was very social and a daredevil. While in Germany, Mike bought a bicycle, so he could peddle around Germany and France taking in all the sights. He got an apartment close to the base, wanting to live amongst the German people. In contrast, Greg lived on the base the two years he was in Korea. He spent most of his spare time at the officer's club drinking with his buddies.

Gregory Paul

1977

Occasionally he would go into the countryside with them to drink at a military-approved local bar.

I worried about Greg's drinking since there was a history of alcohol abuse in the family. When we wrote back and forth, I cautioned him about it.

One day, I received a letter from Greg, telling me he had met a Korean girl named Poksun. She was working at the base, and he'd been seeing her for quite some time. Greg wrote she was beautiful, smart, could speak some English and was studying the English language. He said he asked her to marry him, and after consulting with the army, received approval. They were getting married, in Korea, within the week. He'd just got orders to be stationed in Monterey, California, and was able to take Poksun with him. They planned on coming home on leave, to Phoenix, before his deployment to Monterey.

I was surprised and anxious about the situation but I couldn't do anything about it. Writing back to Greg, I asked him to let me know when he would arrive, and how long they would be able to stay. I told him I planned to give them a wedding reception while they were here. As soon as I got the information from him, I sent out invitations for the reception at my home.

When I met Poksun, I immediately liked her. She was shy, sweet, and willing to help. She never asked, "What can I do?' She just pitched in without a word and we worked well together.

America was a cultural shock for her. She never had a refrigerator and was fascinated with mine. In Korea, in those days, they shopped at the market every day for the exact amount of food they would be eating. They had no leftovers. Water came out of a pipe in the wall. Sinks were not common, so they placed a pan on the floor, crouched down and washed the dishes.

Poksun and I went shopping for a dress for her to wear at the reception. We found a long, pale blue dress that showed off her beautiful, shiny, thick black hair.

For the reception, I had a three-tier wedding cake and served hors d'oeuvres, punch, beer and soft drinks. Everyone had looked forward to meeting Poksun. Friends and family, welcomed her.

Greg needed a vehicle, so after they looked around for a few days, he bought a yellow ford truck. One day, he took it to a car wash, and when the car was going through the automatic cycle, the brushes put a dent in the side of the door. Having had too much to drink that day, Greg knew the door was dented but didn't bother to ask them to have it fixed. When he got home he laughingly told me about it.

Sensing he had too much to drink, I said, "Greg, you should have had them repair it. Why can't you have just one drink instead of so many. I worry about you."

"Don't worry Mom," he said, as he put his arm around me, "I'll never be like Dad. The dents are no big deal."

The morning they left, we said our goodbyes, and I promised to visit them after they got settled.

A few months later, on a week's vacation, Verna and I headed for the California coast to visit them in Monterey. It would be the first of many trips up the Pacific Highway. We got an early start and had a reservation at Motel 6 in Anaheim so we could spend a day at Disneyland. I *loved* going to Disneyland. My favorite ride was the Pirates of the Caribbean. I didn't like roller coaster rides and that was as near to a roller coaster ride as I cared to get. We arrived at the amusement park just before it opened and were the last to leave. Two men, pushing brooms, were right behind us.

We stopped in Solvang, a Danish village nestled in a lovely California valley. It looked and smelled like Christmas even though it was July. We ate some delicious pastry and walked through quaint stores decorated in Danish style.

Arriving in Monterey, we checked in at the army guard station and were directed to Greg's housing on the base. They had a cute little apartment. Greg had purchased furniture from Goodwill, refurbished the items, and they looked like new.

The next day, Greg had twenty-four-hour duty, so Verna, Poksun and I decided to drive to San Francisco, not far from Monterey. Verna and I had never been there, and we thought it would be a good opportunity to go.

Arriving at hilly San Francisco, on the Pacific Ocean, we drove past colorful Victorian houses and crossed the famous Golden Gate Bridge with a view of the notorious Alcatraz prison. Poksun didn't know anything about the prison so we told her its history.

"Can we go through it?" she asked.

"There are so many things to see I don't think we'll have enough time," I said. "I'm sure Greg will take you to San Francisco in the future and you can see it with him."

We rode the colorful cable car down to Fisherman's Wharf with its many shops and restaurants. Sitting outside, at a café on the ocean's edge, we had a delicious lunch of a sour dough bread-bowl filled with clam chowder. We watched some fishermen come in with their catch, and while we were there, we were handed a flyer about a live show at a downtown theater of female impersonators in performance. Never having seen anything like that, we decided to go. Poksun couldn't understand what it was we were going to see. I tried to explain it to her but she had a puzzled look on her face, so I knew she didn't know what I was talking about.

That evening we purchased tickets to the show and got very good seats close to the front. As the show began, the first impersonator appeared. Wearing a long blonde wig, he was dressed in a flamboyant, off the shoulder long dress, with a slit going down the front skirt showing off a gorgeous pair of legs.

Turning to Poksun, I whispered, "That's a *man*."

She looked at me, puzzled, and said, "*No!* Man?"

"Yes, they will all be men in the show, dressed and looking like women."

As the show went on, every now and then, when there were exceptionally pretty impersonators strutting their stuff, Poksun would turn to me and whisper, "Women?"

"No, men," I'd whisper back.

"But they're pretty, and the one on the left looks like they have breasts," she said.

"They must be fake," I whispered back.

It was a fun, colorful show and Poksun was mesmerized.

Late that night we returned to Monterey. When Greg got off duty, Poksun, in her halting English, excitedly told him about the show we saw, "Your mom told me they were men. They looked like women. We don't have pretty men that look like women in Korea."

"Mom," Greg said, with a twinkle in his eye, "what are you doing corrupting my innocent wife!"

"It was girl's night out. It was fun and different. Remember, you don't get harmony when everyone sings the same note."

40

NEVER SAY NEVER

FOURTEEN MONTHS AFTER my granddaughter Stephanie was born, Diane had a baby boy on July 22nd 1978 and they named him Brian James. He was a good baby and had an interest in everything, much earlier than the norm. At three months old, when he sat in his toddler swing, he silently followed conversations by looking back and forth at whoever was talking. It felt like he could understand what was said.

Diane and Steve went to Rocky Point, Mexico, at least once a year and would leave Stephanie and Brian with me. Since I could schedule the shipping of the horticulture material to jobsites around their vacations, I was free to take care of my grandchildren while they were gone. They were sweet, well behaved children and I loved having them stay with me.

When Stephanie was three and Brian two, Diane and Steve went to Rocky Point, for a week. After they dropped the children off, I walked them down the street to the schoolyard, to play on the swings, slides and bars. In those days, the school grounds were open and children went to the schoolyard to play when school was not in session. Today, because of shootings, vandalism, and other crimes, schoolyards are all fenced, and not accessible.

After they played for an hour or two, I brought them home, fed them dinner and gave them a bath before putting them to bed. As I was rinsing off the soap, I noticed raised red spots were coming out over both children. I wondered if they were allergic to the soap. I knew it wasn't measles because measles rash was flat. When they went to bed, they felt a little warm but I couldn't tell if they were warm from the bath or coming down with something.

The doorbell rang. In the doorway, stood my son Mike. He had come home on leave before going to his next Air Force deployment to Mountain Home, Idaho and wanted to surprise me.

After I fixed a chicken salad sandwich for Mike, we sat down to talk. Stephanie started to cry. As soon as she started to cry, Brian began to cry too. Going to the bedroom to look in on them, I noticed the spots had started to look like pustules. Handing Stephanie to Mike, and picking up Brian, I said, "I think they may be coming down with chickenpox. It looks like the same thing you kids had when you were in grade school. With both Stephanie and Brian sick at the same time, I'm glad you're here to help. I'm going to take their temperature and give them a baby-aspirin. After I get them settled, could you to go to the drug store and get some Calamine lotion?"

Holding Brian, I went to the medicine cabinet to get the aspirin. Just then Stephanie threw-up down the front of Mike and she started to wail.

"MOM! I need help here!"

Going back to the room, I saw by the look on Mike's face, he was about to throw up too.

Putting Brian down, taking Stephanie from Mike, I said, "Take a shower and then go to the store. I want to put the Calamine lotion on them so they won't scratch. Get the biggest bottle. Chickenpox is very itchy and I don't want them to be scarred from scratching."

I cleaned up Stephanie, gave them both an aspirin and decided to give them a lukewarm oatmeal bath, which should help with itching. I put a cup of instant oatmeal in the blender on high until it was powder. I ran the lukewarm bathwater, stirring in the powdered oatmeal with my hands. I had Stephanie and Brian sit in the bathtub for about ten minutes while I poured the oatmeal water over them. Brian thought it was fun to splash the water at Stephanie and me, and by the time the minutes were over the bathroom and I were quite a mess.

Coming in with the Calamine lotion, always the tidy one, Mike said, "Wow, what a mess you have here."

Throwing a towel to Mike, I said "Pat-dry Brian, *don't rub*. I'll take Stephanie."

I then put the lotion on all the spots, sat in the rocking chair with the two of them for a while and then put them back in bed. I repeated the oatmeal baths, aspirin and calamine lotion each day. They were fussy, sometimes both wailing at the same time, had a slight temperature, but each day they got a little better.

Mike's leave was up, and as he was saying his goodbyes, his parting words were, "I'm *never* getting married and have kids. That's for sure!"

When Diane and Steve came back, the worst of the chicken pox was over. Diane said, "Someone from grade school at the ranger station had chickenpox and that must be how they got it."

Three weeks later, I got a telephone call from Mike. He said, "Mom, I met the most wonderful girl. I had just arrived at the base when I saw her walking across the tarmac. Her name is Rita. She's so pretty and nice. She's from South Carolina and is in the Air Force too. We're going to the justice-of-the-peace and getting married next week."

"*Mike*, you can't possibly know this girl in three weeks! You should date her for a while so you can get to know her. Please, don't jump into marriage so quickly. Why don't you wait until you both have some leave? We can then have a wedding with the families."

"I've been with her every day and we talk all the time. I know all about her. We don't want to spend money on a big wedding. We have it all arranged."

I'd given him my advice as a mother and knew it was useless to say anything more. He was an adult and had to make his own decisions. I wished him the best and told him to take lots of pictures and send me some. I promised I would visit them as soon as I could.

***

A few months later, Verna and I decided to drive up the Pacific Coast to visit my cousin Marjorie in Oregon and then go to Mountain Home, Idaho, to see Mike and Rita. The trip up the Pacific Coast was remarkably beautiful in the seventies and eighties. In later years, parts of the coastal highway washed away, and now the road turns inland in several places so you lose sight of the ocean at times.

On our way to Marjorie's, we stayed on the beach, in Oregon, in a log cabin. I decided to make a fire in the fireplace. Verna said, "Isn't it a little warm for a fire?"

"I love watching and smelling a fire burning in a fireplace and the night might be cool. I always wanted a fireplace. I've never started a fire before and want to see if I can do it."

After several attempts, I got the fire going and I was so proud of my first fire. However, I had put too many logs on and after a little while it was *blazing*. It was getting *really* hot in the cabin. Then the room began filling up with smoke, so I opened the door. "Verna, why isn't the smoke going up the chimney?"

"I don't know, but it's *so* hot in here and the smoke's getting thicker."

"With my luck, I'll burn the cabin down. How do we put the fire out? Can we throw water on it?"

"*No!* That will make a big mess. It will take days for the fire to burn out with all those logs, so we have to do something. We're only staying one night."

I decided to separate and lay flat the logs that I had so

nicely piled up into a peak. That made a big difference in the blaze. I saw a lever at the side of the fireplace, "Verna, I wonder what this is for?" When I pushed it upward, the smoke went up the chimney. "Let's get out of this hot place and walk on the beach. The fireplace has a big screen across it so I think it's safe to leave it."

After we walked on the beach, evening approached and it started to turn chilly. Back at the cabin, we made sandwiches for dinner and had a glass of wine. The fire burned down, giving the room a golden glow. It smelled wonderful.

When we arrived at my cousin Marjorie's home, her mother, Aunt Bernice flew in from Flint, Michigan. I hadn't seen my cousin or aunt since 1952. It was great to catch up on news of the family. We spent a fun two days together before heading out to Mike's base.

On the way to Mountain Home, we saw buffalo with some little ones, grazing in the distance. Both Verna and I loved to take pictures, and never having seen wild buffalo before, we decided to park on the side of the road and hike across the field to get close enough to take some photos. Later, when I told Mike about seeing the buffalo, taking their pictures, and how close we got to them, he said, "Mom! What were you thinking! You could have been killed. They could have charged and trampled you to death. Especially since they had young."

Mike and Rita didn't live on the base. They had a cozy little house close to the town of Mountain Home. The instant I saw Rita, I gave her a hug and said, "You look just like Meryl Streep, the movie star." Rita was pretty, slim and about five-six with reddish brown hair.

"I've got some news," Mike said, "we just found out Rita's pregnant and due at the end of January."

I laughed, telling Rita, "Just a few months ago he said he was *never* getting married and having children. How quickly things change. I'm excited to have another grandchild on the way. Does this mean you have to leave the Air Force?"

"No," Rita replied. "I'll get a maternity leave just like any other job."

I could tell that Mike and Rita had a lot in common. They were affectionate with each other and did chores and cooking together. We all decided to drive to Boise to see the city and shop. It was a pleasant drive, and we stopped at a pretty wooded park in the city. Two men and two women that looked like gypsies were dancing to music while someone played the flute. The men were dressed in tight, knee length, shiny-black pants, belted white tunics and black headdresses that fell over their shoulders. The women wore full-patterned skirts with pantaloons, full-sleeved white blouses, and wide headbands that pulled back their long hair.

The strangest sight we saw in Boise was a man roller-skating, across a street at a busy intersection, wearing a complete Santa Claus suit, white beard and pointed white hat—*in the summer.* We decided Boise was a very strange city. I bought Mike a shirt and Rita a maternity top, then we headed back to Mountain Home.

After a fun-filled time at Mike's, we started our journey home. As we drove away from their house, I said to Verna, "Rita and Mike seem happy. I like her and I think they make good companions, which is so important. One thing for sure, you should *never* say never."

Mike and Rita

1981

41

THE NEAR-DEATH EXPERIENCE

VERNA AND I went to Chevlon Ranger Station, where Diane and Steve lived, to see our children and grandchildren many times. The Ranger Station, at 6,800 ft., is situated in east central Arizona, in the Apache Sitgreave National Forest. The pine-tree forest has two million acres and magnificent mountain views. In the early 1850's Captain Lorenzo Sitgreave, a Topographical engineer, took the first scientific expedition across Arizona. The National Forest was named after him and the Apache Indian Tribe that lived there.

Verna's daughter, Pam, Steve's sister, who lived in Phoenix, had a baby boy three months old. Chad was a beautiful baby with bright red hair and blue eyes. Verna's mother, Nettie, who lived in Ohio, came to Phoenix to stay with Pam, who was divorced, to help with the baby. Nettie was a widow, in her early eighties, not very tall, a gentle, quiet woman.

In February, Verna and I decided to take Nettie, Pam and Chad to Chevlon to celebrate Diane's birthday. Nettie had never been to the Ranger Station and looked forward to going. We decided to leave on Saturday, at seven-am, so we would have enough time to visit before heading back.

The drive from Phoenix to Chevlon takes four to five hours. You travel on a two-lane paved road until you get to the Mogollon Rim, which is a mountain range of 7,000 to 11,500 ft. You then take a forest service dirt road for a two-hour drive to the ranger station. The narrow dirt road is slow driving, with potholes and vegetation that you have to go around. Many times, you encounter elk and deer so you have to watch out for wildlife.

That Saturday morning was a sunny, warm day in Phoenix. I gassed up my red, 1974, Dodge Dart and went to get Verna. We picked up Nettie, Pam and Chad. They settled in the backseat, with three-month-old Chad lying on the seat between them. Pam set the diaper bag on the floor at her feet, with bottles of formula, diapers and the necessary baby things. There were no child seats or seatbelts in those days. We stopped in the town of Payson for a bathroom break before we headed up the Mogollon Rim.

There was a lot of snow in the mountains and it was a treacherous drive. The car heater was going full blast with the temperature outside below freezing. The sun shone and the big pine trees looked beautiful with white snow glistening on their green branches. The forest service road was difficult to maneuver, but we arrived at Chevlon without incident. Chad slept the whole way which was a blessing.

Diane and Steve lived in a small two-bedroom log house.

It had a large square kitchen, living room and bathroom. The little house was heated by a wood burning stove. Diane had it decorated in a cozy, country fashion. She had lunch ready for us, and Steve had baked her a white cake, her favorite.

After lunch and birthday cake, we chatted and played with the grandchildren. The weather outside began to get cloudy, and the temperature was dropping. Steve monitored the weather and thought we should go home a different route which might save some time and be an easier drive.

He said, "After a short distance on the fire service road, it will be paved all the way. However, you'll travel up a steep, high altitude mountain. With the sun shining on the paved road most of the day, it might be clear."

The sun sets early in the mountains at that time of year, so we decided to leave at three o'clock. Steve gave Verna the directions, and after we said our goodbyes we headed out. The directions were easy to follow and in a short time we started up a steep winding mountain.

There was no traffic on the road, and there were little patches of ice where the road was in the shade. I managed to maneuver around them but as we got higher the ice patches got bigger. I switched into second gear. The drop off on the left side of the narrow road was straight down.

Pam keep saying, "You're doing good Margaret. You're doing good."

Verna and Nettie were silent. Glancing in the rearview mirror, I saw a look of alarm and terror on Nettie's face.

When we were three quarters of the way up the mountain, there was nothing but ice on the road. The car suddenly started to slide backward. I knew from living in

Michigan that you didn't step on the brake when sliding on ice but tried to steer as best you could. We were headed sideways across the road to the edge of the cliff. As we got close to the edge, where there was a patch of snow, I yanked the emergency brake on and the car stopped *right on the edge* of the cliff.

In a panicked voice, Nettie said, "*We're going to die!* We'll fall off the mountain and *freeze to death*."

I thought, 'We're dressed in Phoenix clothes. Living in hot weather you have no hats, no gloves, no jackets, only sweaters. We have no food or water and no way to communicate with anyone.' No cell phones or water bottles in those days. There had been no traffic on the road since we left Diane and Steve's.

"Nettie, it will be all right," I said. "At least the car is headed in the right direction. We're fortunate it didn't spin around. We will get up the mountain. I just need some traction under the wheels."

"It's starting to get dark," she said.

I didn't want her to know that I was worried about the dark too. In the forest when it got dark it was absolutely pitch black.

I said, "Do you think we can get branches or dirt to put in front and behind the wheels so there will be traction?"

"Mom and I will get out and see what we can do," Pam said. "You stay in the car with Grandma and Chad."

"I want to get *out*," Nettie said.

Chad was starting to whimper.

"It's a sheet of ice out there and you'll fall down. You can take care of Chad while we figure this out. That will be a big help. Give him a bottle and maybe he'll go back to sleep."

Verna and Pam got out of the car. I had my window rolled down so I could communicate with them. They slipped and slid across the road, then tried to get some twigs off the trees and ground. They had only their bare hands, and with everything totally frozen, they had a hard time finding anything. They managed to get a few things to put in front and behind the wheels.

"We're going to push as you slowly step on the gas," Pam said. "Ready?"

"Yes. Start pushing."

I stepped on the gas and I could hear them groan as they tried to stay upright, pushing with all their might. Nothing happened.

"*Damn!*" I mumbled. "I have the emergency brake on."

Verna came up to the window and asked, "What did you say?"

Nettie said in a very loud voice, "Margaret said, I have the emergency brake on."

"*What?*"

"Just get back and push," I said.

With the emergency brake off, the car started to slide backward. I quickly pulled the brake on again afraid I'd run over Verna and Pam. They came up to the window and said, "We can't get enough things to put in front of the wheels. Everything is too frozen including our hands."

"We have to think of something," I said.

I thought about what we had in the car. "How about

putting the diapers in front and back of the wheels?"

"Let's try it," Pam said.

Verna and Pam lined up as many diapers as they had, and I slowly stepped on the gas. The car started to move forward. They picked the diapers up and put them down for quite a while until we came to some bare pavement. They got in the car, teeth chattering and shaking with fear and cold, hands scraped from falling on the ice.

The heat was on full blast. After a few minutes of steady motion, Pam said, "I should write to Pampers and tell them how their diapers saved our lives."

It was a miracle that we were able to get out of the situation. With no traffic, icy roads, no warm clothes, the car on the edge of the cliff, and night approaching, it was only a matter of time before it would have become a tragedy.

Afterwards, Nettie talked about her trip to Chevlon and our near-death experience until she passed away at the age of ninety-one.

Pam never wrote to Pampers.

Me?

I was thankful that a great grandmother, a three-month-old baby, a new mother, Verna, me and my little Dodge Dart made it safely up the mountain in the dead of winter.

42

THE MUDSLIDE

FOR THE LAST TWO YEARS the economy had been in a downward slide. Unemployment was high and it was not looking good for recovery in late 1979/1980. I didn't know how much longer I could keep my business. I had to trust the landscape companies and nurseries to make payment on time to the California groves. I worried they would go out of business leaving me to pay the bills. With the market down, people didn't buy homes so new houses weren't being built. Landscape material wasn't in demand. I had a load of big trees going to Metro Center Mall on Wednesday but nothing else for a month.

Monday, the manager of Motorola Insurance Office called. She said, "I understand you previously worked in our office as a claims adjudicator. Are you familiar with computers?"

I didn't know anyone that used a computer at work and I didn't think they were in homes yet. Since I'd seen a picture of one, I said, "Some."

"We're going to start processing claims on computers. We first need to enter the processed claim's manual records. You probably know most of the girls and I think you'll like working here again. Can you come in and talk to me about it?"

"I'm self-employed, but if you're interested in hiring me part-time, I could come in tomorrow and see what hours would work for us."

The next morning, I met with the Insurance office manager and liked her. I told her about my business, and the days I had deliveries I wouldn't be able to come in until late morning.

She said, "That's fine. Two other girls will be doing entries also. We have a computer programmer so he will answer any questions you have. The rest of the adjustors will work on the claims manually."

We came to an agreement on the pay and I'd start work the following Monday.

Wednesday, as I was preparing to leave the house to go to the job site at Metro Center, the phone rang. It was the trucker. He said, "There's a *big* problem. The trees were loaded too high on the semi. On I-17, the overpasses cut the treetops off. The nets that covered them are hanging from the overpass on the freeway." Sounding upset he said, "What should I do?"

Alarmed, I asked, "Where are you?"

"I pulled off the freeway at Northern and I'm parked in the parking lot at Kmart next to the freeway."

"I'm going to call the California grove and the Metro Center job site," I said. "Call me back in an hour."

I talked to the owner of the grove, and he said to send the truck back. They would replace the trees. The trucker could make delivery the next morning. He wanted the telephone number of the trucking company to see what they could work out between them on the cost of the blunder. He indicated that the trucker was as much to blame as his workers.

I called the Metro construction manager and explained what had happened to the trees they ordered. I assured him a new load would be delivered early the next day. He said they had back-hoe and crane equipment ready to go today and someone would have to pay for the rental. He was not happy about the delay in the project.

I then called Arizona Department of Transportation. I told them what happened to the tree delivery, that there were nets hanging from the overpasses on the I-17 freeway and probably tree parts on the road. "That's a first," he said. "We just got a call about it. We'll take care of it."

When the trucker called back, I told him to take the load back to the grove. I drove to Metro Center to talk to the construction boss. With a promise of delivery, the next day, the cost of the rental equipment taken off his bill, he calmed down.

The trees were delivered the next morning and I never heard who had to make things right with the money. I had been so worried that I would end up paying something, I didn't ask how they resolved it.

Monday, when I arrived at Motorola, the girls greeted me warmly. I was introduced to the programmer and asked him if there was a manual. He handed me one, and I walked to my desk where there was a cord telephone with a turn-page calendar next to it. In the center of the desk sat a large, deep, white computer, with square grey-looking glass on the front. Attached to the computer, with a cord, was a keyboard in front of it.

I felt overwhelmed. I thought, *this is going to be hard.* I looked in the thick manual and found how to turn it on. With a whirr the screen lit up with a pale green background and a symbol of something in the center.

Now what do I do? On the left of the computer was a stack of files. Picking one up, I opened it and looked at the computer. The symbol that had been in the center was now moving all over the screen. I wondered what I had done to make it do that. I was afraid I would break the computer. Looking at the keyboard, I saw a key that said enter. Wondering what it would do, I pressed it. A blank page, with a heading, appeared on the screen. Just then the programmer walked over and pulled up a chair. "Let me show you a few things before you start," he said.

I was so thankful! Pointing to a large machine across the room, he said, "If you have to print anything, it will come out over there. Now, let me show you how to consolidate and how much of each claim record you need to input." And so, I began.

***

After two years of service at the base in Monterey, Greg was deployed to Salach, Germany. When his deployment to Germany—and six years in the army—ended, Greg decided not to sign-up for another term in the military.

With an honorable discharge, Greg and Poksun returned to my home.

Greg immediately got a job at Rawhide Restaurant in the foothills of Phoenix. His job was to take a group, on a horse-driven wagon, up the mountain to a Rawhide picnic area. Then he'd build a campfire and cook steak dinners for them.

Brian, my youngest had worked in the Forest Service with Steve for a time. Now he was home again and working for Rick Brown's Studio doing wood work.

Poksun fit in with the family and everything seemed to work well. It wasn't too long before I knew that Greg was drinking a lot, at or after work. When he had too much to drink he became very talkative, what people called a happy drunk. I could tell Poksun wasn't happy.

When I talked to Greg about it, he said, "When I'm working, people buy me drinks."

"Greg, you don't have to accept them, why don't you tell your customers you aren't allowed to drink on the job. You could get a DUI driving home. What if you get into an accident?"

"Mom, don't worry. I have it under control."

One evening, while Greg was at work, Brian came into the family room, sat down and said, "Mom, Greg looked Dad up in the telephone book and went to see him." I was surprised. Brian went on, "Greg said when the door opened, Dad said, '*What do you want, if it's money* I *don't have any.*' Greg told him he hadn't seen him since he was sixteen and just wanted to see how he was doing. He let Greg in and Dad told him he retired, married an alcoholic and sent her to rehab twice. She still drank, so he divorced her. Greg said Dad's house was stacked with junk, every room, from floor to ceiling. There was just a narrow path in each room to get through."

"Brian, do you want to see your dad?" I asked.

"*No*. Why would I? I was fourteen when he left. He never telephoned me, sent me a birthday or Christmas card and never came to see me."

"Well Brian, you're an adult and it's your decision," I said. "But he is your dad."

I thought to myself, 'it was strange that none of Greg's brothers or Diane ever wanted to see their dad. Greg, the most abused, did.'

When I mentioned it to Diane, she said, "In my classes for Special Education, I learned that the severely abused will often go to their death trying to get approval from the parent that abused them."

It made me very sad and worried to think that Greg, if he continued to see his father, would again be verbally abused, put down at every opportunity and ridiculed. I imagined the feeling of defeat and insecurity he would experience *again*. I wondered if his drinking was to cover the hurt and rejection he felt.

As I thought back, I remembered the time Joe told me that if he ever married again he would not marry someone with a Bible-thumping, teetotaling background like I had. He would marry someone who wanted two refrigerators, one for food and one for beer. He got what he asked for.

***

On a September weekend, Verna, Poksun and I planned a trip on a narrow-gauge railroad from Durango to Silverton, Colorado. Greg and Poksun were having problems over his drinking. I thought if I took her on the trip it might ease the tension between them with some time off from each other. It would also give Poksun a chance to see some of our country. Poksun had never ridden a train before and was excited.

The historic narrow-gauge railroad was built in 1882 to haul silver and gold ore as well as passengers on the fifty-two-mile trip to Silverton. Passengers soon realized the views were spectacular going around the high mountains. Their enjoyment has kept the train in service to this day.

Even though Brian and Greg were older, I asked my mother if she could stay at the house until we returned. She was delighted to spend some time with her grandsons.

We left early in the morning to make the seven-hour trip to Durango, stopping for breakfast and lunch. It was a beautiful sunny day and we were happy to leave the hot weather in Phoenix for the cool mountains of Colorado. After checking into our Durango hotel, we walked around the town and found a quaint restaurant for dinner that said "Home Cooking." It was a delightful meal and the freshly baked blueberry pie was the perfect finish.

We boarded the train in the morning and found excellent seats in an open compartment where we could sit or stand and take pictures of the scenery. Across from us were three young university men who were going to hike in the mountains when they got to Silverton. They struck up a conversation with us, asking Poksun about Korea and taking photos of the magnificent views.

We were going around a steep mountain with a drop off that was straight down, when suddenly we heard the brakes screech. Sparks flew. The train began rocking. Passengers screamed. With a horrifying crunch, the train tipped toward the drop, and stopped. Our section had derailed on the side of the mountain. We sat closest to the drop-off! We were told to stay seated and not to panic. We had hit a mudslide. Slowly, very slowly, we exited out the opposite side of the train. Those of us on the side closest to the drop off, left first.

After all the passengers on the train got safely off, the conductor said it would be four or five hours before we could be rescued. The university boys, Verna, Poksun and I hiked around the area together for a little while. Then the boys decided to leave and hike to Silverton. After they talked with the conductor, who wanted them to stay with the train, they said their goodbyes, picked up their backpacks and left.

Dressed in clothes for Phoenix weather, not expecting to be stranded in the Colorado mountains, we were beginning to feel cold, hungry and thirsty. Finally, after about five hours, an engine with men and equipment came from Durango. The men worked for quite a while and finally got the train back on the track. The engine from Durango connected with the back of our train and we proceeded to go backward down the mountains to Durango. Passengers were silent. We realized how close to disaster we had come. We anxiously wondered if it could happen again as we backed down the mountains. (They never gave our money back or a free ticket for a later date.)

When Poksun and I arrived home, my mother said, "Everything went well but Greg called into work sick today. I heard him throwing up last night. He's been in bed all day. When he came into the kitchen to make the call, he looked pretty sick, but when I asked if I could get him something he said no, he just needed to sleep."

Brian looked at me, rolled his eyes and shook his head. I knew Greg probably came home drunk last night. My mother, never having been around anyone who was drunk, probably thought he had the flu. Just then, Greg came into the room.

With a yawn, he said, "I hope you had a good time."

"You won't believe what happened to the train," Poksun said. As the story unfolded, she added, "It was an exciting trip but I don't think I'll ever want to ride a train again."

***

Poksun wanted to get a job but didn't have any idea of what she could do. Her English had improved a great deal, but she worried she wouldn't be able to fit in with the American culture at a workplace.

I thought about Rick Brown's studio. Maybe she could get a job painting DeGrazia figures on wind-bells and plaques. I said, "Poksun, you might be able to get a job where Brian works. You could do oil painting on the merchandise. I know the owner of the studio. They always need artists and I bet he'll give you a job."

"I don't know how to paint," she said. "I've never painted anything before. I don't know anything about art."

Knowing the Oriental culture held older people in reverence, I figured Poksun might take my advice. "Let's go to the studio and look into it," I said. "You're smart and I think you could figure it out. They'll have someone to give you instructions. Nothing will happen if you can't paint and maybe they will have other jobs available. Just give it a try. We could go tomorrow."

That night I told Brian about my idea. I asked him to tell Rick that Poksun and I would come in tomorrow morning to see him. Brian thought it was a good idea. She could drive with him if she got the job.

A very apprehensive Poksun and I arrived at the studio early the next morning. After introducing her to Rick, I said, "Poksun is very artistic and would like a job learning how to paint on the DeGrazia merchandise. Would you have an opening?"

"I can always use artists," he said, "Poksun, can you start now? I have an order I need to get out. One of the girls called in sick."

Glancing at me, with a doubtful look, Poksun said, "I can give it a try."

Later that afternoon, Rick called and thanked me for sending Poksun to him. "She's *great*," he said, "and took to the artwork immediately."

When Poksun came home, she thanked me for getting her the job. She told me she really liked the art-work and was surprised she could do it. She said, "I can't believe what Americans do at work. Can you believe that in the morning and afternoon everyone stops work and goes into a break room for fifteen or twenty minutes? *And* everyone stops working way before five o'clock to put their work away."

"They don't take fifteen-minute breaks in Korea?"

"No, they don't. Everyone starts work immediately when they come in. If you need to set up, you come in early to do that. We work until lunch, which is for 30-minutes, then work right up until the end of the workday. We then put our work away before we leave."

Poksun became one of the leading employees at the Brown Studio. She continues to work there to this day.

Within a few weeks, Greg and Poksun moved into an apartment. After they moved, I only saw them on holidays and weekends but I worried about Greg, hoping they could have a good life together.

Then, Greg lost his job at Rawhide due to his drinking, but he immediately got another job working at "The Point," a five-star resort, as a prep cook. Greg loved to cook, even as a young boy. I hoped losing his job at Rawhide would teach him a lesson to control his drinking.

Months later, after getting drunk too many times, partying on weekends with his friends, Greg and Poksun divorced after six years of marriage. I was afraid Greg was on a path to destroy himself. No matter the cost, I had to help him.

43

THE BLUE BAYOU DRINK

IN JUNE, my high school classmates wrote to me asking me to come to the thirtieth class-reunion being held in July. I never went to class-reunions, not wanting to see Pat, who left me pregnant after graduation. Diane, my best friend from high school, who lived in Kalamazoo, Michigan, called and told me she didn't go to reunions either, but if I went she'd go too.

Talking about the reunion with Verna, she said, "You should go. You need to put the past behind you, and it won't happen until you see Pat again."

"I'll have to look at my business schedule and see if I can make a long trip like that. I'll have to think about it."

Even though the economy had not recovered, I had several bookings for my Desert Shade business in the next few weeks. It would give me money to tide me over. I still worked part-time for Motorola but the work was ending next week. I had a booking for the first week in August leaving me with a free July. If Verna could go with me, we could share expenses.

Calling Verna, I said, "I've been thinking about the reunion. If you can go with me, I'd like to drive to Sault Ste. Marie, Michigan. You know how I hate to fly. I have a month open and would like to leave right after my last delivery. Do you think Bob will let you go and be away for that long? It would be great to see more of our country, and we can stop in Ohio and see your mother."

Verna said, "It's fine with Bob as long as I freeze a lot of dinners for him before I go."

We planned our 8,796-mile trip around the United States in my 1974 Dodge Dart with over 170,000 miles on it.

I called my friend Diane and told her I would be coming to the reunion. I asked her not to tell anyone because I wanted it to be a surprise. She told me Pat was married, lived in Escanaba, Michigan, and had nine or ten kids.

My Aunt May Gordon lived in Sault Ste. Marie, and I told her we were coming and hoped to see her. She insisted that we stay with her. I told her I would phone when we got close to the Sault.

My mother agreed to stay at my house while I was gone. Greg still had the apartment, so only Brian and the animals were at home.

Determined to look my best, I went to a make-up specialist and learned how to apply cosmetics. I went to a gym and worked out every day before our departure. I bought a red dress with a low neckline to show off my cleavage. The first night at the reunion would be casual, so

I bought some well-fitting jeans, cow-boy shirt, cow-boy hat and moccasins. I thought it would be appropriate since I'd been living in the Wild West.

We left early on the morning of June nineteenth and headed for New Mexico to see the Carlsbad Caverns, and then headed for San Antonio, Texas, to see the Alamo. To see the Gulf of Mexico, we went to Corpus Christi and Galveston. We then drove to Houston to get on the I-10 freeway. The sky was dark with heavy clouds, and the rain began to pour. With the rain slanting down, and the streets shiny in the headlights, Verna strained to see the signs as we headed into the round of massive freeways. I concentrated on seeing the road and keeping up with the heavy traffic, relying on Verna to find the right connection. As usual, she came through. With a sigh of relief, we were on I-10.

I'd heard so many great things about New Orleans, we decided to go. It was as wonderful as we'd hoped. We went to the strange over-ground cemetery and walked around, reading the tombstones. Graves had to be over-ground because the caskets, if buried, would float away due to the high water-table underground. It was called The City of The Dead. It's considered the world's most haunted cemetery. We were disappointed that we didn't see any ghosts. Later we ate French pastries at sidewalk cafes and delightful seafood in bars and restaurants, but the highlight of New Orleans was Preservation Hall and the wonderful jazz musicians.

One of the adventures we took that I will never forget was on the "Apple Blossom" paddlewheel boat down the Mississippi River to the Bayou. It was a hot muggy day as we boarded the ship. Standing on the deck, looking at the scenery, taking photos as we glided along, a young boy close to us shouted, "*Dad*, we're going to hit that barge."

"No, son. The captain knows what he's doing. He does this all the time."

A few minutes later the son shouted, "*Dad*, we are really going to *hit* it."

Bam! The captain, trying to turn the ship away from the barge, smashed the paddlewheel and we were stranded. The captain, over the loudspeaker, said, "It will take several hours to get a tug to pull us back to port. We're offering free Blue Bayou drinks until the tug arrives."

I said to Verna, "It's so hot and humid, and I sunburn so easily, I'm going to find some shade to stand in. Can you get us a free drink? I'll walk around the other side of the deck to see if there's a bit of shade."

On the other side, the only shade was under an overhang that was only a few inches wide. I had on white shorts, white shirt with a camera around my neck. I stood plastered against the side, under the overhang. Suddenly, I heard a loud shout from above. Taking a step forward, looking up, I saw a hand, holding a blue bayou drink that slipped out of her hand, and landed upside down on my head, dripping blue bayou down the sides of my face and the front of my shirt. At that moment, Verna came looking for me with a blue bayou drink in each hand.

"*What happened?*" Then she burst out laughing. "What a mess! It could only happen to you."

In the ship's small bathroom, I tried to wash the sticky blue off my face, short blonde hair, and shirt. It didn't do much good and I smelled like a brewery and looked a mess. We didn't get any compensation for the trip or a refund. I think the worst thing was the flies that pestered me until we were brought to port. Every time I hear the name Mississippi, I think of our disastrous trip on the "Apple Blossom."

In the Blue Ridge Mountains, Georgia, we went to Stone Mountain to see the largest bas-relief sculpture in the world. It's of three confederate figures, Stonewell Jackson, Robert E. Lee and Jefferson Davis. The carving was started in 1916 but wasn't completed until 1966. We wondered how anyone could carve such a magnificent sculpture on the side of the large round quartz mountain.

We decided to stay in Gatlinburg, Tennessee overnight and see the smoky mountains. We never made any reservations ahead on our trip because we never knew how long we'd stay in one place. We just decided as we went along, always hoping to find an inexpensive motel for the night. In Gatlinburg every accommodation was booked for many miles. At a restaurant, we asked our waitress why the accommodations were all full.

She said, "There's an open-air free concert tonight with famous performers from Nashville. I'll write down directions. If you want to go, get there very early."

We decided to stay and hear the concert, never having been to a country music performance before, even if it meant sleeping in the car.

The concert was lively, and fun. During intermission, I said, "Verna, you know I don't like to drive on strange roads in the dark, so we'll have to stay in Gatlinburg until morning. Maybe we can find a restaurant that's open late or open all night. That way, if we park there for the night it would be more secure. We could linger over something to eat and we won't have to spend so much time overnight in the car."

A few minutes later, I felt a tap on my shoulder and glanced back at the couple sitting behind us. The man said, "We couldn't help but overhear you say you had to sleep in your car. I realize everything has been booked for some time due to this concert. Where are you from?"

"Phoenix, Arizona," I said. "We're traveling to Michigan and heard about the concert. We decided to stay, even if we had to spend the night in the car."

"Since you are fellow country music lovers, we want to offer you our travel trailer for the night. It's parked at our house. I'll give you our address and directions before the concert ends. We'd hate for you to sleep in your car."

Driving to their home, I said to Verna, "When we were talking about sleeping in the car, I'm so glad I didn't say that country is not my first choice in music. I'd rather it was jazz or blues."

"We really lucked out," Verna said. "Not my first choice of music either, but it was a great concert and I'm glad we stayed."

When we arrived at their home, they showed us to their trailer. It was immaculate, cozy and a godsend. In the morning, they cooked us breakfast and refused to take any money for the accommodation. I will never forget that wonderful couple.

We then headed for Ohio to visit Verna's mother. As we got closer to Michigan and the time of the reunion, I began to get anxious. I wondered why I would put myself through seeing Pat again even though I did want to see friends I hadn't seen for years. "Maybe we should just continue driving around the country instead of going to the Sault for the reunion," I said.

"No-way," Verna replied. "We came this far, so we'll see it through. Besides, your aunt is looking forward to seeing you. We'll have lots of time to see more of the country on the way back."

We spent a couple of days with Verna's mother, Nettie, in Cincinnati, and when we crossed into Lower Michigan, I called my aunt and said we would be there the next day, late afternoon.

We headed toward the Sault, crossed the Straits of Mackinaw and entered the Upper Peninsula. As I drove into the Sault, I thought, 'I don't know what will happen at the reunion. Will Pat be there? Will he talk to me, or ignore me? I'm more than curious about what his wife looks like. I wonder if Pat told her about Diane. Whatever happens I will perservere and not let anything get me down.'

44

THE REUNION

VERNA AND I ARRIVED at Aunt Mae's home three days before the reunion. It gave me time to visit my relatives in Sault Ste Marie, Michigan and across the St. Mary's river in Sault Ste Marie, Ontario, Canada.

"Do whatever you want in the next few days," Verna said. "I'm going to stay with your Aunt Mae. I don't want to go to the reunion with you. I don't know anyone, and you'll be busy catching up on all the news."

While visiting my cousin, Joan, in Canada, her two young children wanted to go bicycle riding with me. They had ten-speeds which I'd never ridden before. As a child, the bike I rode had only one speed and that was your leg muscle. I applied the brake by reversing my foot on the peddle. On the ten-speed, the brake was on the handlebar which you applied with your hand.

We started out and raced down the street at a good clip. Then we had to slow down to turn the corner. Just as I clamped my hand down on the brake, Tim yelled, "Don't press hard on the hand-brake or you'll go over the handlebars."

Warned too late, I flew over the handlebars, picked myself up and limped back to Joan's house. She had a shocked look on her face when she saw blood dripping from my knees and hands.

"Tomorrow night is the first night of the reunion and I'm a mess," I sighed. "The second night is the dinner-dance. I can just see myself hobbling around the dance floor."

Cleaning the wounds, Joan applied anti-biotic and ice to my knees, which had started to swell. "Keep applying the ice tonight and you should be alright. I think it's mostly bad scrapes."

She fixed a lovely dinner, and as we were eating, I dropped my fork on the floor. "Damn," I said as I bent over and picked it up.

Her husband threw down his napkin. "We don't swear in this house," he said.

I forgot they belonged to the Gospel Hall and would never hear that word. "Sorry," I said.

As I drove back from Canada to Aunt Mae's, I decided not to let my injuries deter me. My raw knees would be covered by my jeans on the first night, hose and my dress the second night. I'd just have to grit my teeth and forget the pain.

I told Verna and Aunt Mae about the fall from the bike, and my Aunt made ice-packs for my knees. I didn't sleep well that night. I couldn't help but wonder if Pat would show up. Finally, I thought, 'it really doesn't matter. The past is just that—the past. It can't be changed. The only thing that matters is my family and what I'll do with my life in the future.'

The morning of the reunion, I went to see my childhood friend Diane. She'd traveled from Kalamazoo, and was staying at her parents' home. We made plans to attend the reunion together.

"What happened to your hands?" she asked.

"You should see my knees. I went bike riding with my cousin's kids and took a dive over the handlebars."

"Sounds like something you'd do," she laughed.

"I'm nervous about seeing Pat again."

"Don't be. You've moved on. Maybe the jerk won't come to the reunion. He's not a nice person abandoning you and his child like he did, and not paying a penny for her support."

It was good to see Diane's mother and father again. Diane and I spent many nights having sleep-overs at each other's houses when we were in high school. As the day went on, we had a good time reminiscing and catching up on our family's news. Mid-afternoon, I went back to Aunt Mae's to have dinner and get ready for the reunion.

As I picked Diane up that evening for the first night, I realized how much fun it would be to see all my friends again. It really didn't matter if Pat was there or not. In spite of Pat, I survived. Diane laughed when she saw my western clothes and said, "Margaret, they're perfect. What a great idea and they look good on you."

As soon as we entered the door, we were surrounded by classmates. It was wonderful to be so welcomed. Everyone chatted at once. Suddenly the crowd parted and Pat stood before me.

He looked shorter than I remembered, probably average height and weight. He had a mustache and his hair was snow-white. I didn't like his greying mustache.

"Hello Margaret, I heard you were coming, and I didn't know if I should wear my flak-jacket to protect myself."

Surprised at that remark, the only thing I could think of to say was, "Hi Pat."

I started to turn away, but he put his hand on my arm, turned me toward him and said, "I'm sorry. I've never forgotten you and think about you all the time."

I took his hand off my arm and said, "I forgave you long ago and moved on with my life. I have a beautiful, smart, accomplished daughter that I'm very proud of. Leave the past in the past."

Seeing some of my friends across the room, I started toward them. Pat followed me, trying to get my attention. I ignored him.

"You look great," he said. "I'm living in Escanaba now. I'm the band director at the high school and Escanaba City Band."

Embarrassed because people were watching us and conversation was starting to tone down, I was relieved when Diane came up and said, "Joyce has been looking for you." Grabbing my arm, she steered me across the room at a fast pace.

Pat followed me around the entire night. I finally asked him, "Where's your wife? Did she come to the reunion?"

"She's coming tomorrow night. With all the people around you, we haven't had a chance to talk. I would really like to talk to you. Can you meet me for breakfast tomorrow morning at Denny's restaurant? Please."

Thinking he would follow me around tomorrow night too, I thought I'd better meet him for breakfast. Since everyone probably knew about our past, following me around was embarrassing. Besides, I was a little more than curious about what he had to say.

The next morning, I met Pat at Denny's restaurant. While we were being seated, I noticed his brother, Jim, sitting at the counter staring at us. I figured his brother wanted to see what I looked like after thirty years. I'm sure Pat told him we were coming to the restaurant.

After we ordered, Pat brought out pictures of his many kids and told me about them. He had one son and the rest girls. He then proceeded to tell me all about his life, how he failed law in college because he couldn't concentrate on the subject, due to our situation, and then switched to a music major. His father refused to go to his wedding, but his mother went and wore black. His parents weren't close to his children and didn't see them often.

He told me how, over the years, he would call my telephone number every now and then and hang up when I answered, just to hear my voice. He said he kept track of me over the years.

Listening to him, it sounded like he thought it was my fault he failed at law. As he continued to talk, he never asked me any questions about our daughter Diane, or the two grandchildren. Didn't ask to see any pictures of them.

Never questioned how I got along as a single mother. Never thought to send me money to take care of Diane.

Pat was so self-absorbed, he never really thought about anyone but himself. 'Pathetic!' I thought.

I told him it was best to keep our distance at the dinner-dance. I said, "We had our talk and there is a lot to catch up on with my classmates."

Back at Aunt Mae's, she said, "I was worried about you. Why did you go and meet Pat?"

"I was just curious as to what he had to say after thirty years. Nothing more," I said.

As the time for the dinner-dance approached, I applied my makeup, slid my pantyhose over my sore knees and put my red dress on and applied my makeup. Feeling confident, I drove to get my friend Diane.

We sat at a table with our friends and the music began to play. A classmate, Bob Fowler, immediately came to our table and asked me to dance. He was as good a dancer as he was in high school. When we went back to the table he squeezed in a chair next to me and joined us.

Glancing around, I spotted Pat and his wife sitting at a table across the room. His wife was a little overweight, had brown hair and a pleasant face. Pat was staring at me and gave me a wave. She looked up to where he was waving and gave me a frowning glance. I wondered if she knew about Pat's history with me.

After dinner, everyone was circulating; dancing and drinks flowed. Pat wasn't paying any attention to his wife and drinking a lot. I danced every dance. I noticed Pat didn't dance with anyone, even his wife. He hovered around my table and tried to talk to everyone but no-one paid much attention to him. I noticed his wife walked out and didn't come back.

I had a great time dancing, seeing and talking with my classmates. When the class-reunion ended, I headed for Aunt Mae's. I thought about the two nights, and I was a little more than pleased that Pat didn't appear to be very happy. In fact, it made my night.

45

THE CHANCE IN A LIFETIME

As WE TRAVELED BACK from the reunion, we visited many states. In Idaho, we stayed with Mike and Rita for a few days. I was glad they got along so well and seemed to have much in common. Her Dad had come to live with them and I hoped it wouldn't be a problem. Rita's mother and father were divorced. Rita thought a lot of her Dad, and Mike liked him.

Leaving Idaho, we headed to the beautiful state of Utah and back to Arizona. When I arrived home, my mother said that Greg had moved back in. Everything seemed to be normal. Before she went home, Mama told me she enjoyed being with the boys and had a good time watching sports on television with them.

Greg greeted me with his news, "The chef at the resort gave me a raise and told me I have a talent for cooking. He's going to teach me how to be a chef. A lot of money can be made in that career. I have to buy special knives which are expensive and after a while I will go to culinary school. That's why I wanted to come back home, so I could afford to do it."

"Sounds like a good idea, Greg. Did I get any calls on my business phone while I was gone?"

"No. We didn't take any business calls," he said, "However, someone named Pat called on the home phone and asked for you. He didn't leave any phone number. I told him you were traveling." Surprised, I wondered why Pat had called.

Greg continued to drink heavily. I couldn't help nagging him about it and cautioning him that he could lose his job if he went to work hung-over. I felt he was going to destroy himself if he didn't stop. I would lie awake listening for him to come home, wondering if he would get a DWI or be in an accident. After several months Greg found a cheap apartment and moved out.

Brian moved to Mountain Home, Idaho, where his brother Mike lived. It seemed strange to have all of my children away, but I was sure it wouldn't be long before one or more of my boys would be back home again.

Looking through my mail, I didn't see the check I was expecting from the landscape company in Tucson. They were my last delivery before my trip. When I called them, they told me they paid the trucking company and the California grove, but they didn't have the money to pay me right now. They assured me they would send my money in a couple of weeks. I made several calls to clients, but they didn't have any new orders for me.

I began to worry about how I would pay my next month's bills if I didn't get the Tucson check soon. With the economy still in bad shape, I wondered if any of my future clients would lack the money to pay the trucker or grove when they get a delivery. That would leave me to pay the bills. I couldn't afford that. My home was my only security and I didn't want to mortgage it to pay any bills. After calling the Tucson Landscape Company for a couple of months, asking them to send my check and getting no response, I decided to take my problem to Small Claims Court. I scheduled a hearing, argued my case, and got a decision in my favor. However, I never received any money from the landscape company. That made me worry about future deliveries from other clients and their ability to pay. I'd have to think of something I could do to earn some additional money. I hoped the economy would recover soon.

I thought about Avon, where you went door to door to sell cosmetics, or Tupperware parties in homes. Thinking about Tupperware and how they set up their parties, gave me the idea of having toy parties in homes. Many of my friends complained of not knowing what to buy their children for birthdays and Christmas. Other friends had a hard time finding toys for grandchildren. I called Fisher Price and other toy venders. Although they never heard of toy parties before, I got some ideas and wholesale prices. Calling friends, I learned that most were interested in my idea and I told them they would get a free toy for booking a party. The type of toy they would get would depend on how much was sold at their party.

Getting several bookings, I bought, on my credit card a variety of interesting and educational toys for different age levels. The first party I had was in my home.

I set up a card table in the living room to display the toys. I arranged, next to my sofa and recliner, folding chairs in a semi-circle. I could easily seat the ten people who were coming to the party. After they all arrived, I gave them a sales slip, talked about each toy and the benefit and fun it would be for a child. I served coffee, tea and dessert while they asked questions or went to the table to look at the toys. It was a big success and the profit good, plus I had several months of additional bookings.

Uncle Ray, who told me about Santa Claus when I was four, and changed Christmas in my parent's home forever, died and left a small inheritance to my sister Virginia and me.

A few months later, at a toy party, an elderly woman was lamenting about not taking the opportunity to go to Europe when she was young enough to go. "It's something I always wanted to do," she said. "Now with my arthritis it's too late. My advice to everyone is, go to places you always wanted to go when you're young and able to do it."

I said, "Traveling has been my passion for many years. I always wanted to go to Europe, but I just never could afford to go."

A school teacher attending the toy party said, "Have you ever considered going on the Cultural Heritage Tour?"

"What's that?" I asked.

"It's for school children, from all states, between the ages of fourteen to eighteen. I understand they are short of chaperones this year. It's not very expensive for twenty-eight days touring across Europe. If you're interested in being a chaperone, I'll give you my telephone number. We can meet and I'll give you the information about the tour." When the party ended she gave me her phone number and I told her I'd think it over.

Living on the edge all of my life, I thought hard about the money from Uncle Ray. I could save it, put it in the bank for emergencies, but then, when would I ever again get a chance to go to Europe?

I called Verna. When she answered I said, "Do you think you can to go Europe for twenty-eight days with me?"

"*What?*"

I told her what the teacher said about the European tour. "If you can go, we can meet with the teacher and she'll tell us all about it. She said it wasn't expensive, and with the money Uncle Ray left me I can afford to go."

"It sounds wonderful. We should find out about it and if it's possible, we should do it," Verna said.

After we met with the teacher and found out the details, we decided to go. The Cultural Heritage Tour was called the Odyssey Tour. The cost was $1,959.00 for each of us. It included all airfares, hotels, breakfasts, some additional meals, tour bus and a guide in each country. It also included ferries and a Greek cruise ship to tour the Greek Islands for four days. We would fly on Aer Lingus out of New York City to London on June fifteenth.

We registered and paid our money. We'd travel with fifty kids from many states. None from Arizona. There would only be seven chaperones: two teachers, a teacher's brother from California, a woman from New York and a man from Idaho, Verna and me.

I called my sister, Virginia, and told her I was going to Europe with Verna and fifty kids. She said, "Are you *crazy*? *Fifty kids!* Spending all that money for nothing? What a waste! You should put it in the bank for emergencies.

What are you thinking? You can just look in a book and see pictures of Europe."

"It's a chance in a lifetime. There's no adventure just looking in a book. I'm going in June. I'll send you a postcard."

My mother agreed to stay with the pets and thought it would be a wonderful trip. She was glad I was going while I was able to do it.

I think Mama knew how much I loved to travel—see new places, and experience new adventures. I was excited to be going to Europe, even though I'd be traveling with *fifty* kids.

46

THE ODYSSEY TOUR

BEFORE WE BOARDED the plane for the overnight flight to London, we met in a room with everyone on the tour. The two teachers from California were friendly. The brother looked like a hippie—bald on the top of his head, long hair and a long, full, graying beard. Hardly anyone had beards in 1984, so he stood out. He was very quiet, standing to one side away from the kids. The woman from New York was about fifty, her graying hair pulled back severely. When introduced, she just nodded. The man from Idaho was chubby, probably in his forties, friendly, with a nice, wavy, full head of hair. The kids were all accounted for and very enthusiastic. We were reminded by the airline to be sure to have our passports on our person and not in the luggage. They explained what to do in London when we would go through customs.

When we arrived in London, the young woman who was our guide, never explained what we were seeing as we traveled on the tour-bus to our hotel. During the stay in

London, she didn't point out the history of England as we went to places of interest.

There was an incident when we were at Buckingham Palace to see the changing of the guard that I found amusing. Everyone stood behind barricades, and a police officer riding a white horse kept the crowd in control. A woman tourist kept going outside the barricade to look down the street. The officer rode up to her on his horse, instructing her to get behind the barricade.

She said to him, "Talk to me some more. I love to hear your accent."

He said to her, "Lady, *you* have the accent, *we* are the English."

We spent four days in London and surrounding villages seeing all the historical sights. We went to Canterbury Cathedral where I lit a candle for Uncle Ray. We then boarded a ferry to cross the English Channel to Paris. (The tunnel between the countries wasn't in existence at that time.)

One free afternoon in Paris, two teachers, five of the girls, Verna and I, decided to have lunch at a sidewalk cafe. Sitting outside, we had a tasty lunch as we watched people walk by. Several of the girls wanted to go to the restroom and I went with them. Not speaking French, I went up to the waiter and said in English, "Water-closet?" (Which is what they called bathrooms in Europe.) He pointed to an area down the hall. I opened the door to the restroom. The girls went in first, and I started to follow. I heard the girls squeal and they ran out nearly knocking me over. Inside, there were two men standing at urinals peeing. I thought, 'these little girls are getting more education than they bargained for.'

I went up to the waiter, who had a big grin on his face, and asked, "Water-closet for Madams?" He shook his head and pointed again to where we had been. We decided to wait to use a bathroom.

On a free morning, some students, teachers, Verna and I, took the subway, called the tube, to go shopping in Paris. We had figured out what subway to take. Looking at the board, where the time table was displayed, it was soon time for it to arrive. Walking down the steps to the tracks, I noticed gutters on each side of the steps and a strong stench. There was a young couple, holding hands walking ahead of us. All of a sudden, he turned toward the gutter, unzipped his pants and urinated in the gutter. Two of our girls, walking next to us, stopped dead in their tracks. "*How disgusting!*" one of the girls said. "*Unbelievable!*" said the other girl.

As the tube pulled up, we had the students board first, then the teachers, Verna next, and I was the last to board. As I got on, I was surrounded by five, young, Gypsy-looking people. They jostled me around and my reflex was to raise my arms, to balance myself, to keep from falling. Suddenly, a man, seated in the tube, saw what was happening, grabbed me, and pulled me into a seat. The Gypsies ran out the door. The man pointed to my purse which I'd had over my shoulder. I had been robbed. Fortunately, the only thing they got was a small make-up case that looked like a wallet. It was only big enough to carry lipstick and mirror. My passport was under my wallet, so I was thankful the little makeup case was the only thing they got.

The Eiffel Tower and the Versailles Castle was most impressive. Our stay in France was very interesting: wonderful museums, magnificent statues and beautiful architecture everywhere. The boat trip down the Seine River was fun and Notre Dame Cathedral striking. Our guide in France was informative and friendly. A delightful change from the English guide.

As our tour bus was approaching Germany, we all sent our passports to the front of the bus. The bus-driver then gave all the passports to the customs officer to stamp. One of the boys had put his passport in his suitcase and the driver had to unload all our luggage until he came to the boy's bag. The driver and officer were not happy as vehicles lined up behind the bus.

While we were at a train station in Germany, an old, un-kept woman looked at me across the lobby. She came running toward me shouting, "*ugly American!*" She struck me across my hand with something that looked like an umbrella, and split the top of my hand open for which I have a scar to this day. A policeman nearby pulled her away, and they disappeared into a room. The man from Idaho pulled out a handkerchief and wrapped my hand. We didn't have time to get any other aid. As soon as we arrived at our destination, we went to a drug store to get a bandage. I was surprised that they had nurses on duty at drug stores. She attended to my hand and it didn't cost anything. As I'm writing this, some of the American drug stores now have nurses in attendance, although it's not free.

That evening, I decided to go to the room of the helpful man from Idaho, return his handkerchief and thank him. I rapped on his door, and when he answered, I was shocked. His full head of hair was sitting on his dresser! I tried to cover my surprise, and after thanking him, we chatted for a few minutes about the tour, then I hurried back to my room to tell Verna about his gorgeous head of hair that sat on his dresser.

Germany was a beautiful country. There were flowers everywhere. The countryside, streets and homes were spotlessly clean. I imagined they even manicured their forests. The highlight in Germany was going to King Ludwig's four castles. It was the first time it rained on our trip. I thought the Neuschwanstein Castle the most magnificent. The view from the castle was breathtaking. Hearing the history of King Ludwig fascinated me. He was crowned king at eighteen years old, never married and was considered homosexual, so thought insane. His death was mysterious and there was evidence he was murdered.

In Salzburg, Austria, it started to rain again. We spent the afternoon touring then spent the night in the Austrian Alps. Rain tapped against the window of our hotel room. There was no heat in the room, and it was cold. We were thankful for the soft feather beds which kept us warm. There was snow in the higher Alps, and I hoped the rain would clear in the morning so we could have a good view, and the road wouldn't be treacherous.

It was a sunny, cold day as we went over the Alps toward Venice, Italy. In grade school I learned the history of Venice. I'd longed to see the city built on water. To travel around in boats instead of cars sounded so romantic. I never imagined I would actually go there.

We had to take two bus-boats called Vaporetto to accommodate all of us. Verna and I were lucky to have the Utah kids in our group because they were more interested in history and easier to keep track of. It was a beautiful day, and the boat's driver told us about the historical sites along the waterways. We went to Saint Marks Square and toured the Basilica. The ceilings were gold, the architecture and naked statues amazing.

I couldn't be in Venice without taking a Gondola ride, so when we had a free afternoon, Verna and I hired one. We invited a few students to go with us. The handsome, curly headed gondolier sang a beautiful song as we glided along. Even though we couldn't understand a word, it was delightful.

On a boardwalk, I bought two water-color paintings from a sidewalk-artist of Gondolas and Venice. I held our group up while he put finishing touches on them. The kids didn't mind, but the teachers were impatient because we were scheduled to leave for Florence. Venice was everything I imagined it to be. I was so glad I had the opportunity to see it.

After we arrived at our hotel in Florence we had only a short break before getting on the tour-bus. The highlight of the tour was seeing Michelangelo's "David" sculpture. I didn't expect it to be so large. It was *seventeen feet tall* and the naked statue was very explicit. One of the girls standing beside me, wide eyed, looking at the statue, clutched my arm and muttered, "*Oh my!*"

From Florence, we went to Rome where we toured the Forum and Coliseum. Our guide told us about the bloody, cruel past with thousands watching the killings for their entertainment, cheering it on. One of the girls next to me remarked on how terrible the human race was in those days. I reflected on the past and the world as it is today. *Now,* as well as in the past, the human race can be very cruel.

Our Italian guide took us to a gas station where we had lunch. Most gas stations in Italy had restaurants above them. Afterwards, the girls wanted to go to the restroom. When we entered, we discovered you had to put coins in the stalls. Verna and I had enough coins between us to give to girls that didn't have the right coin. As one girl opened the stall door, I heard her cry out, "I don't know what to do." When I looked in, I saw the outline of a foot on each side of a hole. I told her she had to put her feet in the outline and squat over the hole.

"*Disgusting!*" one of the girls yelled.

"We're lucky we live in the United States," I said. "It makes you appreciate what we have in our country. Other countries are fun and interesting to visit, but there's no place like home."

On a free afternoon, Verna and I decided to walk around neighborhoods to see how people lived in Italy. We took the name of our hotel with us in case we got lost. As we started to walk, we passed the alley next to the hotel where we saw three men, sitting on the ground at the end of the alley holding rifles pointed toward us! We rushed past, looking over our shoulder as we hurried down the street.

We decided to stop for dinner at a restaurant on a residential street. The smells were enticing. Looking in the window, we noticed there were no customers inside. On entering, a little bell softly rang. A middle-aged woman, with a white apron, long hair pulled back with a ribbon, came out of the kitchen and said something in her language.

"Speak English?" I asked.

Shaking her head, she pointed to the clock above the

door and held up five fingers. It was only four-fifteen. I nodded my head, pointed to my watch, and smiled as we left. After we slowly walked around several blocks, we returned to the restaurant just before five o'clock. It was a small, pretty, homey place with white lace curtains on the windows and a red cloth on each table. The woman immediately came out of the kitchen as the little bell rang.

She smiled as she seated us and handed us a menu. We couldn't read a word. Looking at the waitress, I shrugged, shook my head, pointed to her, handed her the menu and smiled. She headed for the kitchen. She and the chef came back, each carrying a steaming bowl of soup. They stood nearby as we each took a sip. It had tiny meatballs, vegetables, and was delicious. I smiled, patted my stomach, made an *umm* sound and they disappeared into the kitchen.

They came back with a bottle of red wine. Soon they came back with a plate of pasta and a large, long loaf of what looked like homemade bread. The restaurant began to fill. As customers came, the waitress chatted to them in Italian. I heard the word Americanos. Everyone took an interest in what we were eating and no one was getting served. The chef continually brought us different plates of food. I was so full I thought I would pass out. As the waitress and chef hovered over us, I shook my head, groaned, patted my stomach and took out my wallet. The chef picked up my wallet and put it back into my open purse, shaking his head. I thought about leaving money on the table but decided it might hurt their feelings. We got up, hugged the chef, smiled, nodded to everyone as we were leaving. What a thrilling experience that was, with no words spoken between us. Something you could never forget.

The next afternoon, we were supposed to go to Pisa. The teachers talked the students into not going, telling them it wasn't worth the ride and they could have more fun at the hotel. Verna and I wanted to go and were disappointed because the bus driver wouldn't want to take only the two of us. The Utah students told us they wanted to go too, so the twelve Utah students, Verna and I, boarded the bus. Of all the students on the trip, the Utah children were the best. They were interested in everything, asked questions, took pictures, never complained and followed directions.

We were so glad we went to Pisa. Pictures of the leaning tower didn't do it justice. It made your mouth drop to think it was still standing. Construction began in 1173 and the tower was completed after 199 years in 1372. There were eight bells in the tower, and the sound was beautiful. The tower was eight stories and you could climb to the top, going up a circular concrete tube. Verna and the kids went up to the top but I stayed on the ground. Verna told me the views from the top were amazing and she was glad she did it even though it was scary to walk up, on a slant, in a tube. In 1990 they began construction to stabilize the tower and people could no longer go up to the top.

Then our tour took us to Pompeii. I thought it was the most interesting city in Italy. It was destroyed by a volcano in seventy A.D. As we exited the bus, the acid smell of burning almost took my breath away. I said to the driver, "I can't believe you can still smell the destruction after all these years."

Shaking his head, he said, "You're one of the few that can smell it. I can't, and if you ask the others on the bus, I'll bet they can't either. A small percentage can. No one knows why."

I was shocked because I could distinctly smell it, wanting to put a hand over my nose. Years later there was a program on television about Pompeii and they mentioned the fact that some people could smell the disaster and no-one knew why.

The restorations were remarkable, the colors vivid. A lot of beautiful mosaic tile decorated the ancient homes. Outside a doorway, in mosaic tile, was a plaque, that said, "Beware of the dog." In the museum there was an actual horse and chariot, well preserved, that had been excavated. It was like the horse was running down a street to get away from the ash.

In a restored home, an artist was sitting in a room that looked like the main room of the house, painting a copy of the border that went around the center of the room. The painting was so much like the border, the colors exact, that I asked him if I could buy it. It was a small picture of a chariot, driven by two deer-like creatures. Riding the chariot was a cherub-angel. When I returned home from Europe, I had it framed, and it's one of my favorite paintings now hanging in my living room. Because I was waiting for the painting to finish and dry, I was in trouble with the bus driver. We were headed to Sorrento on the spectacular Sorrentine Drive. I delayed the bus by twenty minutes and thought, as I entered the bus, 'I can't understand why people want to go on a guided tour. Everything is on a time schedule. The kids are more on time than I am. I'm not being a very good example. I'd better not buy any more paintings in the spur of the moment.' I would have loved to have spent more time in Pompeii.

The Sorrentine Drive went along the coast, a winding,

narrow road with drop-dead views and daring Italian drivers. The color of the water along the coast was turquoise, and the green-swathed mountains above were beautiful. We stayed the night in Sorrento then went to Brindisi, a seaport village at the tip of Italy.

After dinner, we took an overnight ferry across the Ionian Sea to Greece. We stopped the next morning in Corfu, the most beautiful of the Ionian Islands, before heading for Patras in the late afternoon.

The next day we took a ferry across the Gulf of Corinth to see the Temple of Apollo with the 7,000-seat theater. Starting in 586 B.C., athletes from all over Greece would compete in games there. I remembered studying about the temple in my ancient history class in high school. As we all sat on the theater seats, we listened to a wonderful lecture on its history. The kids were mesmerized and asked many questions. That afternoon we departed for Athens.

After settling in the hotel, we toured all the wonderful historical sites. The evening was spent at the sound and light show at the Acropolis, and the students especially enjoyed it. The next morning, we boarded a Greek cruise ship for a four-day cruise of the Greek Islands.

The ship was called the *City of Rhodes*. After seeing the kids settled in their rooms, we went to find ours. It was a tiny room with bunk beds. The bathroom was so small you could hardly turn around in it. It had a sink, toilet and a shower so small that if you were tall, you'd have to shower bent over. We had a hard time making the toilet work. Every time you flushed it, it sounded like an explosion.

A couple of the boys came to our room to see what kind

of room we had. One said, "This room is not that nice. Our room is bigger with a window. If you want, my roommate and I can switch rooms with you."

"That's so kind of you to offer to switch rooms," I said. "You guys enjoy your room. We'll be fine."

The kids on the trip were great. In 1984 they were polite, respectful, interesting and fun to be with. A lot of them hung around Verna and me, going sightseeing with us on free time. There were no cell phones, and the kids actually talked and interacted with what was going on around them.

The first island we visited was Mykonos. We had to go over the side of the ship into small boats that took us to shore where they offered camel rides on the beach with a stepladder to get up to the saddle. I got to the top rung and chickened out. Several of the boys took a ride. Returning to the ship after touring the island, we had a delicious buffet dinner. That night, while we slept, we were to cruise across the Mediterranean Sea to the next island.

In the middle of the night, I heard a *really loud bang.* "Verna, did you hear that? It sounded like an explosion."

"Yes," she replied from the top bunk, "I thought it was the toilet."

Early the next morning, Verna and I stood on the top deck and I said, "There's no wake from the ship, so we're not moving, and there's no land in sight. I wonder why!"

Just then, over the loud speaker, names of all the chaperones for the kids were called to come to the captain's station. He told us that the boiler room had an explosion last night rendering the ship powerless. He told us he'd called for tugs to tow us back to Athens, and it might take several days before the tugs arrived.

"In the meantime," he said, "you need to keep the students under control. There isn't much for them to do so we'll have the social director figure out games and whatever else she can think of. Ordinarily when we dock each day, we pick up fresh food, but we are going to have to improvise with what food we have on hand. Let me know if any problems arise. Thank you for your patience."

With that, he dismissed us. We rounded up the kids and told them what had happened and we were counting on them to be patient and not get into any trouble. There were gambling tables on the ship and they were not to go near them.

The next three days were a nightmare. The toilet smelled terrible, making our room smell bad. The food was awful—watery soup, lots of rice, potatoes and not much else.

The second day, a storm came up, and because the boat had no power the rolling was terrible. We were all seated at a long table at dinner and suddenly one end of the room tipped way up and then tipped the opposite way, like a teeter-totter. Dishes fell off the table and everyone ran out of the room, some throwing up on the way out. Trying to walk in a rolling ship was a challenge.

Keeping fifty kids entertained was a challenge. The social director never organized anything for the students. The kids were great and as concerned about us as we were with them. Walking the deck or sitting in the lounge with them was about all there was to do. We asked them about their lives, what they wanted to do in the future, and had many interesting conversations. The morning of the fourth day two tugs came to pull the cruise ship back to Athens. We never got any compensation for the cruise.

After staying a night in the hotel in Athens, we waited for the bus to take us to the airport to return to the United States. Some of the students had their luggage at the curb as we stood around waiting for the bus to come. All of a sudden two motorcycle drivers came riding up at a fast pace. Each grabbed a suitcase and sped down the street with them. They belonged to one of the girls. She burst into tears. Sobbing, she said, "I don't care about the clothes, it's the gifts I'm bringing back to my little sister and brother that I care about."

The hotel manager told us we should not have put the suitcases near the curb. "We are at a hotel and thought our luggage would be safe. You should have warned us," I said.

As we were flying back to Phoenix, I reflected on our twenty-eight days in Europe. It was a remarkable trip and one I would never forget. The adventure of a lifetime. I'd never regret spending the money on the Odyssey Tour. I hoped Uncle Ray would have been pleased with the choice I made to spend my inheritance on such an adventure.

47

A NEW BEGINNING

When I arrived home Friday morning from the tour, Greg had come home again. He'd lost his job at the resort—being apprentice to the chef—because of his drinking. A friend had taught him drywall construction, and he hoped to get a lot of work.

He said, "One of your clients left a message, and someone named Carmen Hafner wanted you to call as soon as you arrived home." Handing me the telephone numbers, picking up the cat, Kitty, and wrapping him around his neck like a scarf, Greg headed for his bedroom.

I called my client first and took a small order for Whitfield Nursery. They wanted delivery in four days. I had to find a trucker that had a partial load, excluding food, that I could share a semi with. With no computers or cell phones, it took a lot of calling, but I finally located a driver looking for a small load. After I made the arrangements for delivery, I called Carmen Hafner.

"I'm manager of the health insurance department for American Benefit Plan Administrators," she said. "I'm looking for a claims processor. I was at a Phoenix Health Insurance Managers' meeting and asked if anyone knew of an experienced processor looking for work. You were highly recommended by the Motorola insurance manager. She said you had worked for them and might be interested in a job."

"I have my own business and can't work full time. Business is slow right now, so maybe we could work something out."

"Can you come in today so we can talk about it?" she asked. I agreed to see her at one o'clock that afternoon.

When I went to see Carmen, she said, "We handle health insurance claims for all Union workers. Each Union contracts with an Insurance Company and we process their health claims. Right now, I need help processing the Labor Union claims. Since you can't commit to full-time, you could take some work home. All the work is done manually. You could pick up files on the days you're free and return them before the office closes. We have a gal that types all the checks to medical providers, so you only need to adjudicate the claims. We'll give you a calculator to use."

American Benefit Plan Administers business, called ABPA, was very large with many workers. The book-cased walls were entirely covered with colorful files. Each union had its own color, such as, Carpenter Union had green files, Operating Engineers grey, and so forth. The pension department had its office and workers on the same floor as well as the head of each Union.

I agreed to take the job. I liked Carmen. She was my age, attractive, slim, short dark-hair, brown eyes and all business.

We agreed on the pay, and I would start right away. The calculator was large, looking more like a typewriter than today's model which is small enough to hold in your hand. Giving me the insurance guidelines, I took some files home. The process was easy to figure out, and I finished the files and returned them that afternoon. Carmen was pleased with the adjudication.

That night I went to bed at ten, which was early for me. I was tired from both my trip and figuring out my new work. At two-am the telephone rang. It startled me, and I grabbed the phone, worried that Greg either had an accident or DUI because I didn't hear him come home.

"Mom," Greg said.

"Where are you? What's happened?" I asked.

"I'm in the living room. Just wanted to say hi."

Greg was drunk and had called my home phone-line from my business phone-line in the living room.

"Greg, go to bed. Hang up the phone and go - to - bed. I need my sleep. I'll talk to you in the morning. I'm hanging up."

Not able to go back to sleep right away, I thought about my business. I loved my horticulture business, but the economy was not good. Two of my customers had gone bankrupt; new building was slow, so landscape material was not in demand. When I had talked to Carmen about the insurance job, she'd described the benefits of ABPA for full-time employees and they were appealing. Living without health insurance was a worry.

Saturday morning, when I got up, Greg was still asleep and probably hung-over. Monday, I'd need to decide in what direction to go. As I sat sipping my coffee, Brian came in. He'd come back to Phoenix after living in Mountain Home, Idaho. He had his own apartment and worked for Pepsi Cola.

"Hi Mom, how was the trip?"

"Great," I said. "How are things with you? Do you want some coffee?"

"No coffee," he said and sat down. "Well, I've been dating a girl, Lorie, for about seven or eight months now." He got up and began to pace, obviously having a hard time getting something out that he wanted to tell me. Knowing how close-mouthed he was, I waited for him to continue. "Anyway," he said, "She's pregnant and we're going to get married."

Surprised, I asked, "How many months is she?"

"About seven I guess."

'Wow!' I thought. 'Seven months.'

"Why don't you and Lorie come to dinner Sunday, so I can meet her. When do you think you'll get married?"

"We thought in a couple of weeks."

"Brian, you don't have family insurance coverage, so Lorie won't be covered under your insurance for her pregnancy. When you add family coverage after you get married, it's pre-existing so the pregnancy still won't be covered. Is she employed? Does she have insurance?"

"No, she's not working, so no insurance. I don't know what we're going to do. Just save for it I guess. Is having a baby expensive?"

"Yes, you have the doctor and hospital to pay. However, there's a package plan with St. Joseph Hospital that will cover both hospital and doctor for one fee. I'll have dinner about five o'clock tomorrow. We can talk more about your plans then. By the way, Greg is back home."

That night I thought about ABPA and my Desert Shade Company. Whether I should quit my business and go full time with the insurance company. With deep regret I decided it was a financial risk to keep my business. With Brian in the predicament he was in, Greg and his addiction, my need to be covered by health insurance, I decided to see Carmen at ABPA on Monday.

Sunday afternoon, Brian and Lorie came to dinner. Lorie was petite, only about five-feet to Brian's six-two. Very pretty. Large dark-brown eyes, brown shoulder-length hair. You could tell she was very pregnant. I gave her a hug and Brian introduced her to Greg. She was outgoing and we talked about their plans. Lorie was a very heavy smoker, lighting one cigarette after the other. They had their marriage license and planned to get married at the courthouse. I told them I would have a reception at my home afterward, so she could meet the family.

After dinner, as Lorie and I talked, she said, "When I first met Brian, I knew I wanted to marry him, and if I got pregnant Brian would do the right thing and we'd get married."

I thought that was a strange thing to tell me, but didn't say anything. I kept my opinions to myself because the situation would be difficult enough. I had misgivings about their future. If they were going to be able to pay for the pregnancy, Lorie needed to go to work, even if it was for a short time. If she wasn't experienced at anything, she could work at a fast food place and the money she got could go to the medical bills. As it happened, she never went to work.

On Monday, Carmen and I talked about the company benefits. She said she'd be happy if I went full time. She told me I would have to join the Office Workers Union because ABPA was doing the work for all the Unions. When I was in high school, I belonged to the Musician's Union, but never thought I would be a full-time Union worker. The health insurance, vacation and retirement benefits were excellent, so I decided to accept the job. I told her I needed to finish up some details of my business, and I would be able to start full time in September, but would like to continue the part time work until then.

Two weeks later, Brian and Lorie got married and I had a reception for them at my home. Lorie's two sisters, who lived in Phoenix, attended along with my family and friends.

On August 17th, 1984 Lorie and Brian had a baby boy, Brandon Richard. I went to see them in the hospital. The baby was adorable with dark hair and chubby cheeks. The next day, late afternoon, Brian called. "Lorie just got home and her left leg has swollen up twice its size and is very painful. It's really huge."

"You need to go to the emergency room at St Joseph's hospital immediately," I said. "I think she has phlebitis, which is dangerous, but don't tell her that. Drop the baby off at my house. I'm sure they are going to admit her."

Brian and Lorie brought the baby to me and left for the hospital. Lorie didn't want to breast feed so she had enough formula from the hospital to last for about a day.

After a while, Brian came home looking exhausted.

"They admitted her and she does have phlebitis. They thought it was due to her smoking before, during and after delivery. She'll probably be in the hospital for at least a week. They're giving her blood thinners to dissolve the blood clots. I took two days off work for the delivery and I need to go back to work tomorrow. I can't afford to take any more time off with all the bills we're going to have." He sank onto the couch.

"I'll be glad to take care of Brandon," I assured him. "Don't worry about him. Lorie will get good care in the hospital. Go and get Brandon's bed and what I'll need for now. Just get what's necessary for you and the baby. You can get more things tomorrow after work. Lorie will need to come here for a while when she's discharged. With your money situation, you should give up your furnished apartment and stay with me for six months in order to make payments to the hospital." Brian left, and I worried for this young couple.

***

It seemed strange to have a newborn baby in the house. I forgot how much work they were, although it was easier than when I had my four kids. Thank god for disposable diapers. I sent Greg to the store to buy a large package. You could buy formula and not have to make your own like I had to.

Brandon was a good baby, and we got along splendidly. Brian was a great father. When he was home, he took over all the care: changing diapers, bathing and getting up at night. I didn't know how he could work a full day and get so little sleep. I told him I would get up at night, but he said he wanted to do it. When Lorie came home from the

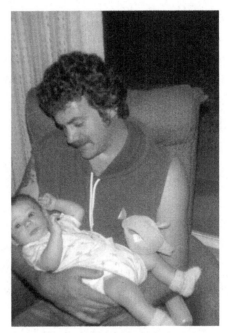

Brian and Brandon

1984

hospital, she would hold the baby and give him a bottle, but she didn't do much else. Brian still had to get up with him at night.

Greg moved into an apartment with a couple of his friends. I wondered how long that would last before he was home again. I decided I couldn't worry about him. I had enough to worry about.

As the first of September drew near, I told Lorie she was in charge since I would be working eight to four-thirty every day. She said she didn't cook, clean bathrooms or do housework. I didn't say anything, but thought, 'poor Brian, what did he get himself into?' She was constantly on the phone. She still smoked heavily, though the doctor told her she should quit.

For their sake, I let them stay six months without having to pay me for anything. I was helpful and friendly to Lorie and hoped their marriage would work. I worried because Brian and Lorie didn't know each other that well. They didn't seem to have much in common. She was outgoing, pleasant and cared about her appearance, but she seemed to expect Brian to do everything while she just talked on the phone, drank sodas and smoked. I couldn't help but wish Brian would have found a better companion. He was a quiet, sensitive, caring man. It made me very sad.

After six months, Brian and Lorie moved to an apartment. The maintenance job for the apartment complex was available and Brian applied. They hired him, giving them free rent. He was glad to get a second job to help pay for their medical expenses.

Sitting down to pay utility bills, I couldn't find the

telephone bill for the previous month. I called the telephone company and asked them why I didn't get a bill and to send me one. They assured me they had sent it and would send another immediately. When I got the bill, it was for over two-hundred dollars. I was shocked. I saw all long-distance calls were to Texas where Lorie's mother lived and Illinois where her brother was. I decided not to say anything to Lorie or Brian because with a new baby and medical bills he had enough to worry about. I knew they couldn't afford to pay, so there was no use stressing over it. I'd just pay it. Months later, moving boxes in the garage, I found the telephone bill hidden there.

My job at ABPA was interesting and I enjoyed working the medical claims. I liked reading the operative reports on difficult surgeries, especially brain surgery. Working as a union employee, was *not* to my liking however. If I was on the phone to the hospital or doctor, and it was break time, I was expected to drop everything and leave my desk. I was written up by a couple of the other processors for not taking my fifteen-minute break or not leaving at the exact time to go home. They said I was breaking union rules. When I was called in to talk to Carmen, she said, "Don't worry, but try and take your breaks and leave on time." Most of the employees were very nice and some became lifelong friends.

Although I hated to give up my horticulture business and the freedom that it gave me to travel, I knew it had to end. I was grateful I had the opportunity to begin again in something new.

48

JAMES

My son Mike and his wife Rita—both in the Air Force— were deployed to Korea, the DMZ Zone, a dangerous area. Their son, James, a year and a half old, had to be left behind. Mike's sister, Diane, and her husband Steve, agreed to become his legal guardians. After a tearful goodbye, James adjusted to his new home surprisingly well. Diane and Steve had moved to Winslow from the ranger station when their children started school. The two little cousins, Brian and Stephanie, six and seven years old, were delighted with James and helped make the situation easier. Diane placed a big picture of Mike and Rita in his room. They talked about his mother and father all the time so he wouldn't forget them.

One morning, before I went to work, Diane called, "I think something is wrong with James's leg. I took him to Flagstaff, to our pediatrician, to have it x-rayed, but they didn't find anything. Every time I change his diaper, he cries out in pain when I move his leg. He also stands on one leg and limps when he walks. If I bring him down to Phoenix, can you take him to a pediatrician? I don't have many medical choices in Winslow."

"Of course! Bring him down. I'll call my doctor this morning and I'm sure he'll recommend the best pediatrician. With a referral, I think James will get right in. I'll take tomorrow off if you can come then. I'm glad you're cautious. I'll call you after I talk to my doctor."

I called my gynecologist, the only doctor I had since I arrived in Phoenix, and told him about the situation. He recommended a pediatrician he considered to be the best in Phoenix. He successfully made the arrangements for an appointment early the next afternoon.

Diane, who was a special education teacher in the Winslow School District, was able to arrange the trip to Phoenix. The doctor took a complete set of x-rays of James's legs. He left the room to view them, and after a long time he returned to talk with Diane and me.

"It's very fortunate that you came to see me as soon as you did," he said. "There's a tumor in the thigh bone that has caused the bone to be so thin that James could have broken his leg at any moment. He would have lost his leg. I'm calling in Doctor Li, an orthopedic doctor, I consider to be tops in the field to operate. James needs to be hospitalized immediately. I've made arrangements for him to be admitted to Good Samaritan Children's Hospital. They will be waiting for you."

"Is it cancer?" I asked.

"I don't want you to jump to conclusions. There is always that possibility; however, I don't believe that it is."

"When will we meet Dr. Li and how soon will he operate?" Diane asked.

"He will see you today in the hospital and tell you when he'll schedule the operation. Diane, I see from the papers you brought with you, that you and your husband are the guardians of James and the parents are in the Air Force stationed in Korea. I suggest you get in touch with your senator and see if the parents can be brought back on a hardship case. In the meantime, do not tell the parents of this development until after the operation. It will only cause anxiety and we don't have all the answers yet."

I called Senator John McCain who I'd met during a campaign, and told him the situation. He said he would set things in motion for a hardship leave.

We took James to the hospital, and he was amazingly good during the many blood tests. Dr. Li explained he would operate in two days. He wanted to get an MRI first and have time to go over all the information. He told us James would be sedated during the MRI because it would be very upsetting to someone that young. James had to be very still during the procedure.

After he left, another doctor came in. He was nice-looking, probably in his fifties, a serious, no- nonsense type. He introduced himself and said he would be at the operation with the surgeon, pediatrician, assistant surgeon and the anesthesiologist.

Alarmed, I said, "I work in medical claims so I recognize your name. You're an oncologist who specializes in cancer. The pediatrician didn't think it was cancer."

"We won't know until we analyze the tumor. It's a

precaution. It doesn't look like it, but until we get in, we won't know for sure."

Diane went home to her family and made arrangements to be absent from teaching. I called my Mother and explained the situation. "If there's anything I can do, let me know," Mama said.

Carmen at ABPA, told me to take the next week off. More if I needed it. She was sympathetic and told me not to worry about my job and to just take care of the little one.

I stayed with James the rest of the day until he fell asleep. I worried about what would happen to him, and how Mike and Rita would handle the news. I was grateful that Diane was so alert to the problem with his leg. A lot of parents would think he somehow hurt it while playing and it would be alright. Especially after a doctor couldn't find anything wrong in the x-ray.

The next day, I went to the hospital early, just as they were wheeling James out of the room to go to his MRI. He saw me, waved, smiled, called to me and seemed happy to be taking a ride in his bed. After he disappeared, I remembered he was supposed to be sedated. Running to the nurse's station I asked why James was so alert and not medicated. She looked at the chart. I could see by the look on her face someone forgot to do it.

"*He's just* a *baby!*" I yelled. "Someone was supposed to medicate him! He will be frightened going through the machine. He's not supposed to move. Do something!"

"It's too late now," she said. "It will not take that long. He'll be alright. They'll strap him to the table."

In tears I continued to rant at her just as Diane was

coming toward us. "Mother," she said. "Stop. He'll be alright."

When James returned from the MRI, he didn't seem traumatized by his experience. I was thankful he was such a good happy baby. Knowing what he would be going through soon, I hoped he'd be able to keep his good nature.

The next day, Diane, Steve and I were there as he was being wheeled into the operating room. When the long operation was over, Dr Li said, "That little boy is going to be alright. He's a fighter and it will carry him through. He had an Eosinophilic Granuloma tumor. It is benign. I was able to save the leg although he will be in a body cast for some time in order for the bone to grow back. He will be out of recovery soon, and you should be at his bedside when he returns."

When James was wheeled back into the room, I wasn't prepared for the extent of the body cast. It started above his waist and enclosed his body, his right leg and foot fully and came down the other leg past his knee. There was an opening between his legs. A large diaper covered the area. His right arm was also strapped to a board so the IVs would stay in place.

Looking at us, James yelled, "*No, no.*"

Diane, ever the patient teacher that she was, distracted him and set up a toy we had brought for him to play with that hooked to the rail of his bed. After she talked to him in her calm, soft voice he immediately smiled. He remained the smiling happy boy that we were used to though out his *long* ordeal.

My mother, who was in her late seventies, said to me, "I think it's best James comes to my house when he gets out of the hospital. Diane has her teaching job plus two little kids; you have to work and shouldn't take any more time off."

"Mom, he has to be diapered and it will be difficult to change him and keep him clean with the cast. He's also very heavy with that body cast on."

"It's the only solution," she said. "I'll be able to handle the situation perfectly well. Now, I won't hear any more about it."

My mother was physically young for her age. She could do almost anything. For example, she decided she didn't want the large pine tree that was in her front yard. She and a lady friend cut down the pine tree with a two-man saw, stacked the wood in neat piles and gave it to, (her words), "an elderly gentleman down the street that had a fireplace." He was probably half her age. A neighbor laughingly told me about it. "We couldn't believe Dorothy would tackle a big tree like that."

It was decided to let her take care of James.

I called my ex-husband, Joe—Mike's father—and told him what had happened. He came to my mother's house to see James and said he could make something for him to lie on. A few days later he came back with a long flat padded board on wheels. It was low to the ground so that James, lying on his stomach, could paddle himself around the house with his arms. The cart was longer than his body and it had a padded wedge-pillow for his head. It worked perfectly.

After the surgery, Senator John McCain arranged for Doctor Li to speak with Mike and Rita in Korea and tell them about their baby. After James was at my mother's home for several months, Rita was sent to Phoenix on leave. A few weeks later, Mike also was furloughed to Phoenix. A few months later they were deployed to a base in South Carolina.

James grew to a healthy adult. His leg healed, and he had the full use of it. When he was twenty, during the Iraq war, while attending the University in Utah, James decided to join the army. He had to get all the medical records regarding his leg before he was accepted. He spent three tours in Iraq before being discharged. When he returned from his last deployment in Iraq, I had a reception for him. He married, became an electrician and lives in the state of Washington.

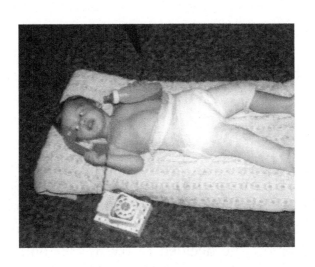

49

THREE SCRUFFY MEN AND A VACUUM CLEANER

GREG SPENT SEVEN DAYS in the Veteran's Hospital for alcohol addiction. While he was at the VA, he took an oil painting class. Although Greg had never painted or drawn anything before, he decided to try it. He found a one-inch square picture, in a magazine of Van Gogh's painting entitled, "A Pair of Shoes," and decided to paint it. While I was visiting Greg at the hospital, I met his art teacher.

She told me, "Greg has unbelievable talent. When I saw the subject, he was planning to paint from such a tiny picture, I didn't think he could do it. When he finished the painting, it was an exact replica of Van Gogh's painting." Greg gave me the large oil painting and I have it hanging in my living room and get a lot of complements on his art work.

He came home after his stay at the VA hospital. I purchased art supplies for him and he began to do oil painting, similar to the work of the artist De Garzia. He showed his paintings at several shops and they took them on consignment. He was commissioned to do some oil paintings for a million-dollar home in Paradise Valley. He did the paintings for inside the house as well as the backyard block walls and gate. He bought a guitar with the money. Although he didn't know how to play the instrument, he kept working at it and could soon play songs. I thought he was recovering, and I felt hopeful.

***

My friend Verna got a call from Ohio that Verna's mother, Nettie, had fallen and broken her hip. In her eighties, Nettie needed to live with someone or go into assisted living. She came to Phoenix, to stay with Verna, but Verna wasn't able to have Nettie live with her for an extended time because her husband objected. She put Nettie on a list at Baptist Community Retirement and Assisted Living Apartments for the next one available. I told Verna that Nettie could come and live with me. Greg was living at home and he was especially good with elderly people. I was sure it would work out. Nettie soon settled in and she and Greg bonded immediately.

Greg, who was a good cook, made special dishes for Nettie. They watched TV at night and he'd make popcorn for her. She loved Long John Silver's fish so Greg would take her to the fast food restaurant. He played records for her and her favorite singer became Neil Diamond who was coming to Arizona State University for a concert. My sister Virginia's son Joe, who attended ASU, stood in line all night to purchase tickets for his Mother, Nettie and me. When we went to the concert, Nettie, who had never been to a concert before was excited. As the loud rock-star concert commenced, Nettie stood with the rest of the young crowd raising her arms and shouting her applause.

Many months later, when an apartment became available at Baptist Assisted Living, Verna told Nettie she needed to take it. She would be among people her own age and there would be a lot of activities. I told Verna her mother could continue to live with me, but Verna thought it would be best for her to be in the apartment.

The apartment was very nice. It had a separate bedroom, small living room, full kitchen and bath. It was on the third floor, and she had a nice view from her window. It was about four blocks from my home and I told her I would walk to her apartment and visit her, which I did several times a week.

The first weekend, after Nettie moved in, Verna and I went to the apartment to take Nettie to lunch. The room was dark, blinds drawn, and Nettie, looking very depressed, was sitting in her wheelchair staring into space. It took Nettie several months to become accustomed to living in her apartment. She told me she missed Greg. He'd been so kind to her.

***

Greg stopped going to AA and I worried about him every time he left in the evening. He never drank when Nettie lived with us, and I was afraid he would start drinking again. It was very hard not to nag him about it.

One summer night, about three o'clock in the morning, I was sleeping with only a sheet to cover me when I felt someone wiggling my toes. Opening my eyes, I saw Greg and an African-American man standing at the foot of my bed. Shocked, I pulled the sheet up to my chin.

"Mom, this guy knows everything about cars, and since you were worried about your car's transmission, he can tell you all about it."

The man proceeded to tell me about transmissions. It was obvious, from their slurred words, they were both drunk.

"Thank you for the information," I said. "It's the middle of the night Greg so you need to call the man a taxi. I don't want you to drive your car. You've had too much to drink. Go to bed."

After that night, I locked my bedroom door when I went to bed. A few weeks later, in the middle of the night, Greg pounded on my door and said, "Mom, Mom, I learned a new song on the guitar. It's one of the Beatles and I know you'll like it."

When I didn't respond to him, he sat on the floor outside my bedroom door and played and sang the Beatles song over and over.

I finally yelled, "Greg, *shut-up*! I have to go to work in a few hours. Go to bed."

***

Greg worked with dry-wall construction. As days went by, he seemed to have a lot more energy than usual. Saturday morning, after he was up for a while, he would cut the grass, trim trees, pull weeds and in a few hours had the yard looking beautiful. He then would tackle cleaning the stove and pull out the refrigerator to clean behind it. On Sunday morning, you couldn't say hello to him because he was very crabby.

When I went to the refrigerator to get some milk, I saw a small piece of paper. It was so small it was only big enough for two words. It said, "*Help me.*"

I sat down and stared at it. My eyes filled with tears. I thought, 'what can I do to help him? What did this mean? Did Greg turn from alcohol to drugs? Is that why he has so much energy and later, he's crabby? Like coming down from a high?' I had to respond to my son's call for help.

I decided to talk to Greg that night. However, he didn't come home, so I went to bed. About two in the morning, I heard a car come to a screeching halt, heard the front door slam open, then someone rang the doorbell repeatedly. Getting up, I turned on the hall light and I heard a car squeal away. When I went toward the door, I found Greg unconscious on the floor, where he had been dumped, just inside the door. I ran to the phone and called an ambulance. They came immediately, and I followed them to the hospital. Greg had overdosed on drugs. After they worked on him for some time, he regained consciousness and they transferred him to the VA Hospital where they admitted him. With only a few hours of sleep, I went to work hardly able to concentrate.

The VA wouldn't let me see Greg for several days. When I did, he wanted me to take him home. I told him he needed to stay until he finished rehab. However, the VA never keeps patients more than seven days and they can always check themselves out, which he did.

Greg promised me he would go to AA again so I let him come home. Then I began to notice some items missing from my house: an antique cigarette holder my uncle Ray had given me and a small Hummel figure. When I asked Greg about them, he said he didn't know anything. I decided to find him a studio apartment. I paid the rent and bought him some groceries. I thought it would be better for both of us, and cheaper in the long run.

Despite my worries about Greg, Verna and I decided to take a week's vacation in Hawaii. When I returned, some of my furniture was gone. I knew Greg had taken them to pay for drugs. Where was he was getting his drugs? I looked at my telephone bills, which recorded what numbers were called and I saw a number that I didn't recognize that was repeated often. Delores's brother worked for the Bell Telephone company. I asked him to get me the address of the number. I drove by and found it was in apartment complex.

After deciding what to do, I went to see my son Brian. He was as tall as Greg, similar in build, both had curly blonde hair, blue eyes and looked somewhat alike. I asked him to go with me to the apartment where I thought Greg was getting his drugs. He was reluctant, saying it was dangerous, but he knew I would go anyway. He didn't want me to go alone, so he agreed. He didn't tell his wife Lori.

"There's a peak-hole in the door," I told Brian. "I'm going to flatten myself against the building, next to the door, so they can't see me. I want you to pound on the door. They might think it's Greg, or someone wanting drugs. I will then jump out and confront them. If they don't seem like drug dealers, I will apologize and say I had the wrong apartment."

I was determined to see this through, no matter what happened. I flattened myself against the wall, and Brian pounded on the door. After a few minutes, the door opened. I moved into view and said, "You can either talk to me or the police, so let me in."

There were three scruffy looking men in the room. They looked like they were in their forties. Brian and I sat on the couch. My coffee table was in front of it. My lamp was in the corner and next to it was my old Kirby vacuum cleaner. The men remained standing. I could tell by the frowning look on their faces they were surprised.

I said, "I know you are supplying my son Greg with drugs and it has to stop. Furthermore, I see you have my furniture so don't tell me I'm wrong. I also have a friend that knows where I am and your address. It will go no further then this if you immediately stop selling my son drugs and *never do it again*. I have no intention of going to the police if you do as I say. It will be your choice."

One of the men, smiling, said, "We didn't seek Greg out. He came to us. Of course, we won't sell him anything. You can count on it. However, he will find drugs from someone else if he has a problem. We don't want any trouble and I'm sure you don't either. You have my word."

"I want my Kirby vacuum cleaner back," I said.

With a surprised look the man said, "Of course. I'll carry it to your car."

I don't know why it was important to get the vacuum cleaner back. It was very old and I got it used. I just felt I had to get it. Looking back, it was a strange thing to ask for and to this day I don't know why I did. Brian, in the meantime, hadn't said a word.

The man carried the vacuum to the car, and said, "You'll not hear from us again and we don't want to hear from you either." He then went back up the stairs, into the apartment.

Brian said, "Kirby vacuum? Why the Kirby vacuum? Why not the coffee table or lamp?"

"I don't know. What do you think? Will they come after me? Do you think they'll continue selling to Greg?"

"I don't believe they'll have anything more to do with Greg. This probably never happened to them before. I don't think they'll want to tangle with you. They sure don't want the police involved."

I dropped Brian off at his place. Getting out of the car, he said, "Don't worry about them, Mom. I think it will be all right. They seemed nice enough. I wouldn't tell Greg what we did. However, if he goes to them, they might tell him about it and why they won't have anything more to do with him."

'Nice?' I thought, 'They should be in jail! At least they won't sell to Greg anymore.'

I carried the vacuum cleaner into the house. At least I did something about the terrible situation Greg was in. His addiction was destroying him, and hurting all of us.

50

ADDICTION

I continued renting the apartment for Greg. When he'd say he didn't have work for a while, and had no money, I'd bring him a bag of groceries. I didn't want to give him money because I was afraid he'd spend it on drugs. One day, when I came home from work, Greg was sitting on the couch with all his things on the floor in front of him. He told me he'd been evicted from the apartment.

"It's not my fault," he said. "It's the old lady in the apartment next to me. I had my friends over on the weekend and we were just jamming when she called the police. The police told us to turn the noise down or he'd take us all in. This morning the manager evicted me because of her."

I sat down beside him. "You weren't evicted because of her; it was because of you and your friends," I said. "You can stay for a while but I don't want any of your friends here. No drugs. If drugs are found on my property, I will lose my house. Verna and I planned to see Diane and Steve at the ranger station this weekend and I need to trust you. If anything happens while I'm gone, you will be on the street. Have I made myself clear?"

"Yes. I promise," he said. He got up and headed with his things toward his bedroom.

"We're leaving on Saturday morning and coming back Sunday afternoon. I mean what I say. Don't do anything you'll be sorry for. Be sure the cat and dog are taken care of, and there's left-overs in the refrigerator."

Verna and I left early Saturday morning. Even though I worried about what Greg would be up to, I couldn't control him even if I stayed home.

When I arrived back from the weekend, and walked into the family room, there was a strange man sitting in *my* recliner, reading *my* newspaper. He looked like he was about forty, short well-groomed hair. He wore slacks with a pressed long-sleeved shirt.

"Who are you?" I asked.

"Who are you?" he arrogantly replied, glancing up from the paper.

"I'm the owner of the house and Greg's mother. Where is he?"

"I brought him home from a party last night. He was pretty much out of it. Nobody else was here, so I decided to stay. He's asleep in his bed and I'd leave him there if I were you."

Knowing that whoever Greg was partying with would probably be involved with drinking and drugs, I said, "Leave my house this minute or I will call the police."

Folding the paper, giving me a smug look, he left.

Feeling discouraged and needing to follow through with my threat to put him out on the street, I called the son of a close friend. He was the pharmacist at the Veteran's Hospital. He knew Greg and often saw him when Greg went to the VA for appointments. I told him what had happened.

"There's nothing you can do for Greg," he said. "He has to reach rock bottom before he'll seriously get help. You should throw him out of the house. You need to go to the courthouse and get a restraining order. I know it's hard, but if you want to help Greg, do it."

As I hung up the phone, tears fell as I realized he was right. With a feeling of hopelessness, I headed for the bedroom to unpack my overnight case.

Early Monday morning, taking the day off work, I went to the courthouse and told the clerk I wanted to put a restraining order on my son. She gave me papers to fill out and told me I would have to go before the judge and would be called soon. I tried to hold back the tears as I filled out the paperwork. I told myself over and over that I was doing what was best for Greg. Why did he do this to himself? Was it because of the constant physical and emotional abuse he got from Joe? Was it the diet pills the doctor gave me when I was pregnant with him that perhaps made him addictive? Many times, I warned my boys about the danger of smoking marijuana and doing drugs.

The clerk called my name and I went into the courtroom.

It was a woman judge, and she glanced up at me as I stood before her. "Can you tell me what has been happening?" she asked.

Hanging my head, the tears I had been holding back, flowed. Sobbing, I just stood there, I couldn't speak.

After a few minutes of silence, she said, "Granted."

As she signed the paper, she asked, "Is he at home now?" I nodded my head yes, as I tried to control myself.

"See the clerk and she will have police officers talk to you. They will evict him and give him the restraining order. You're doing the right thing."

I nodded again as I turned to leave. Too distraught to say a word.

Two police officers approached me, and one asked, "Does your son have any guns in the house?"

"No." Wiping tears off my cheeks, I added, "He was sleeping when I left."

The officers told me they would follow me home. When we arrived, and approached the front door, one policeman asked where Greg's bedroom was. I told them it was the first room on the left.

When we entered the house, one of the police officers, taking my arm, guided me into the kitchen as the other officer went toward the bedroom.

"He has no place to go," I tearfully whispered to the officer who was standing beside me with his hand resting on his weapon. "What will become of him? He has no money."

"It's not your problem," he said.

"If I give you some money, will you give it to him?"

"No, Mam. It's best you don't do that."

I heard the officer tell Greg to get up and get dressed.

He was being evicted and there was a restraining order he had to follow. Greg told him he had to go to the bathroom. The bathroom was across from his bedroom and the officer told him to leave the door open all the way and he would be standing in the doorway.

Greg followed the officer's instructions without an argument. Then they all left.

When I walked past the bathroom, I saw next to the sink a teaspoon, lighter and a rubber band. I thought it was a miracle that the police didn't search for drugs and arrest him instead of just evicting him. I'm sure the officer saw what I saw.

I later learned that Greg had gone to the Salvation Army and they gave him a room.

***

Months later the doorbell rang, and when I went to the door Greg was standing there, thin and dirty. With tears running down his cheeks he pleaded with me to let him come home. I told him to come in and take a shower while I fixed him something to eat. As I made him a sandwich, I reflected on what I might have done differently with Greg.

Was his addiction my fault? I should have divorced Joe long ago despite his threats to kill the children and me. How could I have supported four kids when I had a hard time supporting only Diane? Regardless, I should have left Joe. Was it Joe's severe physical and mental abuse toward Greg that caused him to turn to alcohol and then drugs, or was it me? After I divorced Joe, and only Greg and Brian were left at home, did I worry too much about keeping a roof over our heads and food in our mouths? After meeting Larry, was I going out dancing too often and taking little trips while their Grandma stayed with the boys?

Greg's drinking started while he was in the army and progressed to drugs after he was honorably discharged. He was never in trouble with the law, never threatened me or verbally abused me. Where did it all go wrong? It saddened me to think that a nice, outgoing, talented young man would destroy his life this way.

When Greg sat down to eat, I sat beside him and we talked about how to get him help since AA and the Veteran's Hospital hadn't worked for him.

I said, "You need to stay away from your friends. Only you can break your addiction."

"Mom, I heard the VA in Prescott is better than the one in Phoenix. There are places to stay in Prescott after you're released from the hospital—half-way houses. If I can get there, I want to go. The VA is free but I don't know about the rehab places."

"I'll drive you to Prescott. Don't worry about the money, we'll figure that out after we get there. I'll take tomorrow off and we can leave early in the morning. I think Prescott is a great idea."

As we headed up the highway to Prescott, which was at a higher elevation in central Arizona, Greg was not talkative. It was hard not to lecture him about doing drugs. I wanted to say, 'just quit doing it!' It was difficult to imagine why he wasn't able to. Addiction was something I knew very little about. Reading about it wasn't any help to understand the attraction drugs had to addicts. They didn't have a happy life because of the drugs. They were miserable when the drugs wore off. Instead of talking about the situation, I talked about his brother Brian.

"Brian and Lorrie just had a second baby. It's a girl and they called her Laura. He's still working at Pepsi and managing the apartment where he lives." Greg just nodded. I noticed he was very nervous and almost paranoid. He ducked down when someone passed us on the passenger side as we drove on the freeway, as if he was afraid someone would see him and do something to him.

Arriving in the forested, mountainous small town of Prescott, the VA hospital was easy to find. It was in a beautiful setting, on rolling hills. Previously the hospital had been Fort Whipple which in 1863 was an army post during the Spanish war. It became a hospital during World War I and in 1931 it became the VA hospital of today. The buildings are on the historical registry.

Greg took an immediate liking to the hospital and surroundings. His spirits seemed lifted. After he checked himself in, we talked with the staff about rehab places. They said it was possible to stay in the rehab homes for a year or longer. The homes were not connected with the VA. He would be able to check them out before he was discharged. I told him to just get well and not worry about the money it may cost to go to those places.

As I drove down the mountain to my home, I was relieved that Greg would be away from his friends. Perhaps this time he will be able to come to terms with his addiction.

When I went back to work, a lovely young woman, Jackie, in her early twenties, came to sit by me in the break room during lunch. Because rumors travel in an office, most of the staff had guessed about Greg's problem. Jackie told me she was an alcoholic and had been sober for a year. She said, "Margaret, you should attend AA for family members of alcoholics. It will help get you through this." She got up to throw away a sandwich wrapper, then continued, "My mother is also an alcoholic but won't go to AA. I need to move out and find a place of my own. I'm trying to save money to go to college and can't afford to rent an apartment."

I liked her and immediately asked her, "Would you like to rent a room from me for one-hundred dollars a month?" It seemed like a happy solution for both of us.

Jackie agreed to come to my place after work and talk about it. She was an intelligent, quiet young woman. After seeing my home, she immediately said she'd like to rent a room. I thought it would be good to have her there because Greg would be reluctant to come home with a roomer staying at my house. I'd tell him I planned on getting a second roomer for the other bedroom. That way, knowing there would be no room for him at my place, he'd stay longer in Prescott, which would be good for him. I thought I could handle my problems with Greg myself, as I had to handle all problems in the past, so I never went to AA for the families of alcoholics. Something I should have done.

When I went to see Greg, he seemed to be doing better. We walked around the beautiful grounds of the hospital and he told me he walked around them every day. When I told him that a girl at my office was going to rent a bedroom, that she was a recovering alcoholic, he was surprised.

"Mom, you're taking a chance, she could relapse anytime.

Look at me, I can be without drugs for months and it only takes some little thing and I'm right back doing them."

"She goes to AA faithfully," I said. "If Jackie started drinking she would not only lose her job, but I would evict her. I'm giving her a chance. She'll be able to save her money because she wants to go to college to become a paralegal."

"I hope you're right," he said.

51

DRIVING A STICK-SHIFT

VERNA AND I took many trips together. I planned them around holidays when I could add an extra vacation day. Since most holidays were on Monday, it gave me four days to travel. Our big trips to Europe or Hawaii were scheduled when I had two-or three-weeks'-vacation. I always took a lot of pictures, and when I returned to work at ABPA, I brought my photo albums for everyone to see. Some were so impressed with the places I'd been, they wanted me to chart the same trip for them.

One day, an office worker said, "Margaret, why don't you work for a travel agent? You're good at this. I heard an agency, Travel Registry, wants a girl part-time. It's located somewhere downtown."

After looking up the address, I decided to go on my lunch hour and inquire about it. Maybe I could get discounts on my trips. At Travel Registry, I entered a very small office. It only had room for a large desk, file-cabinet, and two straight-back chairs. A nice-looking man sat at the desk. He had on a pink shirt and purple tie. He was my age, had short curly blonde hair and light blue eyes. His fingers were tangled with a ribbon for the typewriter that sat in front of him.

Raising his hands and trying to shake off the ribbon, in a desperate voice he said, "I can't do this! Do you know how to change a typewriter ribbon?"

"Sorry, I'm terrible at anything that has to do with machines. I'm Margaret Valenta. I love to travel, and I'm here to inquire about the part-time job."

"David Starkman. I'd shake hands, but they're covered in black ink. I do need an outside agent. I can give a percentage of any ticket, cruise or tour that's booked. Are you employed?"

"Yes, I'm a claims adjustor for a health insurance company. The men I work with travel a lot. I might be able to make their travel arrangements. I'm on my lunch hour and have to get back soon."

"Why don't you drop by after work so we can talk about it. I'm here until six o'clock."

"I get off at four-thirty so I'll come then."

David and I hit it off immediately. He had a sense of humor, and was easy to talk to. He came to Phoenix from New York when he was twenty with his companion, Dominik. David owned the travel agency and Dominick was a hair stylist. We agreed on the percentage I would make, and he told me he would have cards printed with my name on them. I told him I'd be able to go to the agency on my lunch hour or after work. He showed me how he was connected on a computer to the Air Lines and how tickets were printed. I was delighted to earn a little extra and be able to travel on a discount.

I soon did all the scheduling for the Union representatives at ABPA, but had to do it on my own time. If my friends, relatives or co-workers needed information on prices and schedules I was able to give it to them and got several bookings. David was pleased with the additional business I brought to his agency.

***

My son, Mike, stationed at an Airforce base in South Carolina, wanted Greg to come and live there. Greg, still in Prescott at a half-way house, decided it would be a good idea. I got him an airplane ticket, and took him to the airport. He soon got a job, and Mike signed on a loan for a Toyota truck for him, so Greg could have transportation.

Mike and Greg had very different personalities. Mike saw everything right or wrong, black or white, no in-between, making him a good military man. If Mike said the loan payment was due at four o'clock, that was when it was due. Not a minute later. One day, on the day Greg's truck loan was due, Greg was at the beach going for a swim with friends. Mike had the truck towed.

Mike called to tell me he had taken back Greg's truck, but he couldn't afford the loan payment because he was paying on a car already. "Since your car is old with a lot of miles, could you come and get the truck and take over the loan? With all the traveling you and Verna do on back roads, a truck would be perfect. It's a few years old, four-speed stick-shift, with a shell over the bed of the truck. I know you'll like it."

"Why did you take it from Greg when you knew you

couldn't afford another car payment? Couldn't you have talked to him before you had it towed?"

"I told Greg when I signed for the truck that he had better be on time with the payment or the truck would be mine. If you don't want it, I'll sell it to someone else. Guys in the military are always looking for a deal on transportation."

"Let me think about it and I'll call you tomorrow," I said.

I decided buying the truck would be a good idea. I called Verna and told her about it. "Would you be able to fly to South Carolina with me to get the truck? I hate the thought of driving back across the country alone."

"I'm sure Bob will let me go. He's been refurbishing an old car for a friend, so he spends most of his time in his shop. When are you planning on doing this?"

"In two weeks. My car mechanic wants to buy my car, and I have vacation coming. David, at Travel Registry, will arrange the one-way airline tickets for us, leaving on a Friday."

A week later Mike called, "Mom, you won't believe what happened! The truck wouldn't start. I checked it over and couldn't find anything wrong with it. I had it towed to a garage and he said the engine needed to be replaced. It's a Toyota! It shouldn't have failed! I called the dealer and they said they'd replace the engine. The problem is they don't have one locally. It's a small dealership. They can't find one right now, and it would take time to get it shipped."

"Mike, I have reservations on the airline next week. My car is sold. I'll talk to a Toyota dealer in Phoenix and see if they can do something about it. I'll let you know what they say."

Calling Verna with the news, I said, "Why do these unusual things keep happening? I have the worse luck."

She laughingly replied, "I think you were born with a black cloud over your head, like Joe Btfsplk, the character in the Lil Abner comic strip. You know, the one by cartoonist Al Capp."

Going to the Camelback Toyota dealer on my lunch hour, I explained my situation, the year and details of the truck. He located an engine in Florida, arranged to have it shipped immediately and a Toyota mechanic to go with the engine to install it. He said, "The mechanic will want to examine the failed engine to determine if it was caused by the owner. If it was, you will be responsible for the replacement."

A few days before I was scheduled to fly to Mike's, he called to say the engine had arrived and the failure was not owner caused. The truck would be ready in a few days. It was a relief. I was amazed at how Toyota came through as promised and backed their product. As a result, I decided in the future I would only buy Toyotas.

Verna's husband, Bob, drove us to the airport. As I boarded the airplane, I began to panic. As many times as I've traveled by plane, I never got over my fear of flying. I just make myself do it. I found my seat on the aisle and Verna sat next to me at the window. I always buckle up tightly as soon as I get seated, and I never take it off until we land. Verna said I always say the same things every time we fly, "We shouldn't be doing this! Why didn't we take a train or drive! Maybe we should get off." She learned to ignore me.

After everyone was seated, the stewardess walked down the aisle glancing right and left to make sure everyone buckled up. She walked by, then walked backward to our seats and asked Verna, "Is she alright?"

"She will be," Verna said. The stewardess looked at me and said, "You're holding your breath. Take several deep breaths. Don't worry, it should be a good flight." To add to my tension the attendant always gives directions before take-off. When she explains that the oxygen masks will drop down when a disaster occurs, and how to use them, where the emergency exits are, I wondered why anyone would want to exit out of a plane way up in the sky. It made me grasp the arm-rests tightly.

Mike picked us up at the airport, and told me that Greg quit his job. He'd taken the bus back to Phoenix. I worried Greg would contact his Phoenix buddies again and have a relapse. Greg knew I had a room-mate, Jacque, so I hoped he wouldn't go home.

When I saw the truck, I liked it. It was pretty. Dark blue with a white strip down from the windows and along the sides. Like a hockey stick. The shell over the bed of the truck had windows along the sides and a white top with a blue strip matching the truck perfectly. Mike had made a wooden partition across the back of the truck-bed, so I could put groceries or suitcases in front of it and they wouldn't slide, making it hard to retrieve them. The drawback was, the truck only had two front seats with the stick-shift in between. I could never have more than one passenger.

On our way back, we decided to see a little more of Florida, stopping at Disney World. Epcot, at Disney World was amazing with its interesting display of many countries— a restaurant in each serving their cuisine. We spent the day going from country to country and wished we had time to go a second day.

As we drove back to Phoenix, we reminisced about the trips we took in the past. Verna said, "Remember our trip to England and the first time you drove a stick shift?"

"Yes. I'll never forget that one. Car rental places in England didn't have any automatic cars. The driver had to sit on the right side of the car with the stick-shift on the left and we had to drive on the opposite side of the road then we do in the US. The dealer explained the positions on the round nob of the stick-shift for first, second, third and reverse which was just below first, and how to use a clutch."

It started to rain, so I turned on the windshield wipers. Still looking back, I said, "Remember, before we left for England, my niece, Linda, who owned a stick-shift car, said, 'Auntie M, when releasing the clutch, remember to give it lots of gas so you won't go jerking down the street.' I'll never forget the look on the dealer's face as I started off, missing the driver-way which I couldn't see from where I was sitting, and we went over the curb."

Verna said, "By the expression on his face I think he wondered if he would ever see his car again. He had explained the Round-A-Bouts they had all over England, which we'd never heard of before, it was only a short time before we came to one. I looked at the street-sign-billboard and thought I'd picked the right street for you to turn onto, Margaret, but I made a *big* mistake."

"You never made mistakes on directions, on any of our previous trips, Verna, but that one was a near disaster. We were going on a one-way street the wrong way. Horns honking, drivers shouting. I saw a driveway that I turned into and stopped. Remember? It was a print shop with the doors open? I told you I was going to back-up and go to the round-a-bout, and told you to be sure to direct me the right way to go. I thought I'd put the car in reverse, giving it plenty of gas like Linda said, and I shot through the doors of the print shop nearly killing the three men at the printing press. You became a master of the emergency brake on that trip."

"I'll never forget the shocked look on their faces," Verna said. "Two Americans with their car in the print shop. You jumped out of the car and said, 'I can't drive this stupid car, I'm nearly killing everyone!'"

"Yes, and Verna, you said, 'I'm not driving the car. If you don't, I'm going home.' I knew then I had to master driving the car or our trip would be ruined."

'It took the men a long time to back the car out of the print shop through those narrow doors," Verna said. "I was amazed there wasn't a scratch on the car."

"Remember, when I saw the first red telephone booth and stopped to call the car-dealer? When I told him, I can't drive a stick-shift and could he please find an automatic, he told me to relax. Stop and get yourself a cup of tea. Everything'll be all right."

"The English and their cup of tea! It's amazing they think a cup of tea will fix everything," Verna said.

"We only went the wrong way on streets twice. The English were so helpful. They even drove the car to head us the right way."

The rain had stopped and I turned the wipers off. Verna continued reminiscing, "Remember when we were in line to take a ferry and the man in the car right behind us offered to drive our car onto the boat? You had gone to his window to ask directions for when we docked, and you told him you were worried about driving onto the ferry and not running over the guy loading the boat."

"Yes, and he offered to drive our car. He told his wife to watch what she was doing when she drove onto the ferry and not bump the back of the car because they place the cars so close together. I crossed my fingers as we were being loaded, not wanting any damages, but she did fine. By the time our two weeks were up, I wanted to take the little car home with me. Now, here I am with another stick-shift. Even though it's been a couple of years since I've driven one, I didn't forget how. The truck is easy to drive. I'm glad I bought it."

"We've had a lot of adventures on our trips," Verna said. "My daughter, Pam, once said before we departed, 'Mom, with as many disasters as you've had on your trips, I hope we get to see you again.' I'm so glad we were able to take as many trips as we did, and I'm looking forward to many more of our adventures."

52

AMERICA WEST AIRLINES

ONE DAY ON MY LUNCH HOUR, I was at Travel Registry to pick up tickets that David had ready for a Union official. David told me that America West Airlines was hiring part-time workers in reservations. Handing me a news clipping, he said, "If you want to pick up some more hours, they pay pretty good and have benefits. I don't know how many hours, or if it would fit into your schedule at ABPA. Maybe you could work on weekends. It would be worth looking into if you're interested."

The job interviews were scheduled for the following Saturday afternoon. In 1990, you had to apply for a job in person. I talked to Carmen, my supervisor, and told her I was thinking about applying at America West for part-time work. She said, "*Margaret*, won't that be too much? Three jobs? You're fifty-seven years old. I don't think even a younger person could work that many hours."

"I spent my spare money traveling, plus helping out my

boys in the past, so I didn't put anything aside for retirement. I will be getting a small pension from ABPA, but I don't think it will be enough. My house is almost forty years old and although I haven't had to make any big repairs, I'm sure it could be something that happens in the future." I handed her the news clipping about America West hiring. "As it is now, I'll probably have to work here until I drop. The girls say they envision me pulling up to my desk when I'm ninety in a wheelchair. I'm only going to inquire. They probably won't want anyone my age anyway."

On Saturday, I arrived at the offices of America West in Tempe. I signed in at the employment desk and was handed an application. I filled it out and waited to be interviewed. Most of the people waiting were half my age. When I was called and shown into an office, a woman, probably in her mid-twenties, was doing the interviewing.

"I see by your application you're working full time. The hours we schedule will be of four, sometimes six hours consecutively. America West wants all employees to have a financial stake in the company. That means you have to buy $2,000.00 of the airline stock. Now, my first question is, do you like to fly?"

"Yes," I lied. "Traveling has been my passion for many years. I've flown to Europe as well as Hawaii many times."

"Although this is going to be part-time work in reservations," she said. "you will have to know how to do all positions except pilot the plane. In this building, we have a two-hour class you must attend every day for six weeks. It starts at seven-am. Will this interfere with your day time job?"

"No, I'm sure I won't have any trouble adjusting my hours."

"You may be required to fill in any position even a flight attendant. That's why I asked you if you like to fly. We require a physical. You have to have good vision, hearing and strength—able to lift fifty pounds." Pausing to look over my application, she continued, "I'm going to have you take the classes. They will start a week from Monday. If you pass the class you will be given a physical, and then you must purchase the required stock in the airline. A variety of shifts will be presented and you'll sign up for the shift you want." She went over the pay and told me I would be able to sign up for the 401K retirement they offer to full and part-time employees plus vacation time depending on how many hours worked. Buddy passes for relatives or friends are given each quarter.

I thanked her and said I looked forward to the classes. As I left the building, I thought, 'I'm really stupid to think I can do this. What on earth was I thinking! It's been years since I went to a class. I've had no advanced education, but more retirement will be great and the pay is good.' As I was driving home, I decided to give it my best. That's all I could do. I hoped Carmen would let me adjust my hours.

I called my son Mike, now stationed in Cheyenne, Wyoming, and told him I was going to work for America West Airline part-time if I passed the class. He laughed. "I can just see you Mom, being a flight attendant. The first air-bump while flying, you'll run to the nearest seat and buckle yourself in. Drink-cart flying unattended down the aisle."

"I'm supposed to work in reservations and hope I'll never have to be a flight attendant. I'd have to quit."

"I'll be anxious to hear how this is going to work out. It'll be interesting," Mike said.

Monday, when I went to work at ABPA, I talked to Carmen about taking America West classes. She said, "We can't adjust your hours. Since you're paid hourly, we'll dock your pay and your time-card will reflect that time. Tempe is a long way from where we are in Phoenix. We'll let you take the class. If your work suffers because of it, we won't allow you to continue."

"Since my class ends at nine," I replied, "I hope I'll be able to make it here by nine-thirty. I'll only miss one and a half hours of work. I don't know if I'll even pass the class. It's been a long time since I went to school. Most were young that applied for the part-time work. One guy I talked to was a student at the University."

Monday, I got up at five-am to drive from Paradise Valley to Tempe because it would take at least forty-five minutes in peak traffic time with no freeway. When I arrived, I quickly found where the class was being held. It was already filling up. There were at least fifty people attending. Most were half my age. Sitting beside me was a nurse and behind me was the university student I had talked to.

The teacher was a woman. Standing in front of a large blackboard, she was probably in her mid-thirties, attractive and unsmiling, making me think she'd be a tough teacher. The classroom wasn't like any I'd ever been to. Instead of seat-desks, we sat in rows of chairs. After introducing herself, she said, "When you arrive each morning, I expect you to have a notebook and pencil to take notes. The first thing that will happen each day, you will be given a test on the previous day's class. When you arrive the following morning, you will go to the cork-board located outside this room to see if your social security number is on it. If it is, you have failed the test and you are dismissed." (In 1990, identity theft was seldom heard of and social security numbers were commonly used for identification.)

She gave a two-hour lecture of the proper way to answer calls, what to do when you get bomb threats, and other problems that can arise. She emphasized the important points on the blackboard. Heart pounding, I rapidly took notes to study in the evening. I didn't want to fail, but I couldn't help thinking I didn't stand a chance. When I got home from working at ABPA, I studied my notes until I could no longer stay awake. In the past, I hated to take tests, freezing up and my mind going blank. The items I thought would be on the test I printed in large letters on paper I could hold in my hand, and read while driving to America West.

The test was difficult and long. My hand shook as I wrote down my answers. Collecting the tests, the teacher stated, "In the future, I will be covering all services of the airline." Then she started her lecture. Again, I took many notes. We had to know the city code names of every airport—like the code for Los Angeles was LAX. Most city codes didn't make sense. We had to learn the proper code word for each letter of the alphabet—such as, b as in boy, c as in Charlie and master the Zulu Time, used in the military as well as aviation.

That night I memorized the city codes and alphabet referral names. On my way to America West, I again held a paper and continued memorizing over and over as I drove. Arriving, I went to the board expecting to see my social security number on it. It was not there. Five socials were on the board and they wouldn't be coming back. The nurse that sat next to me was one that left.

As the classes progressed, each day when I went to the board, I expected to see my name. The college boy left after several weeks so did other students and a teacher. About twenty-five of us remained at the end of the six weeks. I was proud of myself.

I passed the physical, borrowed the money to buy the stock, and my first shift would be five to nine, Monday through Friday. Getting off at four-thirty from ABPA, I had a half-hour to get to America West in rush hour. I learned to weave in and out of traffic at top speed with one eye on the rear-view mirror looking for a police car. I was never late. After four weeks, another shift schedule was offered. I chose the six-pm to one-am. After my shift I got home at two in the morning. Falling in bed, I fell asleep as soon as my head hit the pillow. Getting up at seven after four- or five-hours sleep, taking a quick shower, getting dressed, no time for breakfast, I'd head for ABPA to arrive by eight.

Most reservations were called into the airline from all over the country because computers were not common and the iPhone didn't exist. The only other source to make a reservation was a travel agent. All new reservationists were monitored by managers in a large room.

One day, I went to the reservations area, checked in, put on my headphone and began. After I'd taken calls for about an hour, I received a call from a man. I answered with my usual, "America West Airlines, Margaret specking. How may I help you?"

He responded with, "Just a minute, I'm almost there." I heard a beating sound and I said, "What are you doing? It sounds like you're beating eggs. Are you cooking? Where do you want to fly?" Getting no response, I said, "From what city to what city?"

Still hearing the beating sound, he said in a breathless voice, "Wait, wait, I'm almost there."

"What city will you be flying out of?"

Suddenly, someone came up behind me and yanked my headphones off and disconnected me. Shaking with laughter, a supervisor put a hand on my shoulder—hardly getting the words out—she said, "I can't believe you didn't realize it was an obscene call. I put you on speaker and we all laughed until tears rolled down our cheeks. You kept trying to sell the jerk a flight. Bravo on your dedication."

"Really! I thought he was cooking something while he had the phone tucked under his chin, like I do."

"No, he had the phone somewhere else, if you get my drift. You will get a lot of these calls so just hang up."

"Why on earth would a guy call an airline with an obscene call?"

"They just do. We get bomb threats and you have to push the red button to security. Some people are just crazy."

Working at the airline was interesting, fun and sometimes stressful. When someone calls to book a flight, and you start to assign the seat, and you find three others have been assigned the same seat, you stress as you try to unravel the situation. That can happen when travel agents don't pay attention to their booking. As time went on, stress situations were referred to me by my supervisor making the job very interesting, and challenging as well as a lot of pressure.

Working with the young people was fun. They treated me like an equal. Often, they wanted me to fly with them for lunch on a Saturday or Sunday, to San Francisco, or San Diego. I decided to go with them sometimes, thinking I'd get over my fear of flying. I never did. When the pilots would see me coming, they would say, "And here comes Margaret, the white-knuckle flyer."

When you flew non-revenue, you'd put your reservation in the computer, and keep checking to make sure there were vacant seats. You would be the last to board, showing your badge at the gate. The airline required you to dress in business attire. One day I flew non-rev to San Diego. Sitting beside me was an elderly woman. It was a bumpy flight plus lightning was flashing. When the plane made a considerable bounce as we were flying, I made a gasping sound and grabbed the armrests tightly. The elderly woman laid a hand on my arm and said, "Don't be alarmed. This is the safest Airline to fly on. They've never had an accident." I was glad she didn't know I worked for the airline.

53

MAMA AND GREG

BECAUSE I WORKED THREE JOBS, I never watched television or had time to socialize. Weekends were spent doing necessary chores. Verna and I traveled when I had my vacation. Sometimes we visited my children who had moved to other locations. My son, Brian, Lorie and their three children, lived in Riverside, California with a promotion from Pepsi. While visiting them, it gave Verna and me a chance to visit our favorite place, Disneyland. Son Mike, Rita and the three children were stationed in Cheyenne, Wyoming. My daughter, Diane, Steve and their children, Stephanie and Brian, lived in Winslow, AZ. After Diane got her masters in teaching, she became Principal of the Junior High. Steve worked in Forestry at Chevlon in the Apache Sitgrave Forest. With his father's help, Greg had an Ice Cream-Food-Van and was doing well, and had a contract with Parks and Recreation in Phoenix. Greg had been clean from his drug addiction for nine months.

After my Dad died, Mama, in her mid-eighties, lived alone in their little house in west Phoenix. She kept herself busy tending her flowers, and making crocheted pads for Veteran's crutches. She enjoyed having friends from the Meeting for dinner on Sunday. Because I worked so many hours, I seldom had time to visit my mother and sister, Virginia.

Every day, on my morning break at ABPA, I called Mama to make sure she was all right. I tried to take my break at the same time every day, so she would expect my call and not be outside. I wanted her to know I was thinking of her and interested in what she was doing since I didn't see her that often.

One day, not long after I arrived at the office, my sister Virginia called to tell me Mama was in the hospital with a broken hip, and was soon going into surgery for a hip replacement. "Mama was standing on a chair changing a light bulb in the chandelier, forgot she was on the chair, stepped back, and fell on the tiled floor. She managed to crawl to the desk where the phone was. A coat-hanger was on the desk's chair. Mama was able to pull the phone off with the hanger." Virginia paused to answer a question from the nurse and then continued, "She called me sobbing in pain. She told me she couldn't stand nor sit. I rushed to her house and called an ambulance. We're at Good Samaritan Hospital."

"Oh my god! I'll be right there."

Grabbing my time card, I punched out. I told my boss, Carmen, what happened and I had to leave.

"Take as much time as you need," she said.

When I arrived at the hospital, Mama was heavily sedated. Trying to lift her hand to me, I grabbed it and said, "You're going to be all right. You have an excellent surgeon and he'll fix your hip just like new." She managed a weak smile as she sighed, closed her eyes, and they came to take her to surgery.

After the long surgery, my sister and I were at her bedside as she was wheeled to her room. She was humming a hymn, as if she was in church, still under the influence of the anesthesia.

The surgeon came in a few minutes later to talk to us. He said, "Everything went well. I couldn't believe how strong the bones were at her age. She didn't break her hip due to bone deficiency; it was just a bad fall on a hard surface. Your mother will be in the hospital for a couple of weeks. She'll have Physical Therapy in a few days when she's out of intensive care. When your mother is released to go home, she'll need someone to stay with her for a while."

A few days later, on my lunch hour, I visited my mother in the hospital. The physical therapist was just leaving. He said, "Your mother is amazing. Most of my patients are hiding in the bathroom or pretending to be asleep when I come in. Not your mother, she's waiting for me to walk her down the hall. When I decide we need to turn back, she always says, 'can't we go a little further?' She's determined to walk unaided in the future."

The problem came when Mama was going to be released from the hospital. I knew I wouldn't be able to stay with her because I was working three jobs and would never be there. Virginia couldn't either.

Mama wanted to go home. A lady from the Meeting called and told us she would stay with our mother for a month. Mama healed quickly, worked hard at her exercise-therapy, and was able to walk without aid.

A few years later, Mama's neighbor called my sister and told her that our mother had fallen again. She was outside watering her flowers, slipped and fell on the wet cement driveway. They took her to the emergency room. She'd broken her left wrist and forearm.

After the cast was removed, Mama had physical therapy. In spite of the therapy, she lost the use of her left hand. She no longer could knit and crochet, make jam, can, or help at the Meeting before or after the service. She no longer entertained. Although my mother was in good physical health, she was not able to do what she loved. She stopped eating. My sister would bring her things to eat, and the dog got fat. When we told her to stop feeding the dog her food, Mama threw it in the garbage. She forgot that my sister took the garbage out to the big container in the alley and found the food she threw away. No matter how many times we lectured, pleaded and demanded she eat, she paid no attention to us. She refused to live with anyone and insisted on staying in her own home.

Mama didn't read books, only the Bible. Without a television, she didn't have much to do except read the paper. Even though we knew it was against her religion, my sister and I decided to get her a television. She objected, but we got her one anyway. We told her she watched sports at our homes and she could watch the news in the morning while she sipped her tea. We showed her how to work it and Virginia brought her the TV Guide. She covered the set with a shawl, never turning it on.

One day, when I called Mama on my morning break, she didn't answer the phone, so I called my sister. "Virginia, Mama isn't answering her phone. She knows I call her every morning at this time so I know she's not outside. I'm worried something has happened to her. Can you go to her house and check to see if she's all right?"

"I'm not going alone. You have to go with me. What if she's passed away? What would I do? I can't do it. I'm coming over to get you. You have to go with me!"

Because Virginia had several tragedies in past years, I could understand why she was afraid to go alone. Her son, Dean, at the age of twenty-two, was killed in a motorcycle accident. A few years later her daughter, Linda, thirty-five, a registered nurse, died of a glioblastoma brain tumor, six months after she was diagnosed.

When we arrived, Mama was on the bathroom floor. She'd fallen again and had been sick to her stomach. When we got her to her feet, nothing seemed to be broken. We called her doctor and he said, "Call an ambulance and have them take her to Thunderbird Hospital. I'm at the hospital doing my rounds."

When we arrived, she was admitted, and Dr. Parks was waiting for us. Dr. Parks was my friend and lived in our neighborhood. A gentle man, tall and handsome. He said, "I had her admitted so you can have three days to find a nursing home for her. She can no longer live alone. I know she insists on staying in her own home, but that's not possible, and it will be easier for her to go from the hospital. If she goes back to her home, it will be hard on you because she'll fight it." He looked at his clipboard, then added, "She has lost a lot of weight and is very weak. She should go to a nursing home. We've had this discussion before and now is the time regardless of her wishes. Call me when you decide what to do. It's a hard decision, but it must be done."

As he walked away, we were both in shock. We had been in denial for a long time. Mama always said to friends and relatives that she wouldn't have to worry about going to a nursing home because "Margaret would take care of me. Virginia wasn't the nursing type." I had to work and I couldn't take care of her, and that made me feel guilty and sad.

Virginia and I immediately started going to homes for the elderly. In that time period there weren't many to choose from and most were smelly, and dreary. We finally found a large nursing home not far from Thunderbird Hospital that was better than any we'd looked at. After talking to them at length we decided it would be the best. They had a doctor in residence, a registered nurse on each floor, practical nurses, and it was affordable. They would accept her social security and give back a small amount for personal necessities. We called the doctor and told him where we wanted our mother to go.

I called my children and told them what had happened to their grandmother. Greg was very upset when I told him about it. I didn't know that Greg then went to the nursing home and talked to them. He gave up his food-van and enrolled in their nursing program with the assurance he would be assigned to his grandmother's floor.

After three days in the hospital, my mother was sent by ambulance to the nursing home. We told her she was going to a rehab place for a while to get stronger. We were in her room when Mama arrived, and we could see she was not happy about her situation. I felt she knew we were not telling the truth about why she was there. Her room was on the third floor. It had a big window and her bed was next to it. It was a large room with a bath, and it was bright and cheerful. She had a roommate, probably ten years younger than Mama. Suddenly, Greg walked into the room with a big smile, and said, "Hi Grandma, I'm taking a nursing course and I'm in training here. I'm going to look after you and you gals are going to get the best care possible. Anything you want I'll get for you."

I was shocked that Greg decided to do this. He was always good with the elderly, but I couldn't see him changing diapers, and doing all the unpleasant things nursing required for elderly patients.

The roommate had dementia and Mama was sharp mentally so they didn't make good companions. Greg talked to them both, and when he found out the roommate liked pickles, he'd bring them a couple every now and then telling them a made-up funny story of how he got the pickles.

One of the male patients on my mother's floor, was a middle-aged man that had a stroke. He'd been a professor at Arizona State University. He was bedridden and never spoke. They believed he couldn't. Every morning when Greg went into his room to attend to him, Greg went in the room singing "Popeye-The- Sailor-Man", and ending with toot-toot. Then he'd tell the man a dirty joke and would talk to him constantly as he attended to him. After several months he came into the room with his Popeye song, and the man said, "Toot-toot. What joke do you have today, Greg?"

When Greg reported the incident, the staff was shocked. The man had been so depressed with his situation he refused to speak. His wife and children approached Greg and said, "If you will be his private nurse, we will take him home and we'll pay you well. He responds to you."

Greg told them he would not be able to do it because he only took up nursing to take care of his Grandma.

The staff told me about many other of Greg's kindnesses with the patients. The supervisor said, "Greg is compassionate, and we're lucky to have him. He passed his classes with high marks. He always stays way past his shift, talking to the patients as well as his Grandmother."

Listening to the supervisor, brought tears to my eyes. I always knew Greg was a kind soul and had great potential. It made my heart ache.

When they took Mama in a wheel-chair down to the dining area for meals, she pretended to eat, pushing her food around. Greg did everything he could to make her situation happy, but Mama didn't respond. After about eight months in the nursing home, a week before her ninetieth birthday, Mama was taken to Thunderbird Hospital because her organs were failing. She passed away in a few days. Greg quit his nursing job. He wrote this note for me.

I AM STANDING ON THE
SEASHORE. A SHIP SPREADS HER
SAILS TO THE MORNING BREEZE
STARTS FOR THE OCEAN. I STAND
WATCHING UNTIL SHE FADES ON
THE HORIZON, AND SOMEONE
AT MY SIDE SAYS, SHE'S GONE!

GONE WHERE? THE LOSS
OF SIGHT IS IN ME, NOT IN HER.
JUST AT THE MOMENT WHEN
SOMEONE SAYS SHE'S GONE,
GRANPA, LINDA, AND DEAN ARE
WATCHING HER COMING. OTHER
GLAD VOICES TAKE UP THE GLAD
SHOUT, HERE SHE COMES!

AND THAT IS DYING.

LOVE,
GREG.

54

MICHAEL

ONE MORNING, just before I was going out the door to work, the phone rang. It was my son Mike, who was in the Air Force, stationed in Cheyenne, Wyoming. "Mom, are you sitting down? I have some bad news."

"What happened?" Right away I thought of his three children, and was terrified to think there might have been a terrible accident.

"I was just diagnosed with a large brain tumor. In four days, I'll go to the military hospital in Denver. They're sending six doctors from Walter Reed Hospital in DC to operate. They told me to get my affairs in order. I have about a twenty-five-percent chance of surviving the operation."

Shocked, I couldn't speak for a minute, then said, "Michael! Did you have any signs that something was wrong?"

"I've always had migraines, so I didn't think anything else was wrong when I'd get a bad headache. Then when I needed glasses, I thought I was just getting old. I'm turning forty in a few weeks. I was working at my desk on the base accounts when I lost my vision. I shouted for help, telling them I couldn't see. They transported me to Denver to the army hospital where they did an MRI and discovered the tumor. It must have been growing for a long time it's so large. They won't know if it's malignant, like cousin Linda's brain tumor was, until they operate. Thank-goodness, after a few hours my vision returned."

"Have you called anyone else?"

"No, you're the first. Can you make some calls?"

"Yes, and I'll make arrangements with America West to fly to Denver immediately. I'll call your Dad because he should know."

"I don't want Dad to come."

Diane wanted to go with me to Denver. His brothers, Greg and Brian, weren't able to go, and with Linda's death from her brain tumor still fresh in their minds, they were worried. When I called Joe, he wanted to know if he should go to see Mike. I told him no, Mike would probably be out of it for a while. He should wait until he's stable, and I'd call him after the operation.

I talked to my supervisor at America West, and finding the flights to Denver full, the airline bumped two passengers off to accommodate Diane and me that afternoon. My supervisor at ABPA said to take as much time off as I needed. David at travel registry told me about the free Ronald McDonald House accommodations in Denver for relatives of patients with life threating hospitalizations. Mike said they'd pick us up at Denver since Cheyenne had only a small airport.

After Diane and I arrived in Denver, Mike drove us back to Cheyenne so he could get ready for the surgery. They had told their young children of the situation, and Rita's mother was flying in from South Carolina to take care of them. We would stay at the Denver Ronald McDonald House.

As soon as Rita's mother, Amy, arrived in Cheyenne, we left for Denver. The Ronald McDonald House had twenty-six bedrooms, large kitchen, library, great-room, and a beautiful garden. The staff was kind, attentive and eager to make our stay comfortable. Today, it's huge: seventy-three bedrooms with private baths, three kitchens, laundry facilities, five TV lounges, dens, and indoor-outdoor play areas.

The evening before the operation, Mike insisted we go out to dinner to a fine restaurant. His attitude was amazing. He believed he was going to survive and didn't want to hear any negative thoughts or concerns. Mike laughingly told the doctors if they had to go through his face, he wanted them to make him look like John Wayne, his favorite actor. Early the next morning, Mike was admitted, and they prepped him for surgery. Rita, Diane and I were at his bedside when they wheeled him away. As the pre-medication started to take effect, Mike called out, "Don't worry, I'm going to be ok."

It was a very long surgery. About midway, one of the doctors came out and told us it was going to be several more hours and everything was going as planned. We were relieved when Mike came back to his room and had survived the ordeal. Fortunately, the tumor was benign, Mike could move all his extremities and was coherent.

Before the doctors returned to Walter Reed Hospital, the surgeon showed me the x-rays. He said, "We couldn't get all of the tumor because portions were too close to the optical nerve and carotid artery. The Pituitary Gland was imbedded in the tumor. Without it, he will now have to have medication for most functions of his body. Injections, patches and pills daily. You have to be aware it will make him change over time. Mike will have to have radiation to try to shrink the remaining tumors. I'm referring him to the Naval Hospital in California to have the radiation because this hospital is closing." Rita, Diane and I told him we were thankful for all he did and grateful that Mike had such good doctors.

As soon as Mike was stable and going to be released from the hospital, Diane and I returned to Phoenix. Mike was flown by the Air Force to the hospital in California for the radiation treatments.

During a call from him a few weeks later, he said, "The doctors at the Naval Hospital are arguing about giving me radiation. They said I might go blind or have a stroke. It could kill me. It's been weeks and they've done nothing. I don't know what to do."

"You need to call your doctors in D.C. and tell them what's happening. They will figure it out and take care of it. You shouldn't be making any decisions on your own. Let me know what they decide."

After Mike talked to the doctors at Walter Reed, he was transported to the military hospital in San Antonio, Texas. They did the radiation treatments, and they filmed the unique procedure. Every time, after each treatment, Mike went to the physical therapy area at the hospital and worked out. He said it made him feel better. After they finished the weeks of radiation, Mike returned to Cheyenne and was discharged from the Air Force with total disability. However, the fact that he was totally disabled was omitted in the computer and he didn't get his disability check when it was due. No one seemed to be able to correct the situation, so I called Senator McCain and he immediately got the matter cleared up.

Several months later, Verna and I drove to Cheyenne to see Mike. When I arrived at their house, Rita said that Mike had gone to the store with a friend and would be home soon. A short while later a man came into the room. I asked, "Is Mike with you?"

"MOM!" he said.

I hadn't recognized him. The prednisone he was taking, had made his face, neck and body swell. One evening, when we were playing a game with the kids, Mike went into the garage to get something. After a while, when he didn't return, I asked, "Where's Mike? Shouldn't he be back by now?" James ran into the garage to see what was keeping him. Mike had fallen asleep standing at his workbench. It had happened before, we learned.

Trying to take additional college courses to get a mechanical engineering degree, Mike would fall asleep in class. He could no longer concentrate, so withdrew. His doctors at the VA hospital changed his medication so falling asleep with no warning would stop happening. Sometimes different medications would make him sick, tremble, dizzy, perspire profusely and made him short tempered. He had a constant headache. To keep track of the remaining tumors to see if there was any change, he had to have MRIs. It was a difficult time for the family, and his wife, Rita, handled the situation amazingly well—with loving care.

In the fall, Mike wanted to come to Phoenix for the NFL Cardinal-Redskin game with his ten-year-old son, James. My three boys loved football. Mike and Brian were Redskin fans and Greg a Cardinal fan. Brian and Greg decided to go to the game too, and Brian brought his five-year-old son, Brandon. My three boys talked me into going with them, and I was pleased that they wanted me to go. It was a very hot day in Phoenix, and the game was held outside at the Arizona State University Stadium. I worried it would be too much for Mike, but he persevered. Little Brandon, when the Cardinal cheerleaders came onto the field, shouted, "I like *them!*" making the crowd around us laugh.

As I watched the game, I thought of the many summers my three young boys and I spent at Campland in San Diego. The boys pitched the tent and we had fun swimming in the ocean, going to the zoo, Sea World and museums. Now my sons were men, and I was happy that they wanted to include their mother in their fun times. Michael had survived, and here we are, all together again.

55

JOE'S DEADLY LESSON

JERRY AND SALLY O'MARA, our friends and neighbors back while Joe was in college at Michigan Technological University, corresponded with me throughout the years. Sally and I wrote each other letters a lot about our lives. One day Sally called and said they would like to come and visit me in Arizona. They lived in New Hampshire where Jerry was a civil engineer. I was delighted and we made arrangements for their stay in my home.

When I picked them up at the airport, the years fell away, and I was thrilled to see them again. After spending time going to scenic places in Arizona, catching up with family news, Jerry asked, "Is there a possibility we could visit Joe before we leave?"

"I'll call Joe. I think he would be glad to see you both."

When I called him, Joe said, "Come on Saturday afternoon. I'll figure out where to seat all of you."

I wondered why he would have to figure out how to seat

three people, but I knew better than to ask.

As we approached Joe's house, the yard was nothing but dirt and weeds. It was a ranch style home in not the best neighborhood. Blocking the double garage, was a large rundown boat, which I'm sure would never stay afloat. The station wagon we had purchased after leaving college in 1960, was in the driveway. Now, thirty-five years later, it was completely rusted out. The turquoise color was not visible. There was a padlock hanging from the hood. Next to the station wagon was a white rundown pickup truck. As I passed the car, I glanced inside and the interior was rotted out. A crate was positioned for the driver to sit on.

***

We rang the doorbell and Joe opened the door. "Come on in," he said.

If I thought the outside was a sad sight, I had no idea what a shock the inside would be. Just inside the door were three folding chairs for us to sit on. The entire house was stacked with junk and no place to sit except the three chairs. Model airplane magazines were in tall stacks. There were stacks of egg cartons, meat trays, parts to cars, I had never seen so much useless junk on tables, counters, everywhere you looked, things were piled up. I wondered how he could get around in the house.

Even though Joe knew we were coming, he didn't bother to dress decently. He wore a stained white undershirt and jeans. Joe had a goatee and sideburns. His black hair was turning grey. He told Jerry he was retired from AiResearch.

There was no air conditioning in the house, only a swamp cooler. It was a hot day in Phoenix, and it wasn't long before we were feeling the heat. I couldn't help but wonder why Joe was living like this when he had a large pension from AiResearch.

We sat on the chairs by the door and I asked him, "Is the car still working? Why is there a lock on the hood?"

"Yes, it still runs and I put the lock on the hood to make sure no one would steal it."

I wondered why anyone would want any part of that wreck of a car.

After the O'Maras talked with him for a while, and the heat became unbearable, we told Joe we had somewhere to go. I noticed that when Jerry was getting into my car, he had tears in his eyes. "I can't believe someone that brilliant would end up like this," he said.

***

Several months after the O'Maras returned home, Greg called. He said, "Dad called and said he was ticketed for a DUI and couldn't drive for six months. He wants me to come and stay to drive him around. I'm going to do it. I can't afford the apartment since drywall work is slow right now."

"Greg, you know how difficult your father is and how he treats you. You don't want to be put down and ridiculed like in the past. People don't change, so I doubt if your father has."

"I'll be ok Mom."

Some months later, I planned to go with Adelaide,

a friend and former colleague, who had breast cancer, to the doctor early the next day, so I was staying at her home overnight. We were watching the ten o'clock news, when a man was shown being processed into jail for shooting his son, who was in critical condition at a hospital. Crying out NO, in shock, I realized the man was Joe. The mug-shot showed him with a dirty white undershirt and a defiant look on his face.

"Adelaide, where is your phone book, I need to call the hospitals to see where they've taken Greg."

A few moments later, my nephew Joe called. "Aunt Margaret, I watched the ten o'clock news. Did you see it? Mom told me you were at Adelaide's and gave me the number."

"Yes, and I can't believe he would do it. I'm going to call the hospitals to find out where Greg was taken."

"I found out, Aunt Margaret. He's at John C Lincoln Hospital. I'm headed there right now. I will meet you in the lobby."

Arriving at the hospital, my nephew Joe and I were shown to intensive care where Greg lay in a coma. We rushed to his side, and the attending nurse said, "Don't touch him, we don't want him to wake up yet. The best thing for him is to stay in the coma until he's more stable."

As we stood at his bedside, I looked at my son and wondered how he could end up like this. My heart broke for him. His own father—*shooting* him.

A doctor came in shortly and said, "He was shot in his back. We can't remove the bullet because it's located too close to a vital organ. The next twenty-four hours are critical."

I said, "I have to tell you; my son is a drug addict."

"His blood work on admittance shows no drugs or alcohol in his system. We have to medicate him regardless of his addiction. He can't survive otherwise."

In a few days, Greg came out of the coma. He said to me, "They said someone shot me. Who would do that?"

"It was your father, Greg."

"Why?"

"Can you tell me what you remembered before waking up here?"

"Dad didn't let me live in the house. I had to live in the pickup truck. He had a shell over it, and in the bed of the truck I had a foam mattress with an old rug over it. He put in a fan, attached to a long extension cord, to keep me cool—which didn't do much good. I rode a bicycle to get things for him. I had to pee and poop in a bucket. He did let me take a shower in the house. I remember I knocked on the door and said, "I need to take a shower. I heard him turn the lock on the door so I couldn't get in. I shouted to let me in, and the next thing I remember is waking up here." Then Greg closed his eyes.

With a sigh, he opened his eyes and said, "You know, Mom, I often woke from night terrors, a constant in my life since childhood. Lay frozen with fear, unable to get up and go to the bathroom. I guess my nightmare became a reality."

Joe's brother Don, who lived in Phoenix, got Joe out of jail. Joe called and pleaded with me to help him. I didn't ask how I was supposed to help him, I said, "Why in heavens name did you shoot Greg?"

"To teach him a lesson."

Angrily I said, "What kind of a person are you to shoot your own son! I can do nothing for you. Why didn't you have him live in your house if he was helping you?"

"Because I didn't want him to steal from me."

As I hung up, I wondered why on earth he would think Greg wanted anything in that horrible house.

Joe was put on probation—no jail time. His several guns were returned to him. He was not to have any contact with Greg.

I later learned that Joe had put his stepson, even though he was divorced from his 2nd wife, in an apartment. Joe paid all his bills for years. He wouldn't do that for his own son—making him sleep in a pick-up truck.

When Greg stabilized, he was taken to the VA Hospital. The bullet remains in him. His brother Mike came from Cheyenne, and when Greg was released from the VA Hospital he went to Cheyenne. I was happy that Greg would be away from his father. I thought Greg and Mike would not last in the same house because they had such different personalities. I knew however, no matter what, Mike and Rita would help him when he needed it.

56

ONE DAY I'LL FLY AWAY

THE YEAR IS 1997. I've been working three jobs for eight years and managed to pay off the mortgage on my home. I love my home and feel more secure with it paid off. I still have a car payment on my Toyota Camary and want to put aside money for retirement, so I plan to continue working the three jobs.

***

Phyllis, who I met when we both took a soldering class at Motorola, remained my friend throughout the years. After her husband died, we occasionally traveled together. Retired, she lived in Scottsdale in the winter months and Prescott, a small town in north central Arizona, in the summer. A few weeks before the 4th of July, she called and asked, "Have you any plans for the 4th?"

"Not yet, do you want to go somewhere?"

"I thought maybe you could come to Prescott and spend

the holiday with me. Can you stay for a few days? There'll be lots of things to do."

"That sounds wonderful. I haven't been to Prescott for years. Since the 4th is on a Friday, I'll have Friday through Monday off at my jobs. Give me directions and I'll leave late Thursday afternoon."

As I was going up the mountain toward Prescott, I remembered it was a pretty small town in a beautiful setting, and only a one-and a-half hour drive from Phoenix.

Phyllis lived in a manufactured-home community called Pine Lakes in the Ponderosa Forest. As I entered the community, I noticed a large attractive club house on my left. Next to it was an outdoor swimming pool and a tennis court. I could see two lakes in the background with ducks swimming about. I thought, 'what a beautiful place to live!'

The homes were situated on hills amongst the pine trees. Phyllis had a large home attractively decorated. Having lived on a farm growing up, Phyllis was a great cook. She had a roast beef dinner ready, and I enjoyed every mouthful. We sat on her porch in the cool evening and caught up on the latest gossip. The mountain's cool air in Prescott was a pleasant relief from the extreme heat of Phoenix. I couldn't get enough of the delightful smell of the pine trees. I said, "Phyllis, if I owned a place in Prescott, I'd live here full time. It's so beautiful."

Friday, the 4th of July, we went to the town square to watch the parade. It was a homespun parade, not like the ones you see in big cities. Plenty of horses, cowboys, the high school band, home-made floats and four scotty dogs marching in a row, dressed in patriotic costumes. They stole the show.

Town Square Prescott is the soul of the city. It's surrounded by restaurants, bars, brew pubs, and wonderful little shops. The courthouse is in the center with magnificent trees surrounding it. They were having a craft show, and Phyllis said the Mountain Artist Guild she belonged to had a booth in the show with one of her paintings in it. We wandered around the displays for a while then decided to go that evening to the Sharlott Hall Museum to see the outdoor play, put on by local actors. About forty people attended. It was an old-fashion play with a villain dressed in black and hero dressed in white. Everyone booed the villain, cheered the hero and the noisy cicada insects joined in. The old-fashioned costumes were perfect for the play, and as twilight faded and the stars began to appear, it made a lovely, fun evening.

The next morning, Saturday, Phyllis suggested we go for a hike around the hills of Pine Lakes and then take the forest trails. As we hiked up the steep Midway Street hill, we paused beside a double-carport to catch our breath. Phyllis said, "The home down the hill from here is at the edge of a cliff. It has the best view in the park. I've always wanted to see it, but I don't know the people, so haven't had the opportunity. This is their carport. The home just went up for sale. See the sign? It's by owner."

"Since it's for sale by owner, maybe they'll let us see it. We could pretend I'm interested in buying."

We started down the trail and came to five steps leading down to a square platform with lawn chairs on it. Then we proceeded down six more steps to the back porch of the home. We rang the doorbell and fortunately someone was home. I said, "Could we see your house? I'm up from

Phoenix, looking for a place, and saw your for-sale sign on the carport."

"Please, come in," he said.

As we entered the home, we walked into the kitchen. On the right were accordion doors and behind them was a washer and dryer. The kitchen was a galley-kitchen. Gas stove, large refrigerator, dark wooden cupboards on both sides and a large window over the sink looking up the hill into the trees. Left of the kitchen was a dining room with a large window. When we walked into the living room, it took my breath away. A floor-to-ceiling window, the length of the room, revealed a beautiful forested mountain across a wide ravine. The living room had a patio door on the left, and outside of it, was a large uncovered patio with more spectacular views. There were two bedrooms. One bedroom was small and had a trundle-bed. The master bedroom had an on-suite small bathroom with a tub-shower. Both bedrooms had large closets and windows, making the rooms bright. I asked, "How many square feet does the home have?"

"It's 895 square feet. We also have a large shed attached to the house at the side. We'll look at that later. Let's go out on the front porch so you can appreciate the view."

There was a covered porch the length of the house. The porch was suspended over the cliff and the view was amazing. At the bottom of the wide ravine was a creek, and from there rose a mountain, covered with ponderosa trees.

"Let's go out back and see the shed and side area," he said.

The back-porch led to the large shed attached to the side of the house. Inside the large room were workbenches, shelves, and a big window looking toward the view. A window on the side brought a lot of light into the room. There was electricity in the shed with a wall heater. Next to the shed the ground was level. Lawn chairs faced toward the mountain.

I asked the owner, "How much do you want for the home?"

"We're asking fifty thousand including the appliances. We don't own the land and the land-rental is sixty dollars a month for this space."

"Does the rent go up often?"

"An elderly man owns the property and seldom raises it. Only when he has to make unexpected improvements does he raise it. Never anything big."

I walked toward the edge of the cliff, and looked at the mountain across the way, taking in its beauty. A large bird, like an eagle, flew by. After watching it for a few moments, I thought, 'I'm home.' I turned toward him and said, "I'll buy it."

Phyllis's eyes widened and her mouth dropped open.

The owner said, "Since it's Saturday everything will be closed. I don't own the land, so it's like selling a car. No escrow."

"I'll go to the bank Monday, and give you a check for the fifty thousand if you will include the trundle bed." He agreed. "I just put up my sign early this morning and didn't expect to sell it so quick. We're moving to Tucson and our house won't be ready for three months. Would you agree to rent it back to us until October fourth? We'll pay you 900 dollars a month. That way we won't have to move our things twice and find a rental for that short time."

"That will be perfect. It will give me time to sell my house. I'll see you Monday."

As we left, Phyllis said, "You don't have fifty thousand dollars lying around, so what are you going to do?"

"Since I own my home, I have more than fifty thousand in equity. The bank has checks against the equity in your home to use in emergencies or for large purchases, so that's what I'll use until I sell my house. I couldn't believe how beautifully situated that home was. I love nature, it's almost a religion with me, and I imagine I'll see a lot of wild life and birds. I'll be sixty-five in March, and have worked hard all my life. Now I can just sit on the porch, sip my tea, watch the birds and look at that beautiful view."

"Ha! I can't see you just sitting doing nothing. I thought you loved your house in Phoenix. You have a lot of friends there. All your jobs. I thought you were going to work until you dropped."

"I do love my home. It's been my security blanket. My friends will just have to come and visit. Even though I enjoyed the places I worked, I'm tired. You can't imagine how stressful it's been the last eight years, rushing from job to job, and not getting much sleep. Phyllis, you need to put your home in Scottsdale on the market too. Running two households is a lot of work and expense. It would be wonderful if you could live here full time too."

Driving back to Phoenix, I had a feeling of peace tinged with excitement. I remembered when I moved to Phoenix with my baby Diane. I was nineteen, wishing I could walk out of my life and into another, where I had no past, and no one knew anything about me, and I could be whoever I wanted to be. I didn't know what else to do but go on. Now I've lived at my Phoenix home thirty-eight years, and imagined I'd live there forever.

I thought, 'my life in Phoenix had it's good and bad times. I'm very fortunate to have wonderful friends that saw me through the rough ones. Starting in October, I'll come up every weekend until I come permanently in January. With the trundle-bed I'll have a place to sleep. I can bring a chair to sit on and also most of my linens, silverware and dishes. Each weekend I'll bring more things, like paintings and books. Everyone will be shocked. Especially my friend Verna and my sister Virginia. I wonder what my kids Diane, Mike, Greg and Brian will think about my move to Prescott! None of them live in Phoenix, so I don't think they'll be unhappy about it.'

As soon as I got home, I called my sister and told her about buying a place in Prescott. She was surprised and when I described it, she thought it sounded like a great place to live. I told her I was going to have her son, Joe, a realtor, put my house on the market as soon as I got it ready to sell. When I called Diane she said, "That's great! Phoenix has been getting so big with more crime, a small town will be so much safer. I'm glad you're doing this. I'll come next weekend and help you get your house ready to sell." My boys also thought it was a good move and they too planned to come the following weekend to do any painting or repairs needed. I told them to take whatever they wanted from the house because the house I was going to was very small.

I decided to continue working my three jobs until January. I didn't have to wait until March when I'd be sixty-

five to get full social security benefits. Calling David at
Travel Registry, I told him about my plans. He wished me
well and said, "You've been working for me a long time
and I'm going to miss you." When I arrived at ABPA, I
immediately went into my supervisor's office and told her
I was going to retire, move to Prescott, and my last day of
work would be Friday, January 2nd. When I told America
West Airline, I was going to retire, they wanted me to work
two more years and fly from Prescott to Phoenix on their
small jet, and they would pick me up at the airport. If I
would do that, it would make a total of ten years employed
with the airline, and I'd get free flying privileges for the
rest of my life. I said, "No, I hate to fly, and going over the
mountains in a small plane to Phoenix would give me a
heart attack."

I sold my house, retired and moved to Prescott. I added
a room—an extension of the living room, closing in the
side patio with wall-to-wall windows. On the 4th of July
my family was coming to celebrate the holiday with me.
My grandson, Brian, his wife Tayva, and their three girls,
Madeline, Lillian and Alison were coming from Phoenix,
and planned to stay at my house. Granddaughter Stephanie,
her husband Aaron and their two girls, Alissa and Clara
lived in Prescott Valley and planned to join us. Diane and
Steve were coming from Roosevelt Lake. I thought of my
boys, grandchildren and great-grandchildren who lived far
away and couldn't be there. I wished they could.

The evening before the 4th, we went to the square to put
our folding chairs on the parade route for all of us. It was
something a lot of people did, and in those days, no one
ever touched them.

On the morning of the 4th, we all gathered at the square, sitting, waiting for the parade to begin. As the first horse appeared, with a rider carrying the American flag, my great-grandchildren immediately stood with their hands over their hearts. I was so proud of them. As I gazed at my beautiful, wonderful family, I thought, 'If the things that happened to me in the past hadn't happened, none of us would be here. *They wouldn't exist*. If you could be young again, and were able to undo the things that were done—that were what made you what you are today—but then who would you be?'

Made in the USA
Monee, IL
06 January 2020